Revolution, democratic transition and disillusionment

Manchester University Press

PERSPECTIVES ON DEMOCRATIC PRACTICE

series editors: SHIRIN M. RAI and WYN GRANT

With the ebbing away of the "third wave" of democratisation, democratic practice is unfolding and consolidating in different ways. While state based representative democracy remains central to our understanding of the concept, we are also conscious of the importance of social movements, non-governmental organisations and governance institutions. New mechanisms of accountability are being developed, together with new political vocabularies to address these elements in democratic practice. The books published in this series focus on three aspects of democratic practice: analytical and normative democratic theory, including processes by which democratic practice can be explained and achieved; new social and protest movements, especially work with a comparative and international focus; and institution-building and practice, including transformations in democratic institutions in response to social and democratic forces. Their importance arises from the fact that they are concerned with key questions about how power can be more fairly distributed and how people can be empowered to have a greater influence on decisions that affect their lives.

This series takes forward the intellectual project of the earlier MUP series, *Perspectives on Democratization*.

Revolution, democratic transition and disillusionment
The case of Romania

ANCA MIHAELA PUSCA

Manchester University Press
Manchester and New York
distributed in the United States exclusively by Palgrave Macmillan

Copyright © Anca Mihaela Pusca 2008

The right of Anca Mihaela Pusca to be identified as the author of this work has been asserted by her in accordance with the Copyright, Designs and Patents Act 1988.

Published by Manchester University Press
Oxford Road, Manchester M13 9NR, UK
and Room 400, 175 Fifth Avenue, New York, NY 10010, USA
www.manchesteruniversitypress.co.uk

Distributed in the United States exclusively by
Palgrave Macmillan, 175 Fifth Avenue,
New York, NY 10010, USA

Distributed in Canada exclusively by
UBC Press, University of British Columbia, 2029 West Mall,
Vancouver, BC, Canada V6T 1Z2

British Library Cataloguing-in-Publication Data is available

Library of Congress Cataloging-in-Publication Data is available

ISBN 978 0 7190 9001 1 paperback

First published by Manchester University Press in hardback 2008

This paperback edition first published 2013

The publisher has no responsibility for the persistence or accuracy of URLs for any external or third-party internet websites referred to in this book, and does not guarantee that any content on such websites is, or will remain, accurate or appropriate.

Printed by Lightning Source

To Noel

Contents

List of Illustrations   *page* viii
Acknowledgements   ix

1. Introduction   1
2. Between the past and the future: Romania, seventeen years into its transition   6
3. An anatomy of disillusionment   29
4. Shock and transitions   54
5. The illusions and disillusions of the Romanian Revolution: the case of the Timisoara revolutionaries   87
6. The illusions and disillusions of civil society: the case of the Group for Social Dialogue   137
7. Representing illusions and disillusions: a visual narrative of the Romanian transition to capitalism   174
8. Conclusion   206

Bibliography   214
Index   227

Illustrations

7.1 A young child on a bike in Negresti: Fred Rohde (2000)   *page* 189
7.2 Selling embroideries on a colorful street: Voicu Bojan (2006)   190
7.3 Two men at the "Targul de la Negreni" (Negreni Fair): Gicu Serban (2003)   191
7.4 Poster for the International Film Festival, Transylvania—Romania: Cosmin Bumbut (2004)   192

Acknowledgements

There are several people who made this book possible and I would like to take this opportunity to thank them for their effort, patience and encouragement. Because this book was born out of my dissertation project, I am deeply indebted to my committee members, who have been incredibly supportive throughout the conceptualization and writing process: my committee chair, Prof. Mustapha K. Pasha, for his dedication to research and critical thinking that have inspired me and pushed me to do better as well as for his dedication to this project and my work that has allowed us to work together over several oceans and miles of land apart; Prof. Vladimir Tismaneanu for sharing with me his invaluable experiences and knowledge of Romania and for helping me in the field research process; and Prof. Carole Gallaher, for her unconditional moral support and very sharp advice. I would also like to thank Prof. Patrick Jackson, Prof. Julie Mertus, Prof. James Mittleman and Prof. Paul Wapner for their guidance and support throughout my PhD years, as well as my department, the School of International Service at American University, for allowing me to do this in the first place. I am deeply indebted to all the people that facilitated my field research process as well as those who were kind enough to share with me their experiences related to the Romanian revolution and the period immediately following. Among them are: Mircea Mihaies, Nelu Laslau, Nicolae Badilescu, Lorin Fortuna, Sanda Adrian, Claudiu Iordache, Ioan Savu, Gabriela Adamesteanu, Gabriel Andreescu, Radu Filipescu, Andrei Cornea, Rodica Palade, Alin Teodorescu and Thomas Kleineger. I would also like to thank Prof. Magnus Ryner, the Political Science and International Studies department at

University of Birmingham, UK, and the European Commission, for their support during the final editing stages, and, last but certainly not least, my anonymous reviewer for excellent comments that I hope are reflected in the final manuscript, and of course, my editors, Jenny Howard and Lucy Nicholson, at Manchester University Press.

1
Introduction

The post-communist transition in Romania has been a period rife with high hopes and expectations as well as strong disappointments and disillusions. The engagement with these disappointments or disillusions has mainly fallen along the lines of critical editorial comments by dissidents and intellectuals or academic engagements that connect it to different forms of social and political apathy. What seems to be lacking however, is a more head-on engagement with disillusionment as a self-contained process that is not just a side-effect of political corruption or economic failures but rather an intrinsic part of any transition, directly connected to the nature of the new political, social and economic illusions emerging and old ones subsuming.

This book attempts such a head-on engagement with the process of disillusionment, seeking on the one hand to provide the basis for a theory of disillusionment in instances of transition and, on the other hand, to elaborate on how such a theory could be applied to a specific case-study, in this instance, the Romanian transition from communism to capitalism. By defining disillusionment as the loss of particularly strong collective illusions, the book seeks to identify what those illusions were in the context of the Romanian 1989 Revolution, the period immediately following the revolution—marked mainly by the consolidation of the first political parties and civil society organizations, and the extent to which these initial illusions still play an important role in Romania today, more than seventeen years into the transition.

By seeking to understand the extent to which disillusionment is intrinsic to social change, and more importantly, determine whether it plays an essential role in shaping both the direction and the form of change, the book inevitably places itself at the intersection of a number of different academic literatures: from regional and comparative studies, political science and "transitology" studies, to sociology, psychology and cultural studies. It is of course not easy for a junior scholar to claim an in-depth knowledge of all of these different literatures, and inevitably, comments surrounding the level of engagement with each of these literatures will arise. However, the author hopes that her choice of interdisciplinarity will provide a base for future engagements with the question of disillusionment by more established academics within each of these individual fields of study.

The empathetic tone of the book stems from the author's desire to address the question of social change not only as a theoretical perspective which follows particular rules of description, classification and prediction, but also as an individual and collective struggle that has real and direct effects on the everyday life of millions of people. For those who are undergoing the transitions, democratizations, revolutions, coups, wars and conflicts, social change appears much more confusing than the academic classifications addressing it, and oftentimes with a less concrete and predetermined sense of direction.

Starting with the premise that all societies are built around a series of social myths or illusions, and that social solidarities are inherently connected to these myths and illusions, this book argues that transitions—such as the transition from communism to capitalism—are not only about specific economic and structural reforms but just as much and more about the negotiation of new social illusions as old ones disappear. These illusions, and disillusions—defined as the loss of older illusions—are less abstract than they initially may seem. In the case of the Romanian transition, the illusions and disillusions were directly connected to a series of different expectations at different points of the transition: the Romanian revolution, the period immediately following the revolution, the period of consolidation of major economic and political reforms and the period of critical redefinition and reflection on the past in direct connection to the direction of the future.

These social illusions and expectations and their corresponding disillusions become much more than concepts and terms used to describe a particular state of enchantment or disenchantment that can be either encouraging or discouraging of the reform process, as the case may be. They become the very postmarks of a transition that point to important debates and negotiations about particular choices and directions as well as powerful regrets or critical views of what was and what will come. It is along with these negotiations, choices and regrets that new forms of social solidarity take shape, and the stability of this new solidarity is in many ways determined by the balance between these illusions and disillusions.

As the site that has experienced two of the most powerful political illusions of the twentieth century—communism and the transition to capitalism—Central and Eastern Europe has a unique position in that it has suffered already perhaps one of the biggest disillusionments with a political ideology and yet, has, at least seemingly, been willing to very quickly embrace yet another powerful ideology. This particular trajectory to capitalism that many would describe as "unnatural" and even "forced," opens up the possibility of a more radical engagement with the nature of political illusions and our relation to them, as well as the extent to which a lack of real understanding and commitment to those illusions can undermine not only the relationship between society and the state, but also, the very framework of social solidarity within a state.

The author has chosen Romania as a case-study for a number of different reasons, some more objective than others. Easier personal access to data coupled with the advantage of having lived in transitioning Romania for seven years and studied it from a distance for another ten years has perhaps had much to do with this choice. More objectively though, Romania has faced one of the most difficult transitions to capitalism, being often accused of lagging behind its other Central and Eastern European counterparts in enforcing and managing reforms, as well as in its willingness to accept the new capitalist ideals. Romania is particularly interesting in terms of its transition trajectory given the particular development of the communist illusion in the area, the violent nature of the Romanian revolution, the slow pace of reform, the high levels of pessimism during the transition and the increasing nostalgia and fascination with the communist past simultaneous with the fascination with the possibilities offered by its recent entry into the European Union.

Following this case-study, the book is divided into eight chapters. Chapter 1 provides a short introduction to the book and a justification for its slightly non-conventional tone and approach. Chapter 2 seeks to position Romania seventeen years into its transition, providing a benchmark against which to better understand the historical evolution of the transition. Focusing on the two major debates dominating the headlines in late 2006 and early 2007—the opening of the Secret Security archives and the entry into the European Union—the chapter seeks to point out the extent to which Romania remains caught between its past and its future, equally engaged in both, yet often using a clear line of demarcation between the two.

Chapter 3 attempts to build a theory of disillusionment as a way of understanding social change by examining the important role that both individual and collective illusions play in maintaining social solidarity and building a relationship with the state. The chapter examines the meaning of collective illusions and disillusions in connection to a series of other concepts often used to express similar phenomena: alienation, anomie, malaise, cynicism, apathy. It also examines the larger social impact of positive and negative illusions as well as the extent to which one can consider both communism and capitalism as collective illusions in their own right.

Chapter 4 uses the concept of shock to build a framework for better understanding the transition from the communist illusion to the capitalist illusion. Inspired by Walter Benjamin's understanding of shock, the chapter seeks to argue that there is a direct relationship between the transition from a negative to a positive understanding of the concept of shock and the unfounded enthusiasm with which the transition from communism to capitalism was embraced, along with a number of painful processes of reform, such as the so-called economic "shock-therapy."

Chapters 5 and 6 focus on how these new concepts of disillusionment, collective illusions and shock can contribute to a better understanding of classical studies of social change mechanisms such as revolutions and the formation of civil society. By following the trajectory of the Romanian revolution, Chapter 5 focuses on the initial illusions of the leaders of the Romanian revolution and the extent to which these influenced the fate of the Romanian revolution, as well as the extent to which they were integrated, or not, into the newly built structures of government.

Chapter 6 follows a similar logical structure, relying instead on the illusions of the first members of civil society in post-revolutionary Romania. Following the evolution of the Group for Social Dialogue—the first civil society organization in post-revolutionary Romania—the chapter seeks to challenge the assumption that there are always clear boundaries between the organizations of civil society and political institutions, as well as the assumption that the democratization process can be measured in any way through the "strength" or "weakness" of civil society.

Chapter 7 offers a more creative approach to understanding social change through an examination of the role that the visual plays in the formation, maintenance and destruction of collective illusions. Using the case of a group of photographers who see themselves as social anthropologists studying and tracking the Romanian transition through images, the chapter seeks to better understand how images can be used as an effective tool not only to record different aspects of the transition, but more importantly for understanding how average people relate to the transition on an everyday basis.

Chapter 8 provides some concluding thoughts and wraps up the book with a short summary of the major arguments and findings from the previous chapters.

2

Between the past and the future: Romania, seventeen years into its transition

Two major events marked Romania's transition from the year 2006 to 2007: the publishing of the Presidential Report Analyzing the Communist Dictatorship of Romania and Romania's official entry into the European Union (EU).[1] While many argue that Romania's entry into the EU clearly points to the end of its transition, the controversy surrounding the above-mentioned report questions that assumption by pointing out that the past remains very much a point of contention with serious implications for where Romania will be heading in the future. This chapter seeks to briefly discuss how these two major events have recently played out in Romania and what insight they can provide into further examinations of the origin and the particular evolution of the Romanian transition. Working backwards along the historical timeline, these debates hope to provide an interesting benchmark against which to analyze the events surrounding the 1989 Romanian Revolution, the formation of the first civil society organization and the historical experience of the Romanian transition that the remainder of the chapters will address.

The Secret Security files and the European Union are perhaps the quintessential symbols of the communist experience and the past; and the integration into the "capitalist West" and the future, respectively. That the two would be debated side by side points to the extent to which the communist experience remains deeply embedded into the way in which Romania relates to the "West" and its future. Despite a series of attempts to separate the two and present itself as a new-born nation that has been released of its past, the Secret Security Archives weigh heavily in any and all discussions about political and economic reform, public elites, political corruption, restitution and justice. The following pages trace the debates surrounding the opening of the archives for a comprehensive analysis and seek to underline the importance of the way in which one comes to terms with one's past for the future.

While the Secret Security files—perhaps the most important evidence of the inner functioning of Romania's communist regime—have for the most part remained out of the public eye, gathering dust in a number of different locations, the impetus for change suddenly came in 2006, when the Romanian President, Traian Basescu, decided to launch the Presidential Commission for the Analysis of the Communist Dictatorship of Romania. The Commission was charged with the writing of a comprehensive report meant to establish the criminal nature of the communist dictatorship of Romania.

This was not the first attempt to examine the former communist dictatorship in Romania, and certainly not the first in Central and Eastern Europe. In December 1999, the Romanian parliament voted in a law that allowed access to personal files[2] held by the former Secret Security Police. In May of 2000, the National Council for Researching the Secret Police Archives was created. Controlled by Parliament, the Council remains mainly a research institution, although its creation and leadership have also been met with a certain level of controversy, due to the sensitive nature of the information it examines. In December of 2005, Prime Minister Tariceanu—whose relationship with the president has been very tense, coming dangerously close to several breaking points in the fall of 2006—also established an Institute for the Investigation of Communist Crimes in Romania. The Institute was another research institution funded by Parliament for a period of six years with possibility for extension, under the direct supervision of the prime minister.[3]

Given the previous establishment of several research institutes and councils that had direct access to the Secret Security files and had it in their mandate to investigate and identify the crimes of communism in Romania, one may wonder why the establishment of yet another commission was necessary. In fact, much of the criticism surrounding the Presidential Commission has focused precisely on this point.

Yet, unlike the previous research institutes and research councils, the Commission proved in the end to be highly efficient in its originally stated goal, producing a comprehensive report, of over six hundred and sixty pages, detailing the structure and criminal nature of the communist regime in Romania. Using his strong hand, as he has done on a series of different occasions—at the threat of being called and clearly perceived as somewhat of a bully—the Romanian President did however manage to get what he wanted, and more importantly, managed to initiate a very heated public debate that should have probably occurred much earlier. The controversies surrounding the report, while highly acrimonious, presented the public for the first time with issues surrounding the so-called lustration process—initiated by the Czech and Slovak Republic back in 1990—and questions of individual and collective memory and guilt. Despite their harsh nature, many of the criticisms that were raised against the report speak to a large extent about the lack of any sort of agreement when it comes to the past, as well as about the clear influence that the past continues to have on the way in which present politics is run. A document meant to be mainly historical in nature, opened a Pandora's box of unexpected confessions and in some cases, less unexpected aggressive resistance.

The president personally asked Vladimir Tismaneanu, a Romanian dissident and now a US citizen teaching at the University of Maryland, to establish the Commission and be in charge of structuring the report. Given his long-term interest in the history of Romanian communism, his acknowledged contributions to the fields of history, political science and international relations as well as his personal and direct experience with communism—he grew up in a family that maintained close ties with the Romanian communist apparatus and was early on exposed to a series of political personalities and inside stories—he seemed like a natural choice. As we will see later though, this was highly contested by a number of different people. Whether rightly so or not, is not for us to judge, or a concern of this chapter. What is however a concern, is what these contestations might mean in terms of the way in which people continue to relate to the past and the possibility of ever providing a sense of clarity and calm when it comes to it.

Tismaneanu was directly in charge of forming the team of experts that would do the background research and help write the report. The final chosen members of the Commission were: Sorin Alexandrescu, Mihnea Berindei, Constantin Ticu Dumitrescu, Radu Filipescu, Virgil Ierunca, Sorin Iliesiu, Gail Kligman, Monica Lovinescu, Nicolae Manolescu, Marius Oprea, H.-R. Patapievici, Dragos Petrescu, Andrei Pippidi, Romulus Rusan, Levente Salat, Stelian Tanase, Cristian Vasile and Alexandru Zub. A series of experts also participated in the writing of the report. Among them were: Hannelore Baier, Ioana Boca, Stefano Bottoni, Ruxandra Cesereanu, Radu Chirita, Adrian Cioflanca, Dorin Dobrincu, Robert Furtos, Armand Gosu, Constantin Iordachi, Maria Muresan, Germina Nagat, Eugen Negrici, Novak Csaba Zoltan, Olti Agoston, Cristina Petrescu, Anca Sincan, Virgiliu Tarau, Cristian Vasile and Smaranda Vultur.[4] While these names will not say much to those who are not familiar with the Romanian context, they represent some of Romania's foremost dissidents, writers, philosophers, researchers, historians, political scientists and sociologists. They have each written their own contributions analyzing the Romanian transition since 1989 in light of Romania's past, and their names should be recognized, if only in passing.

The final report produced by the Tismaneanu Commission is by far one of the most comprehensive overviews of the complex repression mechanisms of the Romanian Communist Party, from its very beginning until its collapse in 1989.[5] To my knowledge, no other similar report—comparable in depth and length—has been written in any other former communist country, although there have been several calls for similar reports. The report of the Tismaneanu Commission examines the nature, scope and effects of the Romanian totalitarian communist regime, the context in which it came to power, the different repressive mechanisms used to secure and maintain its power as well as the resistance put up by a series of different dissident movements, the evolution of its structure and role of each institution within the regime, as well as the key people that played an essential role in maintaining this repressive apparatus. The report also looks at key policies that were particularly destructive, such as Ceausescu's economic, demographic and minority policies. The tour de force is concluded by a call for a public condemnation of communism and those who helped support it, for remembering and learning from our communist past, and establishing a prosecution mechanism aimed both at punishing as well as at restoring the rights of those who were abused.

Although highly praised and recognized, the Commission, and its report, has also been met with a series of criticisms that are largely representative of the love–hate relationship that many former communist countries maintain with their past. The criticisms focused on several sticking points: the exceptional interest that the president directly took in forming such a commission despite the existence of several other mechanisms and institutions that were already charged with the investigation of communist crimes; the naming of Vladimir Tismaneanu as the head of the Commission; the choice of members that formed the investigative committee of the Commission and the exclusion of certain key dissidents initially invited to participate; the naming of several political personalities in the text of the final report as close collaborators with the communist regime; and a series of reported mistakes that were made in the text with regards to unchecked research data.

Very few of these critiques were however properly developed, appearing more as personal attacks either addressed to the president, Tismaneanu or other members of the committee. The critiques often left a question mark as to whether their author(s) had even bothered to read the report in the first place, or whether they were simply interested in taking a bite of whatever offer happened to be on the table at that particular moment. The bitter, personal tone of many of the critiques placed people in at least three clearly divided camps: long-time supporters of the president and/or supporters of Tismaneanu; long-time opponents of the president and/or Tismaneanu; and lastly, a series of opportunists who saw in this an occasion to follow their own particular agenda, by positioning themselves sometimes in very unexpected camps.[6]

The exceptional interest taken by the president in the formation of an inquiry commission and the writing of a report that would automatically gain an official presidential decree status was clearly controversial given the high impact of such a report, the one-handed approach to it without approval from Parliament, and more importantly, the fact that the report directly undermines a series of political opponents—conveniently around election time. It is thus no surprise that the opposition would raise its voice against the report, independent of its possible merits.

Perhaps the most virulent critiques were however those directly addressed to Tismaneanu, focusing mainly on his own communist past—or his family's—that, the critics argued, placed him on a shady moral ground, particularly when denouncing other communist collaborators and the regime itself. Yet Tismaneanu's past involvement with the communist regime and his family's interactions with that same regime, have been more or less an open book for many years now. In a series of books and interviews Tismaneanu has directly addressed this question and has responded to criticism by owning up to his family's past while also very openly distancing himself from it. Yet the question that arises then is whether this is enough. For these critics it was clearly not.

The almost obsessive focus on the question of morality and who can stand his moral ground when faced with questions regarding their communist past is an important one. It is again very telling of the unrealistic expectations that the "truth" be told "objectively" and that "pronouncements" be made only by those who have had nothing to do with the "evil" past. These standards would exclude just about anyone who has any stake in the issue at all, for the younger generation—the only ones probably who had little to nothing to do with the old communist nomenklatura—is hardly interested in the issue and would rather see the country move on. The question of who is to be the judge of the past is a very important one. It has been obsessively posed all throughout the former communist countries of Central and Eastern Europe as well as several other places in the world—take post-Nazi Germany or post-dictatorship regimes in Latin America. The answer is never an easy one, for the conclusion seems, for the most part, to be about the same: unless there is a clear social consensus on where and on whom the guilt should fall, the question will always bring about controversy and unrest, without ever necessarily finding the "proper" answer. In the case of Romania, as in all other former communist countries of Central and Eastern Europe, there is no such social consensus.

The critics proposed that a different group would be more fit to run such a commission and write the report: a group that included more dissidents. They picked one name in particular, that of Paul Goma, a famous Romanian dissident, exiled to Paris and still living there to this day. Yet Paul Goma was not the one to receive the presidential call inviting him to lead such a commission. Vladimir Tismaneanu was. While the latter had the courtesy to invite Goma to become a member of the researching team, Goma refused to openly collaborate and sought to discredit Tismaneanu by publishing a series of confidential correspondence, and was thus expelled from the Commission. What some call political games and others petty games, form a very difficult to manage decision-making web in which everything is questioned, likely to be turned into a conspiracy theory and feed directly into the already high level of cynicism that the population at large is experiencing. Yet this should hardly be surprising when so many people are so personally invested in any exploration of Romanian communism and entire identities are built around the issue. One should not underestimate the power of what some may call self-guilt or the need for absolution as well as an often very personal investment in otherwise "objective" investigations of the past. For communist historians and researchers are often very much a part of the past and not the distant observers that some might make them out to be.

Any condemnation of the past thus has important personal connotations that could go either way: a public condemnation with open books (confessions with regards to one's past) may act as an important purification and absolution of oneself, or, quite the contrary: it may raise issues that have been hidden and repressed for a while and often for a reason. Fears of misinterpretation of why one did something, or even changed one's mind along the way, can paralyze someone into denial and a perpetual need to repress the past. The most contested cases have been those in which confessions were only made when the inevitable was about to happen and for one reason or another people found themselves having to reveal things about their past that had been kept hidden for years. These confessions often trigger not only a very negative public reaction but also a deep disappointment, especially in cases where we are dealing with public personalities of one kind or another. The confessions of Mona Musca—one of the most famous female politicians in Romania perceived to be very capable and trustworthy—and later Sorin Antohi—a Romanian Hungarian political scientist and former head of the Political Science department at Central European University—shocked the Romanian public. While immediate reactions seemed similar in both cases, the ultimate repercussions were very different: Mona Musca's ratings went down for a number of months, yet recovered within half a year, while Sorin Antohi lost his post as head of the Political Science Department at Central European University and found himself isolated and repudiated even by close friends. Which road of the two others are likely to take, one can never know, but the incentive to guard one's past can certainly be strong, given the powerful repercussions it can have on one's life.

Yet the search for "justice" and "truth" continues and these are questions that we will be forced to grapple with until one conclusion or another is reached, for as long as there continue to be high stakes in the issue of the past, it will continue to be pursued. Calls to leave the past alone and focus instead on the future are simply unrealistic, for the future is always built on the past. Romania's transition, its recent entry into the European Union, its current political arrangement and international positioning are all directly connected to the past, even while often standing in direct opposition to it. This intricate relation between the past, present and future is perhaps what makes it so difficult to condemn one's past, for in the process, one is also condemning the very process that led to where and who we are now.

Despite all the criticism, perhaps one of the most important achievements of the Commission has been to gather enough momentum and energy in order to start a real discussion on how to deal with the past. While the Commission's report will remain open to criticism, it continues to be one of the most comprehensive documents on the history of the Romanian Communist Party. It is the first such comprehensive document to be put together and published online for everyone to access. Whether one agrees with everything that is in the report or not, it would be difficult to dispute its contribution to history. More than anything, these controversies surrounding the report have signed off the final days of glory of a generation that still finds itself more connected to the past than the future, for in ten or twenty years' time, the debates will have changed, the memories of our communist past will have become museum pieces and concerns will have shifted towards realms whereby the excuse of our communist past can no longer be used to justify lacks, inefficiencies or resistance to change.

Despite their claim to originality, the Tismaneanu Commission and the Report, while unique in their comprehensive overview of the former communist dictatorship of Romania, were certainly not unique in terms of their fundamental endeavor: that of settling the past. In fact, many Central and Eastern European former communist states have dealt with the question of the past and the so-called process of lustration much earlier, sometimes immediately following the fall of their respective communist regimes. The former Czech and Slovak Republic was the first to initiate and name the process of lustration—the term's initial meaning was that of purification by ritual sacrifice, but was later used to describe the process of weeding out members of the old communist nomenklatura and agents and collaborators with the former communist regime.[7] As in Romania, the lustration process in the former Czech and Slovak Republic proved to be very controversial. As early as the 1990s, prior to the first free elections, lists of former collaborators with the communist regime, coming out of the now open Secret Security Archives, resulted in the denunciation of several politicians, leading to an investigation that demanded a more comprehensive analysis of the archives and a clear set of instructions as to what to do in such cases. This set the basis for the most comprehensive lustration law in Central and Eastern Europe that allows for prosecutions, rehabilitation of victims, restitution of property and so-called decommunization. The new lustration law raised a series of local protests, similar to the ones we have seen in Romania, as well as a powerful international opposition: international institutions such as the Council of Europe and the International Labor Organization compared the new lustration law with Stalin's purges and argued that this was no way to get to grips with the past.[8]

Despite its strong words, the law has had, for the most part, little consequence for many members of the former nomenklatura, who are still enjoying a privileged position in public live and oftentimes in political office. None of the leading criminals of the former communist regime were brought to justice and, to this day, there still is no major systematic study of the history of Czechoslovak communism, which, Rupnik argues, is much needed. The law did however provoke a series of tensions that helped weaken the newly elected post-communist regime leading to a series of important questions as to whether this was really a search for justice or revenge. The title of an important article revealing a dialogue between Adam Michnik and Vaclav Havel, the question of whether a lustration law is really a search for justice or an opportunity for revenge is an important one. Havel approaches the issue by explaining that his own personal position on this is somewhat split: on the one hand, as a private individual he leans towards forgiveness, while on the other, as a president, he has to acknowledge the injustices and the need for some kind of compensation. When he discusses the issue of the lustration law and the controversies surrounding it—coming from those who saw it mainly as an act of revenge—Havel argues the following:

> I think that the essence of these changes—if you prefer, we do not have to call them revolutionary—lies in introducing law instead of lawlessness, and not in introducing new lawlessness. The only problem is that social pressures have been caused by the old lawlessness, whose impact is still felt. For example, try to picture the case of one of my friends, Standa Milota, who was persecuted for 20 years and could not work; today he has a pension of one thousand Czech crowns because he could not be promoted and therefore his salary will always be low. Meanwhile, the person who persecuted him and prevented him from having a normal job today has a pension of five thousand Czech crowns, a house, and many other goods. People observe such cases and say that it is true that the "top" officials have changed, censorship has been lifted, and newspapers may publish whatever they want, but the real, material, everyday wrongs and results of the old lawlessness have remained unchanged.[9]

What Havel calls lawlessness others may call injustice, yet the story that Havel tells is very representative of hundreds of thousands of other similar cases. How one repairs this wrong is certainly questionable, for even restitutions only work to a certain extent, and given that many of the former communist countries are still struggling with their transition, money or other benefits are not exactly easily available to restitute. The point to Havel's story however, seems to be a certain inability to help such forms of "injustice" and a sense that, contrary to expectations, the "real, material" world has hardly changed if not gotten worse for many, after the fall of communism. Repairing the public damage—individual or collective—is thus very difficult to do, if at all possible. If even a comprehensive lustration law, like the one passed in the Czech and Slovak Republic failed, then who is to say that it would not have the same fate in other places. In fact, the criticisms to all and any attempts to promote such policies in any form or shape have proven to be more controversial than helpful. This has however not stopped people from trying.

A more successful approach has been to disconnect attempts to recover and comprehensively understand the history of Central and Eastern European communism in respective countries from lustration laws. When initially announced, the Tismaneanu Commission stated that it would only pursue an academic and historical role, not seeking to blame any one individual or seek prosecution. If it had perhaps kept its initial promise, it might not have been faced with so much controversy as was the case in the end. Examples of other Central and Eastern European countries pursuing lustration policies and failing abound.

In Poland, the Chief Commission for the Prosecution of Crimes against the Polish Nation broadened its mandate in 1991 to include not only Nazi crimes but also the crimes committed by Stalinists and Ukrainian nationalists. The Olszunski government, which was the first to pursue a clear policy of decommunization, began by replacing a series of military personnel proven to have been involved with crimes of the former communist regime and moved on to attack other politicians who were discovered to have been former collaborators with the communist regime. This led not only to a series of controversies in the press, but more importantly, to the very collapse of the Olszunski government. The message was clear: anyone who even attempts to pursue such policies is likely to fall into public contempt and lose their place in office. Why would this necessarily be the case? Probably because it was 1991 and many careers stood to be ruined by serious decommunization policy and also because perhaps there was no broad commitment and public backing of such a policy.

The case of Bulgaria also speaks to the same conclusion. Although some prosecutions of former communist criminals were made in 1992, the issue pretty much disappeared from the public agenda after a series of controversies surrounding the open access to data of the former state security in 2001 and then the sealing of those same documents later in 2002. Although a Commission on the Disclosure of Documents and Establishing Affiliation with the Former State Security and Intelligence Directorate was formed, the Commission maintained a research position, one that was hardly perceived as threatening to anyone. In fact, as Bertschi argues, issues of lustration and prosecution were put on the back burner as more pressing issues of economic instability and increasing poverty were on the public's mind.[10]

Countries like Hungary and Slovakia were not much different in their own failed attempts to pursue different kinds of policies of lustration and decommunization. In fact, probably learning from its neighbors, Hungary's Office of History, which deals with issues regarding its communist past, made it very clear that they do not deal with processes of lustration. Although in October of 1994, there was an attempt made at a screening process conducted by independent courts in Hungary, it is not clear to what extent this screening was successful in dealing with the larger problem of many former communist party members maintaining important positions in the public realm. Overall, the lustration and decommunization policies in post-communist Central and Eastern Europe seem to either have failed completely or made very little difference, given their initial mandate. The causes for this were varied, yet most of the time, it had to do with a series of controversies that risked to either tip the political balance or completely destabilize the country if one were to stay the course when it came to decommunization.

In light of these examples, a series of important questions arise: Why exactly has the process of lustration proven to be so controversial, given that most people will agree on the need to condemn, in one way or another, the communist past and those who supported it?; Should one support a particular way of remembering the past, and can the entire communist experience be put under the same banner?; Can we even trust the evidence that exists with regards to former communist collaborators?; To what extent can communism be considered the result of a collective wrongdoing as opposed to an individual one?; and perhaps last but not least, What would a lustrated society look like?

The first question seeks to discuss the apparent contradiction between the criticism of lustration and its apparent high level of public approval. Although all different attempts at lustration policies, or different versions thereof, have proven more or less ill-fated, the majority of the public at large in Central and Eastern Europe will probably agree that a sense of justice is needed and that former communist elites should not be allowed to parade in and out of the public domain without any sort of restrictions. Perhaps the answer might lie in the fact that the majority of the population had little if anything to do with such controversies that were raised and sustained by people who had a direct stake in the issue. Much of the public debate on the issue thus appears either as direct political instigation or as a purely intellectual debate that for the most part excludes the public at large. The latter seeks answers to the more pressing economic issues that immediately affect their wellbeing and thus locates these debates within that specific context.

Another answer may lie in the fact that none of these policies of lustration occur within a context of political vacuum. As Maria Loss argues, lustration discourses are often very loaded, as they almost always involve a call for the release of privileged information that has up until now been used as a political prerequisite of immense strategic importance.[11] Information that has been used to secure important positions and break others, to keep people in line and blackmail others into otherwise inconceivable alliances, is clearly a key political capital. The extent to which the Secret Security files being used to blackmail people is more of a political myth or reality, is easily tested, I believe, by some of the reactions that one can easily see in the press and the political domain when such information is revealed or risks being revealed.

The second question with regards to the particular ways in which the past can be remembered and the attempts to label the communist past under one particular banner—usually criminal or evil—pertains to a series of different debates that have occurred around the topic of remembrance and rewriting history. The Tismaneanu Commission was accused of rewriting history, almost as if the process of rewriting is evil in itself: it somehow assumes that history has once been written in an objective form and that someone else is now attempting to erase that and replace it with something else. One may argue that indeed history is in a way "written" metaphorically, as it occurs, yet it is written in the eyes and minds of many, and thus the text of what is "written" is not one, but rather many. It is without question that a series of important studies in the field of historical research have already established the role that a particular retelling of history plays in the weakening or strengthening of particular identities, policies or legacies. The search for an "objective" history, in light of these studies, seems to a large extent almost futile. And yet this search continues, for when the past involves cruel tortures, unfair jail sentences and the suffering of millions of people for over forty years, one needs to find a solution which inevitably involves being able to clearly identify the victims from the criminals.

Labeling the past criminal or evil—which is what most condemnations of communism seek to do—can be somewhat questionable to the extent that communism involved a lot more than a political apparatus. It was an entire lifestyle and described a period of time that involved a lot more than just purges, crimes and wrongdoings. In fact, many people continue to maintain fond memories of communism: the sense of security that it offered them and in a way, the simple lifestyle that they once had. The extent to which this nostalgia is triggered by the difficulties of the transition more so than the actual overall positive feeling left by the communist period, is certainly questionable. After all, nostalgia is known to be a selection of overly positive memories, all brought together with clear gaps between the segments of the timeframe in which they occurred. The repression of negative memories is probably only natural, as Esbenshade argues,[12] particularly in a place like Central and Eastern Europe, where the ghosts of several pasts are still haunting the area; where several acts of erasure and reconstruction have left the same place imbued with a series of sometimes contradictory meanings. He calls this process the dialectics of memory: the constant process of negation and reinvention, something that Milan Kundera has been able to so nicely capture in his novels by pointing out that what we choose to remember and to forget is often nothing but a complex mechanism of self-defense, one that does by no means seek to do justice to "real" history, if such a thing exists.

Esbenshade's example of the East German entrepreneur seeking to open a communist theme park where people would be able to experience "real" communism: drive Trabant cars, have little cash to use, stand in line for everything and be treated really badly when sitting down to eat in a restaurant or requiring any other type of service, is very telling of the complex ways in which nostalgia can be exploited for actual profit. The film "Goodbye Lenin" explores similar themes in which nostalgia is used as a mechanism of survival for those who are too old and fragile to adjust to anything radically new. In his view, memory appears less as something that can be coagulated into a unitary story, such as a "real history" and more as something that can be exploited—as in the case of nostalgia—and also something that can only be captured in pieces: which is why he calls it "collected history" as opposed to "collective history." More importantly, Esbenshade wonders whether remembering should necessarily be considered a good thing—thus questioning in many ways the role of history as well. Quoting Nietzsche, he argues that without forgetting, it would be impossible to live at all. Yet the question then becomes: What is one to forget? How does one choose what to remember and what to forget?

If this does not complicate things enough, even when one chooses to remember, the evidence of the past is not always straightforward. In fact, much of the criticism of the lustration process lies with the lack of a clear and straightforward prosecution mechanism when individual and collective guilt cannot so easily be determined, and when the material on which the prosecution is to be based is not always to be trusted. Several lawyers have pointed out the difficulties of prosecuting people for crimes that for example were not illegal at the time—what we now consider a crime was oftentimes in the past considered not only to be legal but also encouraged by the political apparatus[13]—or prosecuting all those who were guilty of associating with the former communist regimes: for that would include sometimes more than a quarter of the population of the country, many of whom are essential for its functioning. Others wondered about what would happen if the same logic applied to prosecuting people in the public sector were to be extended to the private sector: thus applying prosecutions to informers and people who were not officially employed by the party.[14] Others yet wonder about the extent to which the Secret Security files are to be trusted, given that many of them have been tampered with on several occasions.

Added to this are concerns as to whether communist crimes can be considered individual or collective: to what extent the silent bystander was also guilty of the crime just as much as the criminal. Lustration policies, as they have been attempted up until now, have not been able to recognize any sense of collective guilt given the relatively small number of mechanisms that can be used to prosecute collectives. People like James Booth do however argue that despite institutional shortcomings, justice needs to be directly connected to remembering, and that it is essential to at least recognize the victims, even when prosecution is not possible, for forgetting can mean a second death.[15] Public condemnations that are not necessarily followed by prosecution either, because of lack of sufficient mechanisms or sometimes lack of evidence as required by the law, have played an important role historically, in cases like the Nuremberg trials, the Rwandan and Armenian genocide, and what some call the Sudan genocide.

That people are now able to visit a Rwandan genocide memorial or a Holocaust museum is most certainly not without consequence. Yet one need not forget that these public acts of condemnation are more than just important lessons for others to learn: they also play an important role in helping those who lived through the genocide or the Holocaust to renegotiate their past and their particular role within it. Some are more ready than others to do so. Visiting the Holocaust museum for a Holocaust survivor, just like visiting a genocide museum for a genocide survivor, is highly traumatic. People are sometimes shocked speechless for days, fall into dangerous trances where they relive the past as if it was happening right there and then, or simply break down and cry. For many, it is a part of their lives that they prefer to shut out of their memory and ignore for years on end. Going back to it is inevitably painful and while a sense of justice is often needed and demanded, trials and personal condemnations have only been able to erase some of the pain, if any.

If one can consider post-Nazi Germany or post-genocide

Rwanda as examples of lustrated societies, then they could provide us with a glimpse of what this kind of society would look like. Yet unlike Central and Eastern Europe, where lustration has often been associated with very negative connotations and described using terms such as hell, chaos, evil, witchhunt, absurd, surreal or Kafkaesque,[16] in these societies one can speak of a sense of social consensus on the issue of lustration—even if in some cases it has been forced by a formerly discriminated minority on the majority. Even with this sense of consensus, the past is far from being settled even in these lustrated societies, and in fact, it continues to threaten to burst out again in dangerous forms.

The question of whether people need to come to terms with the past in order to move into the future carefree remains on the table. The debate as to whether it is better to leave the past untouched for a while or whether it is essential to uncover it and bring it out into the open is still there, although our contemporaries seem to clearly lean towards the latter. The latest story surrounding the resignation of Polish Archbishop Stanislaw Wielgus—along with several other Polish priests—for his involvement with the Polish Secret Service[17] has certainly reinforced the need to reconsider what to do about Central and Eastern Europe's communist past. Although it is unlikely that we shall ever arrive at the straight answer to the question of what to do, perhaps the compromise that we will be able to arrive at is that we will need to continue to attempt more complex investigations into the nature of the different communist apparatuses, such as was attempted by the Tismaneanu Commission, despite the controversies that this will most likely spur.

Yet while doing so, we must not forget that beyond the newspaper articles, criticism and controversies lies an audience, and that this audience will certainly be affected by what is being said. The fact that the population at large seems tired to a point where it is willing to simply forget about the past is worrisome. The fact that they are turning a deaf ear to these arguments is either a sign of profound cynicism or distrust, as many of these arguments are viewed as yet another attempt at manipulation. The ability to trust has run short and, just like a traumatic experience that needs to be blocked out of our system, the communist past is both consciously and unconsciously rejected, and, as if to make up for it, the future is embraced with more enthusiasm than may be warranted by circumstances. One thus needs to learn to tread lightly on this issue and be concerned not only with larger issues of justice, truth, and memory, but also with the more direct impact that this will have on the Central and Eastern European population at large, that we can easily say has paid more than its fair price for this democratic transition.

The controversies surrounding the Tismaneanu report did however subside within enough time to allow the Romanian media to celebrate the country's official entry into the European Union. After such a long wait—Romania officially applied to join the EU back in 1995—the celebrations however seemed to lack the enthusiasm that one would expect, almost as if Romanians took this event for granted and quickly moved on with their everyday lives. Of course, this may also be because the accession, at least in the short term, has few direct implications for the majority of the population: except for the UK now opening its borders to Romanian citizens and talk of how the structural funds are to be spent, in all actuality, little change is expected to become visible in the immediate future. As the government prepares to spend the structural funds, the investments are not likely to be seen until 2009 or later, while Romania's "free" access to the EU labor market is still limited by a number of cumbersome restrictions that are not likely to be lifted until 2010, or later in some parts of the EU.

Perhaps the most visible celebrations of Romania's entry into the EU appeared in a series of publicity campaigns that monopolized the event in order to promote a number of different products. Ursus and Bucegi, two local beer producers, competed with each other by offering two very different projections of what Romania's entry into the EU meant for the population at large. While Ursus focused on the accession as opening the door to the West and bringing a whole new continent to our doorstep—as if Romania were not already part of that continent—the Bucegi campaign exhibited both excitement and a certain amount of hidden cynicism when it came to the accession, making fun of a series of EU regulations that will now come into effect—particularly those regarding the management of small family farms that still house a large percentage of Romania's population (over 30 percent). These two campaigns are, I believe, highly representative of the particular approach that Romanians have taken towards the EU accession: on the one hand a clear excitement over the opening of horizons; on the other hand, a certain amount of hesitation over the extent to which the EU's policies—particularly its agricultural policies—are necessarily fit to deal with the complexities of Romania's rural communities, considered to be the main location of poverty within the country. What these two campaigns reveal is both the nature of Romania's enthusiasm, as well as the extent to which the entry into the EU is very much seen as an economic benefit to be exploited by all those who can—hence the use of the very image of the EU to increase sales of a number of different products.

Silviu Nedelschi, the head of Copy Publicis—the company who directed the Ursus campaign—explains their choice for focusing on the accession moment in light of its historical symbolism as well as the need to rejoice in something that the country had been working towards for the past seventeen years. The Ursus advertisement does indeed reflect precisely this effort, by depicting hundreds of people pulling on a thick cord which brings Western Europe closer to our borders, enchanting us with images of the Eiffel Tower, the Leaning Tower of Pisa or Big Ben. The message is twofold: "Ursus beer flexes its muscles and brings the Eiffel Tower closer" and "Celebrate with Ursus Romania's success."[18] The attempt to appropriate Romania's success in joining the European Union is certainly not limited to beer companies, for this accession has been used and abused by a number of different people and companies to raise their profiles, almost as if without them, this accession would not have been possible.

The Bucegi campaign, although also centered around the moment of the EU accession, struck a series of different chords. As Alexandra Tinjala, General Manager of Sister—the publicity company that developed the campaign—explains: "Our public has a very healthy way of looking at this accession, a very Romanian, positive way of accepting a series of realities that are not exactly 'pink', and that is why I am not sure whether we necessarily chose this particular approach or whether it chose us."[19] What Mrs. Tinjala seems to be arguing is that their publicity spots were nothing but an accurate reflection of scenes and images that one might regularly encounter in everyday attitudes towards the EU. Staying close to the image of the simple Romanian, oftentimes the Romanian peasant, the advertisements supposedly exploit the true image of Romania, with the good and the bad. In fact, the Bucegi slogan has long been—even during the time of communism—together for better or for worse. And yet the slogan has now changed, slightly: they have added "from now on, for the better." If during communism it was fairly clear what the "for better or for worse" implied, today's hope for the better, following the EU accession, is also very straightforward and certainly reinforced by the theme of the new commertials: "Of all the moments in life, this time, Bucegi prefers the happy ones."

The new, accession-oriented advertisements focus on how the Romanian peasant, for example, will deal with the new EU regulations with regards to farm animals. One of the spots presents a visit to the parents, living in the countryside, and a meal conversation over a glass of Bucegi as to how they are going to deal with allocating enough square meters per chicken, given that their yard is not quite large enough to support them all—according to new EU regulations. The advertisement makes fun of what are perceived to be ridiculous farm regulations, instituted by people who have obviously never lived in a traditional farm and have in mind only the large, commercial farm model. If implemented, the new EU agricultural regulations will forever change the face of Romanian villages and along with them Romanian traditions, by challenging many common sense rules and habits that have until now been passed on from generation to generation and that will, from now on, have to be controlled by agencies and people over whom the peasants have little or no control.

To use Milan Kundera's metaphor, this is another instance of the "unbearable lightness of being," whereby difficult issues are tackled with a shrug and a glass of beer. And indeed, this seemed to be exactly how the new accession was celebrated: with a glass of bitter yet cold and well-deserved beer. While it may seem highly unconventional to use beer commercials as one the best metaphors of Romania's accession to the EU, this is in many ways highly representative of the state in which Romania finds itself now: for the most part eager to settle its accounts with the past—although not without a fight as to how exactly those accounts should be settled—and ready to plunge into the unknown with a certain amount of unbounded enthusiasm and a pragmatic—often bordering on the cynical—attitude towards its new community: the European Union.

The fact that Romania continues to contest its communist past and look for a "truth" about what happened even while it has officially stepped into the EU, is in many ways a direct result of the way in which the transition has been managed. The sense of secrecy and deceit still dominates most people's perception of the former communist party, the 1989 Revolution, and the institutional, political and economic reforms undertaken ever since. This sense of secrecy that is often said to hide rising instances of corruption and shameful behaviors may however overstate the actual relevance of the "secret" itself by transforming it into the holy grail that promises to deliver not just "the truth" but also an easy solution to political and economic struggles.

The following chapter seeks to understand how illusions such as the existence of a "truth" behind the veil of secrecy and deceit came into existence in the first place; why people insist on holding on to them despite evidence that their deliverance clearly does not meet expectations; and more importantly, what happens when people finally give up such illusions. While not necessarily focusing on the question of "secrecy," the chapter does propose to look at communism and capitalism as two different types of grand social illusions that are in turn sustained by a number of smaller illusions. The collapse of communism is thus seen not only as the collapse of a political and economic system, but more importantly as the collapse of a particular way of understanding the world and one's role within it. The consequences of this collapse of disillusionment are perhaps more daunting than one would imagine.

Notes

1 After this chapter was already finalized, another major event shook the Romanian headlines: in April 2007, the Romanian parliament voted to impeach President Basescu for unconstitutional behavior on the basis of a hand-written note that supposedly pointed to his attempt to interfere in the judicial process. Thirty days later, a popular referendum was held

on whether the president should be allowed to serve the remainder of his mandate. An overwhelming 75 percent of those who voted supported the president. The impeachment was to a large extent interpreted as an attempt of the opposition Social Democratic Party to regain power and stop the reform and anti-corruption process that President Basescu had initiated. While publication time-constraints will not allow for further elaboration on this event, suffice to say that the language in which the entire event was portrayed and examined often hinges on similar questions surrounding past involvement with the communist party, thus offering further support to the line of argumentation that this chapter follows with regards to the opening of the Secret Security Archives and the publication of the Presidential Report.

2   These files have been the center of many controversies given that they contained information about the entire underground system used by communists to identify enemies, spy and intimidate opponents.

3   For more details on this see: Ioana Borza, *Decommunization in Romania: A Case Study of the State Security Files Access Law*, 2007, available at: www.polito.ubbcluj.ro/EAST/East6/borza.htm (accessed March 29th, 2007).

4   These names appear at the beginning of the report itself.

5   The report is available online yet has not yet been translated into English. The Romanian version can be found on the site of the Romanian Presidency at: www.presidency.ro/?_RID=htm&id=82 (accessed March 27th, 2007).

6   For more information see: Vladimir Alexe, "Agentul Volodea," *Ziua* May 13th 2006; Administrator Asociatia Civic Media, *Ucis De Comisia Tismaneanu*, 2007, available at: http://civicmedia.ro/acm/index.php?option=com_content&task=view&id=63&Itemid=1 (accessed March 29th, 2007); Victor Roncea, "Tismaneanu Contestat De Dobre," *Ziua* January 15th, 2007; Maria Bercea, "Condamnarea Communismului Romanesc: Comisia Prezidentiala," *22* April 28th-May 4th, 2006; Ilarion Tiu, "Crimele Comunismului 'Marca' Tismaneanu," *Jurnalul National* December 20th, 2006.

7   C. Charles Bertschi, "Lustration and the Transition to Democracy: The Cases of Poland and Bulgaria," *East European Quarterly* 28.4 (1994).

8   Jacques Rupnik, "The Politics of Coming to Terms with the Communist Past: The Czech Case in Central European Perspective," *Transit online* 22 (2002), available at: www.iwm.at/index.php?option=com_content&task=view&id=286&Itemid=464.

9   Adam Michnik and Vaclav Havel, "Confronting the Past: Justice or Revenge?", *Journal of Democracy* 4.1 (1993), 27.

10 Bertschi, "Lustration and the Transition to Democracy: The Cases of Poland and Bulgaria."

11 Maria Los, "Lustration and Truth Claims: Unfinished Revolutions in Central Europe," *Law & Social Inquiry* 20.1 (1995).

12 Richard S. Esbenshade, "Remembering to Forget: Memory, History, National Identity in Postwar East-Central Europe," *Representations* 49, Winter (1995).

13 Luc Huyse, "Justice after Transition: On the Choices Successor Elites Make in Dealing with the Past," *Law & Social Inquiry* 20.1 (1995).

14 Helga A. Welsh, "Dealing with the Communist Past: Central and East European Experiences after 1990," *Europe-Asia Studies* 48.3 (1996).

15 W. James Booth, "The Unforgotten: Memories of Justice," *American Political Science Review* 95.4 (2001).
16 Los, "Lustration and Truth Claims: Unfinished Revolutions in Central Europe."
17 Celia Chauffour and Henri Tincq, "Les Fantomes De L'eglise Polonaise," *Le Monde* February 1st, 2007.
18 Alina Stanciu, "Publicitatea a Aderat O Data Cu Romanul (The Publicity World Acceded to the EU Along with the Romanians)," *Cotidianul* January 19th, 2007.
19 Stanciu, "Publicitatea a aderat o data cu Romanul (The Publicity World Acceded to the EU along with the Romanians)."

3
An anatomy of disillusionment

Why illusions and disillusions?

The word that has been perhaps most often employed to express the effects of the changes brought about by the collapse of the Berlin Wall and the 1989 revolutions across Central and Eastern Europe is disillusionment. People have generally used it as a way to describe a certain state of being—a sense of hopelessness—that had significant effects on both the physical and psychological ability of individuals to tackle the changes at hand. Disillusionment was mentioned in a number of different contexts, from studies on political and social apathy,[1] to studies on political and intellectual elites,[2] to medical and psychological studies[3] as well as journalistic reflections.[4] The conclusion was more often than not that disillusionment was pervasive and it interfered with citizens' ability and willingness to participate in the newly founded democracies of Central and Eastern Europe.

Attempts to engage with the issue of disillusionment in a more theoretical manner, as opposed to a purely descriptive one, have already been made, the latest and most notable one being perhaps Henri Vogt's book *Between Utopia and Disillusionment*.[5] In a similar move to the one attempted in this book, Vogt suggests that post-communist disillusionment was not only a result of dealing with corruption, economic collapse and communist elites returning to power: it was directly connected to particular revolutionary utopias, utopias of freedom and utopias of the future—whether it be entering NATO or the European Union. Defining utopias as a series of dreams and aspirations, Vogt focuses on how people have struggled to come to terms with the problematic nature of many of these utopias that became more and more visible in time. Basing his analysis on a series of interviews conducted in Estonia, East Germany and the former Czechoslovakia, he uses the transcripts of these interviews to underline both the differences in these utopias from country to country as well as a similar set of challenges that turned these utopias into disillusionment: a lack of a sense of justice following the 1989 revolutions, an increasing sense of individuality and social fragmentation, and rising post-revolutionary and postmodern ambivalence.

What this study adds to Vogt's engagement with the question of disillusionment, is both the empirical richness of yet another case-study—Romania—as well as a more focused attempt to understand not only what were the post-revolutionary utopias or illusions but also who helped define them and in what contexts. To do so, the study focuses on the Timisoara Revolutionaries—the first leaders of the Romanian Revolution—as well as the Group for Social Dialogue—the first civil society group to emerge immediately after the revolution—seeking to understand the basis on which the democratic future of Romania was built and questioning the extent to which these original ideals or illusions match up with later assumptions about what people wanted and how they envisioned the democratic transformation. The study also offers an alternative explanation and classification of utopias or illusions by turning towards the fields of sociology and psychology, in order to better understand the way in which individuals and collectives use these illusions to navigate instances of social change.

By arguing that disillusionment is an inevitable part of any process of transition or social change, the following seeks to understand both the positive and negative aspects of disillusionment, and explore the extent to which the concept can be used to offer an alternative way of interrogating and theorizing the changes in post-communist Central and Eastern Europe. By choosing a concept such as disillusionment as the entry point of analysis, the study consciously seeks to place the focus of the analysis on the people undergoing these transitions as opposed to the institutions and processes managing them. The choice to borrow more from the field of sociology and psychology should not be seen as an attempt to avoid engagement with the, by now, very rich literature on "transitology" and post-communist studies, but rather to point out that perhaps the current debates on how post-communist studies should be conducted within the fields of political science and comparative and regional studies have run dry precisely because of a lack of engagement with other literatures as well as other methodologies.[6] It should be no surprise then that more and more young scholars of post-communist Europe are turning towards fields such as cultural and visual studies, studies of everyday life or multi-disciplinary approaches in order to explore alternative methodologies for engaging the question of social change.[7] While the risk of being labeled as an "under-theorized" study runs higher with some of these approaches, taking that risk has already proven worthwhile in light of the wealth of highly intriguing empirical research and the development of new theoretical frameworks for studying transitions: such as study of nostalgia, emotionality and popular culture in transition.

There are a number of classical writers and established scholars that have in one way or another pointed out the intrinsic connection between disillusionment and social change, the most famous of which is perhaps Durkheim, with his studies on suicide[8] as well as his most famous work, the *Division of Labor in Society*.[9] His notion of anomie captures both the physical and psychological impact of radical social change on the individual, while also offering a way of understanding the breakup and re-establishment of social solidarities. But like other scholars of his time, Durkheim mainly saw disillusionment—or in his case anomie—as a negative side-effect of transitions, one that could be overcome in time, but had to be endured during the actual transition. Marx's concept of alienation falls, in many way, along similar lines of thought, pointing to yet another negative consequence of the formation of capitalist relations: the precedence of consumption and production over all other forms of social relations.[10]

The transition towards a possible positive understanding of disillusionment came only later, with social scientists associating periods of social change with increasing possibilities for self-reflection and reassessment of one's social and political environment. Peter Sloterdijk's studies on cynicism are one such example,[11] along with Jose Ortega Y Gasset,[12]

Erich Fromm,[13] Ghita Ionescu[14] and Charles Taylor's[15] work on disillusionment and self-reflection in modernity. The recent engagements with the question of hope within the Central and Eastern European context should also be seen as a direct result of the increasing understanding of disillusionment as a dual concept: one that includes not only the negative aspects of the loss of particular illusions but also the positive aspect of building new ones.

Alina Mungiu-Pippidi, Katherine Verdery and Vaclav Havel are among the few Eastern European writers to attempt to conceptualize the role of hope in transition societies. Mungiu-Pippidi coined the terms "hope capital" and "negative social capital" to underline the fact that hope should be seen as an essential political and social resource that can make or break transition societies.[16] Havel also points out in several of his speeches that without hope, freedom and democracy would simply not be possible. If hope is the modern faith that is required to build modern societies, then hope needs to be cultivated and encouraged. Katherine Verdery takes a slightly different approach to the question of hope, focusing on the issue of excessive or unfounded hope, which, she argues, can easily lead to irrational and highly detrimental behaviors, such as investing in bound-to-collapse pyramid schemes, or attributing god-like characteristics to key people and politicians who are perceived to be the only ones able to provide relief.[17]

In the field of psychology, Stanley Teitelbaum also focuses on some of the positive aspects of illusions,[18] particularly on what he calls positive and necessary illusions. Positive illusions are the illusions that help improve your image of yourself and thus positively impact your life through a change in attitude, while necessary illusions are illusions that act as a buffer or protection mechanism from realizing the true nature of things. Each of these illusions plays an essential role in organizing the reality of our everyday life as well as fulfilling a set of essential wishes and expectations even in contexts of adversity. In fact, Teintelbaum goes as far as to argue that without these positive illusions, society could not exist as we know it today. Building on his analysis of individual illusions, this study seeks to argue that collective illusions are essential for maintaining a particular organization of society—institutional as well as ideological—

and that the loss of these collective illusions necessarily corresponds with the construction of new ones.

The response patterns to the loss of illusions that Teitelbaum draws out are important to understanding processes of disillusionment at the collective level. Teitelbaum identifies a series of common response patterns to the loss of individual illusions: 1) acceptance of reality; 2) denial and distortion of reality; 3) the formation of replacement illusions; 4) defensive hyper-vigilance; and 5) despair. Each of these response patterns could also be applied to the collective level and in fact, many of these responses do correspond to a series of important phenomena noted throughout post-communist Central and Eastern European states. The type of response could thus be connected not only to a particular communist legacy—that helped shape a particular set of illusions—but also to the extent to which the social organization, the social routine, was dependent on those illusions.

Thus, a country with strong collectivist measures will be particularly resistant to privatization, just like a country with strong state institutions and strong attachment to ranks within those institutions will be particularly resistant to institutional reform. A country where the level of dependency on state institutions is particularly high—high rates of employment in state industries, complete reliance on the state for the provision of different social services such as education, health care, retirement—will put up resistance to reforms that challenge that routine even in situations where the overall goal of the routine may prove to be harmful. Under this interpretation, behaviors such as support of liberal parties combined with demonstrations against job loss caused by privatization, no longer appear contradictory, but rather consistent with a particularly defensive way of dealing with lost illusions and the construction of new ones.

These defensive attitudes, often expressed through what many label as disillusionment, should not necessarily be interpreted as negative, for as Paul Kwon,[19] Julie Norem and Nancy Cantor,[20] and Phebe Cramer[21] argue, not all forms of disillusionment are negative. Focusing on concepts such as defensive hopelessness or defensive pessimism, they argue that setting unrealistically low expectations in a risky situation can be constructive in some cases, given that it forces one to work harder in order to avoid failure. On the reverse, they also argue that not all forms of positive illusions are constructive in the long run. In fact, some may turn out to be dangerous, as setting unrealistically high expectations risks making even a relatively positive result look like a failure.

Making the distinction between positive and negative disillusionment is particularly important for understanding that not all instances of post-communist disillusionment can be interpreted under a similar framework—generally one that suggests negative consequences, such as interference with the democracy building and reform process, weak participation in civil society or antisocial behavior. It is by now clear that certain aspects of disillusionment have proven to be quite beneficial, with intellectual disillusionment providing a critical understanding of social transformations in general as well as toning down the initial enthusiasm about the transition to a Western capitalist-style democracy, and collective disillusionment lowering the general level of expectations, thus releasing the weak post-communist states from pressures that they would not have been able to withstand.

Understanding the extent to which disillusionment is an intrinsic part of any large process of social change, or transition, could also help relieve some of the panic that tends to surround these periods, while pushing us to focus not only on the cause of disillusionment, but rather on the way in which new illusions are built. As expressed before, it is essential to look at disillusionment as a double process—one in which old illusions are lost, but also one in which new illusions necessarily have to emerge.[22] It is unfortunate that during times of transition, new illusions are often embraced without question—at least until much later, thus often leading to unrealistic expectations that cannot be met or checked. A clearer understanding of the process of disillusionment as connected to social change would hopefully alleviate such tendencies.

Classical studies on the purpose-giving role of traditional illusions—often labeled as myths—provide a basis on which a theory of emerging illusions during periods of change could be built. Mircea Eliade's contributions in the *The Sacred and the Profane*[23] are particularly relevant for discussions on differences between traditional and modern illusions, focusing on the way in which societies are organized along time and space coordinates[24] while Levi-Strauss's contributions in

Myth and Meaning[25] are also particularly important for understanding the role of illusions in forming different types of social solidarity, often based on a common understanding of the universe. Freud's study of illusions as different forms of escape in *Civilization and Its Discontents*[26] helps us understand the need for new illusions as a form of releasing feelings of collective guilt and finding comfort, while Zizek's work on the role of illusions in modern ideological regimes—communism and capitalism—is also an essential starting point for understanding not only the manipulation of illusions, but more importantly, the way in which they are silently integrated into our everyday activities.[27] While a proper development and engagement with these studies would necessitate a book in itself, the remainder of the chapter attempts a humble approach to understanding the illusions on which the modern ideologies of communism and capitalism were built, as a way of framing later discussions on the Romanian Revolution, the emergence of the first civil society groups and popular perceptions of the transition.

The communist versus the capitalist illusion

In her book, *Dreamworld and Catastrophe*, Susan Buck-Morss refers to communism (socialism) and capitalism as the two dominating mass utopias (we could call them mass illusions) of the twentieth century. The dreams of these two illusions were powerful enough to justify the complete restructuring of the societies that chose to dream them in hope of harmony and prosperity for all:

> The construction of mass utopia was the dream of the twentieth century. It was the driving ideological force of industrial modernization in both its capitalist and socialist forms. The dream was itself an immense material power that transformed the natural world, investing industrially produced objects and built environments with collective, political desire. Whereas the night dreams of individuals express desires thwarted by the social order and pushed backward into regressive childhood forms, this collective dream dared to imagine a social world in alliance with personal happiness, and promised to adults that its realization would be in harmony with the overcoming of scarcity for all.[28]

Turning these two utopias into reality, Buck-Morss argues,

allowed for the creation of two of the most disruptive and violent social projects, one of which so far has collapsed under its own weight. Buck-Morss however, is quick to point out that while it may seem like the end of the Cold War has already designated the victor in the unspoken competition between the two utopias, the fall of the communist illusion does not point to the strengths of capitalism, but quite the contrary. Given that both utopias were based on more or less similar promises of collective happiness and materialism through the sovereign structure of the state, Buck-Morss warns that they may be more similar than we think, not only in their functioning but also in their ultimate effects. That communism collapsed first is not necessarily an indication that capitalism might not do the same one day.

Borrowing Walter Benjamin's notion of dreamworlds to describe the illusion of communism and capitalism, Buck-Morss seeks to understand the turning point at which dreamworlds become negative or dangerous:

> Dreamworlds become dangerous when their enormous energy is used instrumentally by structures of power, mobilized as an instrument of force that turns against the very masses who were supposed to benefit. If the dreamed-of potential for social transformation remains unrealized, it can teach future generations that history has betrayed them. And in fact, the most inspiring mass-utopian projects of mass sovereignty, mass production, mass culture—have left a history of disasters in their wake. The dream of mass sovereignty has led to world wars of nationalism and to revolutionary terror. The dream of industrial abundance has enabled the construction of global systems that exploit both human labor and natural environments. The dream of culture for the masses has created a panoply of phantasmagoric effects that aestheticize the violence of modernity and anaesthetize its victims.[29]

The dream becomes dangerous when concrete mechanisms are set in place to turn it into reality, when the entire energy of a society is consumed in seeking to achieve the dream, when no sacrifices are big enough for the ultimate goal and more importantly, when the political and economic structure that sustains the dream becomes too strong and too important in our daily routines, that a change, or an awakening from the dream, seems impossible. Perhaps the awakening from the communism dream was only made possible by the existence of an alternate dream: the dream of capitalism.

Were it not for this, would people have been so willing to go through yet another social restructuring? And yet the dream is essential to our modern existence. Dreams give people the illusion that they are special, they give them a sense of identity and a sense of purpose in a world that would otherwise seem to be spinning completely outside of their control. The energy that dreams can gather—easily seen in the monumental projects made possible by these dreams—is testimony to both the power of dreams as well as the necessity of dreams.

The collapse of the dream, according to Benjamin, as well as Buck-Morss, is the moment of awakening from the dream, or if one were to allow a parallel between the concept of a dream and that of an illusion, it is the moment of disillusionment. Negotiating the loss of a powerful social illusion is certainly not easy. The awakening takes time and is often dependent on the existence of a safety net, another dream to fall back on. The idea that one could remain awakened without entering a new illusion or dream seems questionable in at least two different ways: is such an awakening ever possible and is such an awakening desirable?

The discussions concerning the possibility of a "third way" in Central and Eastern Europe live under the illusion that not only would a "third way" be possible, but also that the "third way" would be free of the dangerous dream-like nature of the other two ideological possibilities. Given that much of the intellectual community of Central and Eastern Europe was hoping for a more creative approach to what was to come after the fall of communism, the Bulgarian philosopher Ivailo Ditchev argues that the lack of such a creative approach has had a devastating effect on the spirit of these societies:

> Looking West for the natural, post-communist countries see nothing. There exists a vast number of means to solve problems of situations but no representation of ends, no idea of the meaning of the whole [...] Post-communist countries today are haunted by the idea that there was nothing symbolic in the defeat of communism.[30]

And yet some of these creative approaches were at least imagined by a series of different Central and Eastern European writers: people like Agnes Heller, G.M. Tamas, Gyorgy Konrad and Vaclav Havel all hoped that the fall of communism would signify more than an awakening from the communist dream, and hoped for an awakening from the dream of modern ideologies in general. Agnes Heller provides the option of pursuing a capitalist illusion in which the technological imagination can be combined with what she calls the historical imagination. While the technological imagination supports the idea of progress and justifies any and all sacrifices required to achieve it, the historical imagination questions costs that appear too high: hopelessness, poverty, unemployment. She seems to propose a more tame capitalism, one that would fall more along the lines of a social democracy, in which progress—technological progress mainly—would not always carry a positive connotation independent of its consequences.[31]

G.M. Tamas, Gyorgy Konrad and Vaclav Havel all propose different versions for the development of a third way, yet agree that it would need to be based on something similar to an apolitical democracy. Agreeing that the Eastern European understanding of democracy was significantly different from that of the West and that the democratic ideal in Eastern Europe was essentially antipolitical, they each propose different systems that would accommodate this. In his most famous work, *Antipolitics*, Konrad imagines a society in which politics is devoid of power and becomes instead a forum of discussion in which leaders naturally emerge and replace one another.[32] Havel imagines a similar society in which the guiding force is not representative democracy, but rather a naturally emerging form of morality—what Tamas calls commonplace morality—whose main principle is "living in truth."[33] This morality that Havel imagines seems to be both a bottom-up as well as a top-down morality, in which society controls the moral direction of the state and vice versa. Tamas is perhaps the most pessimistic of the three, arguing that while an apolitical third way would be desirable, this third way is not likely to be achieved because the thirst for power will always be too strong to make politics any different from what they have always been. Perhaps the saddest thing about the transition to capitalism, according to Tamas, is that it may simply be the default solution to the failure of socialism rather than the victory of liberal democracy.[34] Tamas's warning about the moral exhaustion of the liberal regime across the world is something that requires serious consideration, for today's circumstances have created a situation where, despite our awareness of the shortcomings of this regime, we continue to embrace it without the due criticism.[35]

Building the communist illusion—an insider's perspective

To better understand the nature of the ideological illusion in the Central and Eastern European context as well as the consequences and trajectory of its birth, acceptance and later collapse, a closer examination of the communist illusion is required. As the only modern ideology that has experienced the full cycle of birth, mass acceptance, collapse and some would now argue even revival or reform, the communist illusion is perhaps our best case-study for understanding both the appeal as well as the dangers of modern ideologies. Looking at the communist illusion through the eyes of an intellectual who has personally experienced both its appeal as well as its rejection—Arthur Koestler—gives us an insider's perspective to how the illusion was built, sustained and, after long struggles, rejected in its structure. While many others have written about the nature of the communist illusion,[36] Koestler's account very gracefully emphasizes the extent to which seemingly strong collective embracing of the communist illusion was built on contradictory and often very shaky individual commitments, thus providing an interesting perspective for understanding the dual natural of the process of disillusionment and illusion formation. Koestler's account, while clearly not exhaustive of all other accounts, is particularly relevant to the positive and negative aspects of disillusionment.

The idea that the power of the communist illusion lies in propaganda alone is simply mistaken. People were not necessarily fooled into accepting communism. Its appeal went beyond its promises or rationale. As Arthur Koestler explains, communism was like a religion, a faith that was much needed at the time. Communism did not just promise to heal the wounds of a war. It captured people's imagination and fed their need to have the world around them redefined, to find new meaning in it, to find new roles for themselves in it. Reason alone cannot explain its origin. The revolutionary appeal is attractive in itself, precisely because of its uncompromising, radical and purist nature. The promise of a complete break with an unwanted past and embracing an ideal is often too difficult to resist.

> A faith is not acquired by reasoning. One does not fall in love with a woman, or enter the womb of a church, as a result of logical persuasion. Reason may defend an act of faith—but only after the act has been committed, and the man committed to the act. Persuasion may play a part in a man's conversion; but only the part of bringing to its full and conscious climax a process which has been maturing in regions where no persuasion can penetrate.[37]

Koestler places the attraction to communism between two poles: the devotion to some form of pure utopia and the revolt against a polluted society. His justification for joining the communist movement is very simple: "I became converted because I was ripe for it and lived in a disintegrating society thirsting for faith."[38] Disintegrating societies are thus particularly prone to new forms of illusions or ideologies. For when all resources are wasted, the only one that is left is hope, hope against all hope, hope even when the promise of that hope seems and often is impossible to achieve. In a polluted society, the need for purity, for the ideal, is perhaps more intense that the rationale that clearly states that it is impossible to achieve.

Communism appealed to those who needed hope the most: those highly sensitive to change—artists and intellectuals, the poor and the minorities. That Koestler was an intellectual coming from a family that had lost its fortune leaving him to struggle at an early age is no coincidence. Yet Koestler's engagement with communism, like the engagement of most of those who truly believed in it, went beyond its intellectual appeal.

For even early on, communism exhibited a mix of openness and closure, of exploration and secrecy, of trust and distrust of structures. As a critique, communism seemed open to any and all experimentation, as reflected by many of its supporters in the theater, literature and the arts. As a political apparatus however, it left little room for creativity, stifling it through secrecy, the obvious lack of trust, the over-reliance on set rules and organizational structures that did not always seem to make sense, and the reticence to allow any form of self-criticism.

Just like love and faith are often blind, so was communism. For as Koestler explains: "Faith is a wondrous thing; it is not only capable of moving mountains, but also of making you believe that a herring is a race horse."[39] The process through which this belief was often channeled was "dialectical thinking." The idea of dialectical thinking was used to confuse and justify by the same logic as the "divide and conquer" technique. The challenge of previous thought structures, as well as social and political structures, served two roles: to destroy what was before and to reinforce the party as the only stable and trustworthy structure. Dialectical thinking came to mean that everything and anything could be justified as long as it came from the party. And perhaps the most powerful mechanism of indoctrination was allowing people to each find their own different justification for otherwise unexplainable acts. Thus, as Koestler explains, communism was not only addictive but also forced you to play Wonderland croquet with yourself.

For a while, the party actions allowed for many doubts to seep in. Even in the most doubtful moments, the party still seemed like the only mechanism for reform, and thus all faults had to be addressed from the inside, without destroying the overall structure for "once you stepped out of it [...] nothing which you said or did had the slightest chance of influencing its course."[40] The idea that communism could be reformed, that it continued to be the best alternative even when it was obvious that its means were doubtful, is what allowed it to survive for as long as it did. That communism worked like a faith, meant that giving up faith involved much more than simply stepping out of the party structure: it involved a deep personal struggle, an empty space left behind, a hollowness and a deep sense of disappointment not only with the party but also with oneself. When faced with such a desperate choice, one is often willing to accept lies and treat them as hopeful relief from a present that would otherwise be dry of all hope. Comparing communism to a walk through the desert, Koestler seeks to explain his own inner struggles through his "fictional" character in his novel, *Darkness at Noon*:

> History has taught us that often lies serve her better than the truth; for man is sluggish and has to be led through the desert for forty years before each step in his development. And he has to be

driven through the desert with threats and promises, by imaginary terrors and imaginary consolations, so that he should not sit down prematurely to rest and divert himself by worshipping golden calves [..] We are doing the work of prophets without their gift. We replaced vision by logical deduction; but although we all started from the same point of departure, we came to divergent results. Proof disproved proof, and finally we had to recur to faith—to axiomatic faith in the rightness of one's own reasoning. That is the crucial point. We have thrown all ballast overboard; only one anchor holds us: faith in one's self. Geometry is the purest realization of human reason; but Euclid's axioms cannot be proved. He who does not believe in them sees the whole building crash.[41]

It seems that reason and faith have to go together for modern societies to exist, for social structures to survive. The co-dependence between the two—reason often seems to require faith for people to follow an idea while faith often seems to require reason for the modern individual to follow through as well—has created a modern society like no other: one that requires a much deeper level of maturity and knowing itself in order to truly understand the best choices and directions to go towards. The equal need for freedom and protection forms a love–hate relationship with the state that neither the communist nor the democratic, capitalist state has truly been able to address. The swinging back and forth between the two is perhaps a sign of just that. Maturity requires understanding and yet a full understanding of the social consequences of our actions and progress may not be possible in the amount of time that we have allowed ourselves. As Koestler explains, we may have outdone ourselves, reaching a point where our scientific discoveries have pushed us into a world that we are simply not ready for, emotionally or rationally:

A people's capacity to govern itself democratically is thus proportionate to the degree of its understanding of the structure and functioning of the whole social body [...] Every technical improvement creates a new complication to the economic apparatus, causes the appearance of new factors and combinations, which the masses cannot penetrate for a time. Every jump of technical progress leaves the relative intellectual development of the masses a step behind, and thus causes a fall in the political-maturity thermometer [...] The peoples of Europe are still far from having mentally digested the consequences of the steam engine. The capitalism system will collapse before the masses have understood it.[42]

There are several essential aspects of this testimony that need to be underlined in support of arguments presented earlier in the chapter: 1) Koestler's clear support for the necessity of illusions and hope in the construction of new forms of social organization; 2) his argument that oftentimes the need for illusions and hope is stronger than the logical justification for their particular functioning; 3) his emphasis on the fact that doubt and desperate choices often lead to unwanted compromises; and 4) his conviction that our ability to understand the development of new illusions often lags far behind on the timeline of events. The significance of this will be addressed in the chapters to come, while the remainder of this chapter seeks to underline precisely how a similar framework can be applied to understanding the development of Romanian communism, through the eyes of another insider, Prof. Vladimir Tismaneanu.

The construction of Romanian communism—another insider's perspective

Just like any other national brand of communism, Romanian communism had its own particularities that cannot be ignored when attempting to discuss this particular case-study. The initial dependence on the Russian communist party, the initial appeal to an elite group of people who were the ones to take much of the blame after the fall of communism, the cult of personality developed around Ceausescu as well as the swift nature of reforms introduced in order to sustain the powerful industrialization pushed forward by communism, are among some of the most important particulars that one needs to keep in mind when examining post-communist Romania and more importantly, what is often labeled as disillusionment in post-communist Romania. So how was the communist illusion built in Romania? Vladimir Tismaneanu, a Romanian historian and political philosopher, attempts to answer this question in his latest book entitled *Stalinism for All Seasons*.[43] The product of twenty-five years of research and writing, the book is perhaps one of the most comprehensive studies of Romanian communism ever to be written, and thus an important account to discuss.[44]

Perhaps the most important characteristic that the book focuses on is the tenuous relationship between Romanian communism and Russian Stalinism. While fiercely upheld at first, Russian Stalinism was later rejected in order to make room for the local consolidation of power and for an alternative route to development, one that while equally violent, tended to experiment more with ideas coming from other communist regimes like China or North Korea. During the sixty-eight years of Romanian communism however, there is little indication of any true, widespread intellectual and philosophical fascination with communism. While idealized, communism was introduced as a political model of social organization as opposed to a critique of history and philosophy. The model under which the Romanian communist party developed was clearly the Russian model, one that imposed itself as superior, as a disciplinary father figure, as one that could not be crossed, questioned or by any means surpassed. The Romanian communist "child" thus grew up with a deep feeling of inferiority, illegitimacy to a certain extent, and fear. As Tismaneanu well puts it:

> Romanian communism developed a peculiar political culture with characteristics deriving both from the national character and the international Leninist tradition: suspiciousness, a deep inferiority complex, a sense of illegitimacy, political narcissism, sectarianism, anti-intellectualism, and an obsession with political and social "transformism."[45]

The obsession with social "transformism" that Tismaneanu talks about is perhaps what motivated the very radical transformation of Romanian society in these sixty-eight years: starting as an agricultural society that maintained many of its medieval practices and features of local organization, Romania went straight into the deep industrial era with impressive projects and a relatively high rate of development. The optimism associated with these transformations became obsessive, particularly in its representations in connection to two of the main leaders of the Romanian communist regime: Gheorghe Gheorghiu-Dej and later, Nicolae Ceausescu. While the outside was beaming with images of success and optimism, the inside was lurking with political intrigue, a clear lust for power and quite a bit of fear, doubt and self-doubt that needed to be controlled with an excessive confidence on the outside. Romanian communism was thus embodied by these two main characters, coming to life through their actions, reforms and policy choices. The illusion of communism was thus an illusion concerning the strength of these two characters to provide hope and deliver their promises. Hope, they certainly did provide.

Ceausescu's charisma and his unprecedented understanding of the importance and efficiency of propaganda, allowed him to demand sacrifices that would otherwise have seemed inconceivable. His ability to portray the final goal in a glorious manner, to build in Romanians a sense of confidence and superiority that was for the most part unfounded, created a society that was able to fool itself into thinking not only that it was progressing at higher speeds than many other countries, but also that truly believed—and in many ways continues to believe—itself to be superior to everybody else. The loss of the communist illusion thus meant a lot more than the loss of the illusion of a glorious future—now to a certain extent counterbalanced by the promises of capitalism and entering the EU. It also meant a loss of confidence, a confidence that was essential to how an entire generation defined itself and thought of its role in the world.

The sense of sacrifice needed to propel the Romanian society into the future demanded in many ways similar reforms—in their radical nature—to the ones experienced during shock therapy after the fall of communism. The process of nationalization, collectivization, and rapid industrialization quickly transformed the Romanian landscape into something almost unrecognizable, forever changing the way people were going to live their lives, breaking up traditional family units, creating an over-reliance on the party and the state, tying people to jobs and homes that were not necessarily the best fit and pushing them into a routine that was inescapable outside of short trips to the countryside. The country was transformed to a point where these changes appeared almost normal, where resistance could mainly be imagined in the form of demanding better life conditions as opposed to a change in ideology. Ceausescu and the Romanian communist party seemed to have managed the impossible: to get the pauper to believe to be king, the beast to be beauty and the Romanian to be happy. And yet that was not the case.

As strong as the Romanian illusion may have appeared on the

outside, Tismaneanu points out that the party remained quite controversial throughout its lifespan: initially very weak, with a very small mass base and weak appeal to both masses and intellectuals—who seemed more concerned with the question of nationalism than that of class struggle—the party was also deeply affected by a series of other weakening factors like the socio-economic structure (agrarian character) of Romanian society, the non-Romanian ethnic origin of many socialist and communist leaders (Jewish and Hungarian), the disregard displayed by the Romanian Communist Party (RCP) towards traditional national aspirations, and perhaps most importantly, the fact that the Romanian socialists were campaigning for a virtually nonexistent class—there was no working class in Romania at the time, just farmers.[46]

The need to build up a working class required quite an effort, allowing the party to play off the intellectuals and the minorities against the masses and to later reject and punish its initial supporters—the Jews and the Hungarians—in order to appease the nationalist sentiments that dominated the masses. The first disillusionment with Romanian communism thus came much earlier than 1989, for it became clear to many of those who were on the inside that this was just a game that needed to be played in a way that would mostly benefit the leadership and help them consolidate power. The intellectuals and the minorities—often part of the same group—were thus the first to be alienated and harshly punished for any form of resistance. Their awakening could not be made public or else it would risk awakening everybody else.

The Romanian Communist Party's relationship with intellectuals was thus significantly different from that of other communist parties. The RCP counted few intellectuals, who for the most part were distrusted as being part of the traditional upper classes in Romania (the only ones who could be educated). By placing workers in charge of all the important positions within the party, there was more of an assurance that there would be little resistance and that infighting for power would be restricted to insider games and political maneuvers that would remain at most opaque from the outside. This also ensured that there was no or little written history (institutional memory) outside of a few members entrusted with writing often pre-approved slogans and lines of thought.

With no intellectuals to denounce the nonsensical decision-making process of the party, the construction of the Romanian communist illusion moved ahead unobstructed, guided by the official line of thought and action of the RCP and later, of the Romanian party elite. Tismaneanu describes the communist ideology in Romania as being dominated by two separate and yet clearly interdependent trends: national communism and national Stalinism. National communism repudiated universal recipes and theoretical ossification, by maintaining the right of each party to pursue its own strategy regardless of Soviet interests. It questioned the dogma of the dictatorship of the proletariat and asserted that reform, including party reform, was inevitable. National Stalinism opposed any form of liberalization, let alone democratization. Reactionary and self-centered, it valued autarky and exclusiveness; it clung to a number of presumably universal laws of socialist revolution and treated any deviation from these as a betrayal of class principles; it played on sentiments of national isolation, humiliation and panic. The difference between the two was skillfully used to portray whatever image of Romania seemed more desirable at the time for those on the outside, yet on the inside their effects turned them into one and the same.

The smart political maneuvering between national communism and national Stalinism, depending on the situation at hand (national communism when the Russian influence was beginning to threaten the authority of the party and its leaders and national Stalinism when Russia had taken the road of reform and was encouraging all its allies to do the same), allowed the RCP to play off the national pride of Romanians and maintain the illusion that they were protecting the country's best interests. Maintaining a clear separation between the Romanian Communist Party and the Russian Communist Party was probably one of the policies that allowed for the continued support of the RCP at a time when resentment for anything foreign was growing. This resentment also made it easier for the country to be sealed off from any Western influences without much protest from the inside (other than some of the minority communities that suddenly found themselves separated from their mother countries, cultures and populations).

There are thus several things that allowed the Romanian

communist illusion to be maintained for as long as it was: the ability of the RCP to play their cards right when it came to maintaining power in all circumstances (with or independent of Russia's actions), the lack of a stronger intellectual class to denounce what was happening, the dependency of the working class on the party and the state, the formation of a necessary routine that governed all aspects of social life, and the normalization of sacrifice to a point where it was no longer perceived to be unusual. The collapse of the communist illusion, while sudden in its unfolding, was not necessarily intended as such, as we will see in the following chapters. The strength of the communist illusion lay perhaps in its ability to establish a strong sense of routine, which even when painful, provided one with a certain peace of mind and reasonable expectations of how the future was going to unfold. For the majority of the population, life under communism meant that one knew exactly the steps one needed to take: pursue a career that would likely keep one close to one's home town, benefit fully from all forms of social security, form friendships with the proper food and clothes distributors, and life was not so bad. The party membership guaranteed you a job upon graduation, an apartment that often came with the job, a series of other benefits including free healthcare, childcare and education. That none of these allowed for much individual choice or provided the best quality care is a different issue. These benefits however did succeed in providing an important sense of stability that is still longed for seventeen years into the transition.

As long as one embraced the ignorance and routine imposed by the party, there was no reason to fear any punishment. And the population at large was, for the most part, ready to do just that. The lack of alternatives, the constant indoctrination, the few rewards, the sense of stability and the normalization of the process of immiseration, allowed the communist illusion to set on the Romanian population like an invisible net, with just enough room to breathe, mate, and survive. Any break in the net was quickly fixed and covered, any movement from one side of the net to the other was carefully controlled, and the obstacles were perceived as natural steps that one had to take to achieve some form of satisfaction. Providing one's kids with enough to eat, warm clothing and an education, was enough to make most families happy.

This guaranteed the survival of the illusion at the mass level. The political infighting at the top remained for the most part invisible and did not affect the sense of stability that was hanging by a thread.

Any threats to this stability—like the Targu Jiu (later the Valea Jiului) and the Brasov demonstrations that will be discussed later—were quickly covered up, signaling however the slow erosion and collapse of the party mechanism. While preparation for an inevitable collapse was probably taking place at the top, the majority of the population remained engulfed in their routines. Only a change to this routine could challenge the party. The ideational forces played little role in bringing about the mass demonstrations that ultimately led to the collapse of the system. Most of the people that were out in the streets in December 1989 were not there to fulfill any high ideals of democracy or freedom, but because this was a change in the routine. People came out into the streets because others were out in the streets, because they were excited to do so and were curious to follow these exciting new developments. People yelled out "Down with Ceausescu!" because others were yelling it, because it suddenly seemed right to do so in public, not because they had planned to do so anytime in the past. Once the routine was broken, the spell of the party was broken along with it and the organizational system collapsed in an instant.[47]

The collapse of the communist illusion in Romania was a direct result of the collapse of the organizational mechanism that guided the actions and routine imposed on the population at large. The indoctrination process seemed in the end to simply convince people to accept a stable routine rather than make them truly believe in the superiority and importance of the party. No arduous belief in the tenets of the party seems visible beyond mere recitation or sporadic excitement brought about by party-organized public demonstrations of allegiance to the party and its all-powerful leader. This however, is not to say that there was a strong sense of what the alternative to the party would be. Democracy and capitalism were clearly misunderstood, being often confused with a certain standard of living that did not necessitate any sacrifice or radical change in the social, economic or political structure. Embracing democracy was thus probably more random than we would really like to accept. While there was a sense of what people did not want, there was certainly not a clear sense of what they did want, something that became fairly obvious in the days, weeks and months following the revolution.

As we were soon to find out though, the routine of communism was not something that would be quickly erased. Its logic continued to govern the way in which Romanian society functioned, following the immediate chaos of the revolution. When many of the structures that sustained the routine simply collapsed, people had nothing to fall back on, no familiar ground, no guarantees, no calm. Freedom and democracy meant little when one could not properly use them or understand them. The learning process meant that Romanian society had to undergo perhaps an even deeper series of changes than those initially required by communism, in order to adapt to the reform process. This process of transition from one illusion to another was deeply marked by a series of different shocks, some labeled as "positive" or "negative shock," some as "shock therapy," and others as "collective culture shock."

Among these different labels, shock emerges as an essential concept for understanding the transition from one political illusion to another, and more importantly the intricate justification system that transformed individual and collective pains and sacrifice into a masochistic process of enjoyment that awed and traumatized at the same time. The following chapter describes the shock of the transition as both painful and thrilling, a means of experiencing as well as negotiating change, an opportunity for self-reflection and a way of absorbing increasing levels of change that characterize not only so-called transition societies, but all modern societies.

Notes

1 Mikolaj Czesnik, "Voter Turnout and Democratic Legitimacy in Central Eastern Europe," *Polish Sociological Review* 4.156 (2006); Jan Culik, "Profound Disillusionment," *Central Europe Review* 1.20 (1999); Charles H. Fairbanks Jr., "Ten Years after the Soviet Breakup: Disillusionment in the Caucasus and Central Asia," *Journal of Democracy* 12.4 (2001); Alina Mungiu-Pippidi, "10 Years of Illusions," 22 January 25th–31st, 2000.

2 Andras Bozoki (ed.), *Intellectuals and Politics in Central Europe*

(Budapest: Central European University Press, 1999); Beata Barbara Czajkowska, "From Tribunes to Citizens: Polish Intelligentsia During and after Communism," unpublished dissertation, University of Maryland, 1999; Vaclav Havel, *The Power of the Powerless: Citizens against the State in Central and Eastern Europe* (New York: Palach Press, 1985); Arthur Koestler, *Darkness at Noon*, trans. Daphne Hardy (New York: MacMillan Company, 1941); George Konrad, *The Melancholy of Rebirth: Essays from Post-Communist Central Europe 1989–1994*, trans. Michael Henry Heim (New York: Harcourt Brace & Company, 1995); George Konrad and Ivan Szelenyi, *Intellectuals on the Road to Class Power*, trans. Andrew Arato and Richard Allen (New York: Harcourt Brace Jovanovich, 1979); Vladimir Tismaneanu, "Dialectics of Disenchantment," *Debates on the Future of Communism*, ed. Vladimir Tismaneanu and Judith Shapiro (New York: St. Martin's Press, 1991).

3 Brittney Beck, Steen Halling, Marie McNabb, Daniel Miller, Jan O. Rowe and Jennifer Schulz, "Facing up to Hopelessness: A Dialogal Phenomenological Study," *Journal of Religion and Health* 42.4 (2003); Phebe Cramer, "Defense Mechanisms in Psychology Today," *American Psychologist* 55.6 (2000); Paul Kwon, "Hope, Defense Mechanisms, and Adjustment: Implications for False Hope and Defensive Hopelessness," *Journal of Personality* 70.2 (2002); Stanley H. Teitelbaum, *Illusion and Disillusionment: Core Issues in Psychotherapy* (Northvale: John Aronson Inc., 1999); Richard Stone, "Stress: The Invisible Hand in Eastern Europe's Death Rates," *Science Magazine* 288.5274 (2000).

4 See Jan Culik's editorials in the *Central Europe Review* or the political editorials in *Jurnalul National, Cotidianul* and *22*.

5 Henri Vogt, *Between Utopia and Disillusionment: A Narrative of Political Transformation in Eastern Europe* (Oxford: Berghahn Books, 2005).

6 See Jordan Gans-Morse, "Searching for Transitologists: Contemporary Theories of Post-Communist Transitions and the Myth of a Dominant Paradigm," *Post-Soviet Affairs* 20.4 (2004); Charles King, "Post-Postcommunism: Transition, Comparison, and the End of 'Eastern Europe'," *World Politics* 53 (2000), for two very interesting discussions on the state of the literature, particularly the debate between the more classically trained political scientists and comparativists and the so-called "transitologists" as well as the interventions of sociologists and anthropologists.

7 See Denise Roman, *Fragmented Identities: Popular Culture, Sex, and Everyday Life in Postcommunist Romania* (Lanham, Boulder, New York, Toronto and Plymouth: Lexington Books, 2003); Adele Marie Barker (ed.), *Consuming Russia: Popular Culture, Sex, and Society since Gorbachev* (Durham and London: Duke University Press, 1999); Don Kalb and Herman Tak, "The Dynamics of Trust and Mistrust in Poland: Floods, Emotions, Citizenship and the State," *Postsocialism: Politics and Emotions in Central and Eastern Europe*, ed. Maruska Svasek (New York and Oxford: Berghahn Books, 2006); Svetlana Boym, *Common Places: Mythologies of Everyday Life in Russia* (Cambridge: Harvard University Press, 1994).

8 Emile Durkheim, *Suicide: A Study in Sociology*, trans. John A. Spaulding and George Simpson (New York: The Free Press, 1951).

9 Emile Durkheim, *The Division of Labor in Society*, trans. W.D. Halls (New York: The Free Press, 1984).

10 Karl Marx, "Economic and Philosophical Manuscripts," *Karl Marx: Early Writings*, ed. T.B. Bottomore (New York: McGraw-Hill Book Company, 1963).

11 Peter Sloterdijk, *Critica Ratiunii Cinice*, trans. Tinu Parvulescu [1983] (Iasi: Polirom, 2000).

12 Jose Ortega Y Gasset, *Omul Si Multimea*, trans. Sorin Marculescu (Bucharest: Humanitas, 1980).

13 Erich Fromm, *Man for Himself: An Inquiry into the Psychology of Ethics* (New York: Henry Holt and Company, 1947).

14 Ghita Ionescu, *Politica Si Cautarea Fericirii* (Bucharest: Bic All, 1999).

15 Charles Taylor, *The Malaise of Modernity* (Toronto: Anansi Press, 1991).

16 Alina Mungiu-Pippidi, *Politica Dupa Comunism* (Bucharest: Humanitas, 2002).

17 Katherine Verdery, "Faith, Hope, and Caritas in the Land of the Pyramids: Romania, 1990 to 1994," *Comparative Studies in Society and History* 37.4 (1995).

18 Teitelbaum, *Illusion and Disillusionment: Core Issues in Psychotherapy*.

19 Kwon, "Hope, Defense Mechanisms, and Adjustment: Implications for False Hope and Defensive Hopelessness."

20 Julie K. Norem and Nancy Cantor, "Defensive Pessimism: Harnessing Anxiety as Motivation," *Journal of Personality and Social Psychology* 51.6 (1986).

21 Cramer, "Defense Mechanisms in Psychology Today."

22 For a better understanding of this double process of disillusionment, see Zizek and Stavrakakis's discussion on what they call the connection between fantasy and reality in Yannis Stavrakakis, *Lacan and the Political* (New York: Routledge, 1999).

23 Mircea Eliade, *The Sacred and the Profane: The Nature of Religion*, trans. Williard Trask (San Diego: Harcourt, 1987).

24 According to Eliade, traditional societies organized space and time in a more fluid manner with social space—the space that certain collectivities would call theirs—being chosen and delimited based on its connection to what certain myths described as "the center of the world, the main source of energy, the entryway to heaven." The concept of time was also directly connected to a series of events in the collectivity as opposed to a mechanical clock. The passing of time was thus marked by a series of different festivities that would be repeated in a cyclical manner at particular intervals determined by weather patters or life cycles. The fact that traditional societies kept such a fluid notion of space and time allowed them to easily integrate change into their belief system, using contradictions as revelations or signs from the gods.

25 Claude Levi-Strauss, *Myth and Meaning* (New York: Schocken Books, 1979).

26 Sigmund Freud, *Civilization and Its Discontents* (New York: J. Cape and H. Smith, 1930).

27 Slavoj Zizek, *The Sublime Object of Ideology* (New York: Verso Press, 1989), 21.

28 Susan Buck-Morss, *Dreamworld and Catastrophe: The Passing of Mass Utopia in East and West* (Cambridge: MIT Press, 2000), ix.

29 Buck-Morss, *Dreamworld and Catastrophe: The Passing of Mass Utopia in East and West*, x.
30 Ditchev quoted in Buck-Morss, *Dreamworld and Catastrophe: The Passing of Mass Utopia in East and West*, 242.
31 Agnes Heller, "Between Past and Future," *Between Past and Future: The Revolutions of 1989 and Their Aftermath*, ed. Vladimir Tismaneanu and Sorin Antohi (Budapest and New York: Central European University Press, 2000).
32 George Konrad, *Antipolitics* (San Diego: Harcourt Brace Janovich Publishers, 1984).
33 Havel, *The Power of the Powerless: Citizens against the State in Central and Eastern Europe*.
34 G.M. Tamas, "The Hungarian Revolution," *The Spectator* 1989.
35 G.M. Tamas, "Victory Defeated," *Journal of Democracy* 10.1 (1999).
36 See Verdery's work, particularly Katherine Verdery, "Anthropological Adventures with Romania's Wizard of Oz, 1973–1989," *Focaal: European Journal of Anthropology* 43 (2004); Vladimir Tismaneanu, *Condamnati La Fericire: Experimentul Comunist in Romania* (Sibiu, Brasov: Fundatia Exo, 1991); Vladimir Tismaneanu, *Reinventing Politics* (New York: Free Press, 1992).
37 Koestler quoted in Richard Grossman (ed.), *The God That Failed* (New York: Harper & Brothers Publishers, 1949), 15.
38 Koestler quoted in Richard Grossman (ed.), *The God That Failed*, 17.
39 Koestler quoted in Richard Grossman (ed.), *The God That Failed*, 45.
40 Koestler quoted in Richard Grossman (ed.), *The God That Failed*, 65.
41 Koestler, *Darkness at Noon*, 99–100.
42 Koestler, *Darkness at Noon*, 167–70.
43 Vladimir Tismaneanu, *Stalinism for All Seasons: A Political History of Romanian Communism* (Berkeley: University of California Press, 2003).
44 While this remains a particular perspective that cannot claim to be entirely exhaustive and comprehensive, Tismaneanu's contribution has been assessed by many others as one of the most authoritative voices in the field of Romania studies: see for example Robert Levy, "Review of Tismaneanu's Stalinism for All Seasons: A Political History of Romanian Communism," *East European Politics and Societies* 18 (2004).
45 Tismaneanu, *Stalinism for All Seasons: A Political History of Romanian Communism*, 13.
46 Tismaneanu, *Stalinism for All Seasons: A Political History of Romanian Communism*.
47 See testimonies in Paul Cernat, Ion Manolescu, Angelo Mitchievici and Ioan Stanomir, *In Cautarea Comunismului Pierdut* (Pitesti, Bucharest, Brasov, Cluj-Napoca: Paralela 45, 2001); Gheorghe Cionoiu, *Procesul Tranzitiei Sau Punctul Meu De Vedere* (Bucharest: Editura Brumar, 1996); Claudiu Iordache, *Romania Pierduta* (Bucharest: Editura Irini, 1995); Eduard Pamfil, "Comunismul S-a Nascut Pe Malurile Nevei Si a Murit Pe Malurile Begai," *Victoria* Anul I, Issue I 1989; Ruxandra Cesereanu, *Decembrie '89: Deconstructia Unei Revolutii* (Bucharest: Editura Polirom, 2004); Tamas, "Victory Defeated."

4
Shock and transitions

If the previous chapter has tried to understand and explore both the positive and negative aspects of disillusionment as a particular framework for looking at transitions and periods of great social change, this chapter tries to better understand the initial point of change or transition, generally characterized by a so-called period of shock. By seeking to answer the question of how transitions came to be understood as generally positive times, the chapter explores different understandings of the concept of shock, arguing that perhaps the transition from a negative to a positive connotation of shock might provide the answer.

Modern transitions (generally from a state of totalitarianism to attempted democracies) have been celebrated with great enthusiasm in different parts of the world: from Latin America, to Eastern Europe and some parts of Asia and Africa.[1] Critics of the transitology literature have pointed out that this enthusiasm was largely due to the inherent assumption that modern transitions (post-communist transitions in particular) always had democracy as an endpoint.[2] Questioning the extent to which that was true, these critics point out not only the problematic attempts to study transitions through specific "democratic reform" processes but also the need to redirect our attention towards local reactions to change and processes of adaptation. This chapter seeks to understand how people adapted to the shock of change following the Romanian Revolution as well as how they were pushed to understand this process of change as something positive.

The transition from negative to positive shock

Larger social transitions have traditionally been connected to some notion of shock, particularly contemporary ones which have made explicit use of the concept of shock to describe everything from economic transitions—shock therapy—to social and cultural adjustment to those transitions—collective culture shock. The concept of shock can thus be used to mark more clearly the transition from one illusion to the other. Through an examination of what constitutes shock in modern transitions, its effects and the reaction to those effects, one can perhaps more clearly understand the nature of modern transitions and what, if anything, separates them from past transitions or large social transformations.

The concept of shock is very rich in its meaning, having been associated with a series of different phenomena, from the rise of technology, to the increase of stimuli in modern societies, from the devastating experience of war to the experience of harsh economic reform. Perhaps what has been most interesting in the evolution of the concept of shock has been the relatively swift transition from a negative connotation of shock to a positive one. An analysis of why this change in connotation occurred in the first place, might give us important insights about how and why people approach change differently.

The first authors to address the concept of shock in more detail were Freud,[3] Baudelaire,[4] Simmel[5] and Benjamin,[6] who focused on the significant increase in stimuli in modern environments and the way in which these stimuli affected the modern individual as well as the fabric of modern society. In its initial conception, shock was understood mainly in relation to modern technologies and particularly the technologies of war. Shock was thus closely associated with the notion of trauma: physical trauma as a result of war and later psychological trauma as a result of a series of different modern technologies and transformations that significantly changed the structure of society and the individual experience within this structure. Walter Benjamin, in his renowned essay on the storyteller,[7] gives an excellent example of the extent to which the shocking experience of war can challenge traditions that are thousands of years old, such as storytelling. For Benjamin, it becomes clear that the experience of war has shocked not only soldiers, but also their families, into a silence where conversation is much more comfortable through the medium of books and other publications as opposed to the age-old tradition of storytelling.[8] Shock thus takes its toll not only on the individual but also on society as a whole, changing the way in which people relate to one another by changing a series of practices, of which storytelling is just one example.

While Benjamin was amongst the first writers to discuss the concept of shock within a political context, he was perhaps also the one who marked the beginning of the transition from a negative to a positive connotation of shock, by acknowledging that shock was a necessary part of modernity, one that was not likely to go away soon and one in which the individual could even be able to rejoice. Slowing down the process of shock and absorption of shock can allow the individual important insights into the nature of change and modern society and create a space where shock becomes a period of revelation, of awakening and realization of one's own ability to adjust to shock. Adopting the concept from Baudelaire's poetics of urban shock, Benjamin suggests that one the ways to absorb shock is to adopt the attitude of the melancholic flaneur, the constant urban wonderer, who views shock less as an aggressive set of stimuli, and more as an interesting pattern of transformations that can be set within a historical framework. The melancholy of the flaneur provides an essential protective shield that separates the self from the aggressiveness of the stimuli, allowing them to enter consciousness without necessarily hurting it or overwhelming it. By slowing down the perception of time, melancholy essentially cancels the aggressiveness of shock and allows it to be properly absorbed and interpreted, creating a situation where change becomes a natural, less painful transition from one state to another.

Benjamin provides an important alternative to Freud's assessment of shock as something negative, that forces consciousness into a defensive position, allowing the trauma to settle into our unconscious and cause unexpected and often dangerous side-effects. For Benjamin, when shock enters consciousness, it need not necessarily encounter a defensive reaction: instead, it can help trigger the so-called *memoire involontaire* allowing for what he calls an *auratic* experience. This auratic experience gives objects a new significance, allowing them to transcend their otherwise common existence and become signifiers for something much larger. In a world dominated by material production, this means that objects and buildings themselves become entrusted with fragments of history and revelatory experiences that can intellectually and spiritually enrich those who can unveil them. Carl Cassegard, a writer also fascinated with Benjamin's treatment of shock, describes this auratic experience as:

> that which makes an object or a human relationship appear unique and in possession of a "tradition" of its own. The aura arises from an awareness of the unique history of the perceived object. This being the case, it is intrinsically vulnerable to modern techniques of reproduction and to the objectifying and "linear" mode of perception associated with sensation [...] "The disintegration of the aura in the sensation of shock," he [Benjamin] believed, was the price for which modernity was to be had. The objective which he set for himself ever since the mid-1930s was indeed to search for forms of experience which would survive this disintegration [...] Shock is the catalyst, not only of the disintegration of the aura and of experience, but also of the birth of a mode of perception in which sensation and intellect play a predominant role.[9]

Shock is thus positive to the extent that it can trigger an auratic experience or what Terry Eagleton calls a "privileged inwardness" that allows subconscious marks and untraceable memories to come back to the surface and reveal new meaning to what would otherwise appear as common.[10] It is within this interpretation of shock that Benjamin gives us for the first time the ability of think of it as something positive, as an ability to negotiate our experience of modernity and possibly transform the otherwise greedy culture of consumption into an enriching experience.[11]

Benjamin's treatment of shock as something positive made room for other interpretations of the positive nature of shock, allowing contemporary treatments of the concept to focus on shock as not only desirable but also essential to how the modern self is defined. Shock thus became directly connected to the thrill and speed of modern experience, to pleasure sought in reaching new extremes and surviving the impossible. It also became connected to the increasing stimulation of the senses particularly through different kinds of illusory experiences made possible by the manipulation of the visual through photography, film, and other recording and distortion devices. The rise of the media and publicity industry in modern societies has allowed for the creation of a virtual world of images and emotions triggered through images that can be used to manipulate want and desire, goals and images of the self. The modern auratic experience can thus be triggered not only by involuntary memories but also by manipulated images that appeal to the senses through comforting techniques and desirable fantasies. Through these images, the modern individual is pushed to new extremes, enticed to try new things and seek pleasure in achieving the impossible and setting himself/herself up against different sets of challenges.[12] Masochistic endeavors in which people attempt to change their physique, aptitudes and even personalities, have become, in many ways, mechanisms of adapting to the increasing rate of change in the modern world: by putting the experience of shock on a pedestal one can simply ignore its traumatic effects and dispel concerns over its implications for society and the individual.

Using shock as the new standard for measuring whether one is living life to the fullest, whether one is truly alive, the modern lifestyle imposes a culture of over-achievers, of constant work with little reward, of learning to push oneself even in activities that would otherwise be considered relaxing: traveling, extreme sports and even amusement parks, where trying something new and shocking becomes a must. If "doing" gives the modern individual a sense of meaning, then shocking experiences are meant to augment that meaningfulness and take it to yet another level. Extremes such as climbing to the top of Mount Everest or reaching the moon, even at the cost of extreme physical or psychological damage, are more and more common. In our search to redefine meaningful experiences[13] by taking them to different extremes, we may have forgotten that shock continues to carry traumatic side effects and that, in our constant rush to try new things, we forget to take care of ourselves, to acknowledge the importance of calm and routine. The repression of the trauma of the modern existence may be spilling out in unexpected ways. The seemingly irreversible nature of change pushes many of these concerns aside or tries to tackle them by recreating a sense of tradition and values that is strangely anchored in a selective acceptance of the past.

Shock and the experience of time, remembering and nostalgia

As transitions from one political and economic system to another are expected to occur almost overnight, new timelines are imposed on change: two or three years will be enough to put an entire society on a radically different path and ten or fifteen years will transform that society into something unrecognizable. These often unrealistic timelines are part of a tendency to connect development with time, and not just any time, but fast-time. Ideas of fast-capitalism, the compression of time and space and chrono-politics have slowly made their way into the social sciences literature establishing an important connection between shock and time.[14] Time is faster and speedier today than it was in the past. Abstract time has become completely disconnected from the natural cycle of day and night allowing for night shifts, twenty-four hour services, and the outsourcing and manipulation of time differences in order to provide round-the-clock customer service. These have become an essential part of any modern economy. Time is thus not something that just happens and runs its natural course: it is something that can be manipulated, changed, dictated, distributed across the globe, maintained with atomic accuracy.

Speed has become such a positive and desirable quality that anyone who is viewed as too slow or too calm is someone who does not quite fit in. Speed in everything from communication, transportation, processing and work process is essential to modernity and modern competition. One who refuses to wear a watch is viewed as rebellious, while people who dare to show up late to meetings are viewed as unreliable. Time and adherence to a schedule are essential features of the modern work experience as well as interpersonal relationships: you need to know at all times where you are and what you are doing within a particular timeframe that is often dictated to you. Time thus becomes intrinsically connected to trust: respecting the timeframe means that one is reliable and trustworthy. Anyone outside of it, is not. The increasing importance of time and of compressing as much as possible in a short period of time, means not only that everything speeds up but also that along with that speed people need to be better able to adapt to and process new kinds of stimuli. Thus, from an early age, we are exposed to these stimuli and taught how to maneuver them, with our success often tested in terms of how we are able to cope with them: everything from exam taking, to job applications, to advancement is determined by our speed at certain tasks and our ability to have as many different experiences as possible, yet combined with in-depth knowledge of one particular field.

As time becomes not only a measurement of success but also a measurement of trust, reliability and predictability, modern shock as connected to time—fast-time—puts more and more pressure on the modern individual. Changes in our concept of time have a deep effect not only on our efficiency levels but also on the way in which we relate to the past. As time becomes faster and faster, the past seems further and further away, separated not only by long distances in time but also by radical shifts in conceptions of time: the modern individual begs for more time, for shorter working weeks, for more vacation, time to spend with one's family, while also asking for more efficiency, increased turn-around time, more profit. We want time to go faster and run slower at the same time. And yet, as more and more gets packed into less and less time, the moment gains a different significance, the present seems overwhelming, the past distant and the future closer than ever. The very experience of living has changed to a point where one stops interpreting things through the prism of past experiences and traditions and more through the prism of future possibilities.

This intense experience of time and sharp increase in stimuli is not without consequences. As our relationship to the past changes, the nostalgia for past times is expressed in new and modern ways. In Romania, commercials and movies appealing to childhood times and grandparents' villages are making a strong comeback, with more and more youth in their late twenties finding it more and more important to recall the times of their childhood, the times of the transition. An increasing number of emails are circulating among the Romanian community abroad about the "good old days" of playing outdoor games that now hardly anyone remembers, of collecting empty beer cans and cigarette cartons, of wearing the first blue jeans and Adidas shoes, or of enjoying our first jar of Nutella.[15] Nostalgia is more and more prevalent at all different levels of society: grandparents, parents and youth remember their past with an increased longing for those days that suddenly appear a lot more positive than the actual past experience might warrant. And yet, while nostalgia and the longing for the past is said to be normal in highly unstable times such as transitions, this particular nostalgia has turned into a social melancholy that sees that past not only as something that is irretrievable, but as something that has a higher worth and emotional value that what may be experienced today.

The sadness over never seeing their children experience the same freedom and love for the outdoors, the same fearless exploration of their environments, the same carelessness up to adolescence, is making people more and more aware of the nature of the changes that their society is undergoing. Increases in drug use and crime, instances of depression at a younger and younger age, higher rates of divorce and increasing financial pressures are all making children mature much faster than they should. The increase in stimuli, shock and speed of time are stealing away childhood, innocence and carelessness. As the scars of shock are starting to become more and more visible in Western societies, with the rise in so-called existential shocks, dependence on anti-depressants and treatments for attention deficit disorders, transition societies are becoming more and more aware of the road that they are embarking on and while attempting to fit in the best they can, they are also trying to negotiate a more stable future for themselves. Despite the shock of communism, these societies are still closer to the experience of calm, the charm of the rural and many careless childhood years. And for as long as that calm retains visual reminders in the villages spread throughout Central and Eastern Europe, in the old courtyards and toys, the nostalgia will persist.

In her essay on Walter Benjamin, Susan Sontag argues that nostalgia is more than the art of remembering but rather, the art of rearranging time according to a more random order than the chronological one. This selection of positive experiences triggers not only a longing for the past, but also the realization that the longing is made more intense by the fact that the present situation is so far from the positive nature of these memories. Losing the linearity of time in remembering, in nostalgia, allows one to re-experience one's past through idealized moments alone, creating an interesting mechanism of escape from the present and possible projection for the future. Nostalgia is however more than a momentary escape from the present: it is an indisputable critique of the present that for one reason or another, fails to deliver similar positive experiences as the past.

Seeking to explain Benjamin's fascination with daydreaming experiences and what he called wish images, Susan Sontag argues that Benjamin was a nostalgic by birth. "Born under the sign of Saturn," Benjamin always showed a sensibility towards the past and works that chose to recall the past. His fascination with seventeenth-century baroque drama and Proust's *À la Recherche de Temps Perdu* became an integral part of his larger work on history and how the experience of time can be read into space. The connection between time and space that fascinated Benjamin points to a new way of perceiving time: through the way it reflects in space, architecture and the urban experience. If history merges into the setting, then melancholy is directly connected to space: nostalgia is triggered by space. The process of remembering is however more than just simple nostalgia. For as Susan Sontag explains:

> Benjamin regards everything he chooses to recall in his past as prophetic of the future, because the work of memory (reading oneself backward, he called it) collapses time. There is no chronological ordering of his reminiscences, for which he disavows the name of autobiography, because time is irrelevant [...] Memory, the staging of the past, turns the flow of events into tableaux, Benjamin is not trying to recover the past but to understand it: to condense it into its spatial forms, its premonitory structures.[16]

Disconnecting time from its linearity might thus be necessary for a backward examination of the self or of the past. Looking at nostalgia or melancholy from this perspective, allows it to become more than just a longing but rather a direct expression of what one wants independent of the restrictions at hand. The nostalgia for certain fragments of the communist past may thus be nothing more than a different way to express the desperate need for security, stability, calm and carelessness, or an attempt to reconstruct a certain identity that is now made to seem more cohesive. What triggers this nostalgia is often a present that is in one way or another destabilizing or unwanted. The shock of the transition, in the case of Central and Eastern Europe, can act as a powerful trigger of nostalgia that is often associated with communist times.[17] Rather than see this as a threat or a desire to reinstall a communist government, we could treat it as simply an attempt to renegotiate the past, to rewrite it in a way that provides more consolation and escape.

Shock can act as much more than a trigger for remembering, nostalgia and longing, according to Carl Cassegard's reading of Yasunari Kawabata: shock can also play a very important revelatory role.[18] The revelatory function of shock is sustained by what Cassegard calls the aestheticization of shock, the drawing of shock in a positive light, whereby the thrill of shock breaks the continuity and fluidity of experience, revealing something that lies beyond its linearity: an original state of "nothingness," a state that is closer to nature, more open-ended, in which a breakdown of expectations and abolition of context occurs. In Kawabata's novels, shock is welcomed because "consciousness knowingly makes itself defenseless against the shock that will free it from spleen."[19] Playing on Freud's argument about consciousness automatically blocking out shock, Kawabata argues that the modern individual can control this reaction, making himself/herself fully susceptible to effect of shock, in the hope that it will erase the so-called spleen.[20]

Benjamin would perhaps in many ways agree with Cassegard's positive depiction of shock, for his association of shock with nostalgia and remembrance is nothing but a similar escape into the realm of idealized memories in a timeless world-frame. Yet shock, as described by Benjamin and even Cassegard, is momentary shock—a shock created by a particular encounter or a particular event. Perhaps what is different about modern shock is the fact that it appears to be constant: shock is no longer just a moment in time, an event, but rather an entire period, an entire lifestyle. One can hardly separate shock from non-shock any more, as the overwhelming assault of different kinds of stimuli has made its way into every aspect of our modern lives: from the home environment to the office, from the street experience to our vacations. The revelatory function of shock may thus be numbed to a point where the escape itself becomes yet another form of shock. The tendency to view shock as a positive experience, however, persists not only in narratives that associate it with the concept of time or change but also with the increasing technologization of modern societies.

Shock, technology and normalization practices

The concept of shock has often been connected to modern technologies, particularly the technologies of war. Yet other apparently harmless technologies also add to the level of shock in modern lifestyles. Given that some of these technologies have become so integral to everyday existence, the element of shock associated with them has often been neutralized by what some have called normalizing technologies.[21] In his article on shock in modernity, Tim Armstrong argues that modern shock does not necessarily require a literal wound, that in fact modern shock is more often linked to everyday life and the technologies of the urban such as the telephone, trains and tramways.[22] The modern shock is thus the shock of the technologies associated with industrialism and capitalism. Some of these technologies are more integrated than others, and while the process of normalization has turned the shock of these technologies into something minuscule, much of the world still struggles to adjust to simple things like remote controls, computers and even moving escalators.

On my recent trip back from Rwanda, in the modern Addis Ababa airport, an interesting scene could be observed: Rwandan businessmen dressed in suits and carrying briefcases, fitting perfectly in the modern environment of the airport and the image of the well-traveled capitalist, were crowding in front of the escalator and testing the moving stairs as one would test water to see if it was good for swimming, and hesitating as to whether to get on it or not. The rest of us, a little confused, made our way through the crowd and naturally got on the escalator with the confidence gained from years of riding escalators and other types of moving technologies. Following our example, and with hesitating steps, the rest of crowd followed us, holding on to the banister and swaying slightly as if they were about to fall. At the top of the moving escalator, yet another trial awaited them: stepping off it with enough control to prevent them from falling. Hesitating again and stumbling on several occasions, everyone made their way to the top, laughing happily and patting each other on the back as if they had just returned from a testing journey. Lesson learned: appearances can be deceiving after all and suits and briefcases alone do not make one look and feel natural in any environment.

Simple technologies such as escalators can be a challenge in many developing societies. And just like escalators take time to learn how to properly ride, so do other technologies, which we often take for granted. The speed with which some of these technologies are entering our societies and becoming an integral part of our existence, separating us from others who do not have access to similar technologies, is creating more than a technological barrier: it is creating different understandings of the "normal" where one is pushed to accept the shock of any technology not only as desirable but also as part of the normal. The thirst with which the developing world desires modern technology: from TVs to CD players, to computer games and modern cars, shows the extent to which they seek to be included into the "normal." And yet, in this normalization process, we fail to acknowledge that adjusting to modern technologies may take more than time, and that perhaps the most difficult part of the process is learning to deal with the shock of these technologies as an integral part of our lives.

In his critique of technology and what he calls fast capitalism, Timothy Luke argues that perhaps one of the main ways in which people deal with the shocks of modernity, capitalism, globalization, and the increasing techonocratization of everything, is through a series of normalizing techniques that seek to present changes, technologies and transformations as natural.[23] Through a normalizing discourse that seeks to absorb shock, technologies such as the internet, wireless phones and computer programming that until even ten or fifteen years ago were cutting edge, have now become part of the normal lifestyle of just about every individual in the Western world. Within the course of a few years, the use of such technologies is by no means perceived as extraordinary but rather as something necessary and quite average. The ability to learn how to manipulate these technologies within a short period of time—whether it be typing at a certain speed or learning how to manipulate more and more computer programs that have become an integral part of any office experience—is something that is simply taken for granted and by no means viewed as a struggle or a stretch.

This process of normalization is perhaps made even easier by the apparent speed and lack of effort with which these technologies seem to integrate themselves into the average lifestyle. Whether this is indeed as effortless as it seems is questionable. As Timothy Luke well points out, this process of normalization also tends to hide the realities of the production process, focusing only on the end result.[24] The production process here need not only be the literal mechanisms of production, but also the mechanisms of integration, of learning and of struggling with understanding different sets of technologies that have become such an integral part of the modern lifestyle.

Looking at what we now consider to be very basic technologies, such as electricity or refrigeration, Luke points out the disconnect that exists between understanding how these technologies actually function and simply learning how to manipulate them. Not understanding the life-threatening risks of each of these technologies puts us in a position of naivety, whereby many of these machines are viewed as harmless and almost naturally present in our households. Luke is particularly intrigued by our treatment of what he calls "normal accidents"—accidents involving these "simple" technologies, whether it be someone getting electrocuted or burnt—whereby even life-threatening situations are treated with incredible lightness and forgiveness. Our willingness to live with risk points to the extent to which shock has become an integral and necessary part of our lives. Our increasing dependence on simple technologies like electricity, Luke warns, is not something to be ignored, for a mere power outage—such as the electrical blackout experienced along the US's East Coast in 2004—can literally act as a natural disaster, significantly affecting our ability to go about our daily lives, to function and survive.

Smaller accidents surrounding modern technologies often go unnoticed in transitioning societies, despite their devastating effect on those who are experiencing them. In

Romania alone, hundreds of people die yearly from improperly installed natural gas-fuelled heating installations. After the collapse of the state-owned heating companies, many families were left to their own devices to face the often cold winters. The heating installations seemed like the perfect solution, given the low subsidized price of natural gas, yet proved to be quite dangerous due to gas leaks and frequent fires, often affecting entire buildings.

Playing on Foucault's idea of grids of normalization, Luke argues that this normalization process creates a system whereby living within the grid means that you are part of the "normal" while anything outside the grid means something that is either "abnormal", antisocial or pre-modern. The struggle of much of the developing and transitioning world to catch up with these technologies and build a similar infrastructure to that of the West is very much a struggle to be accepted as part of the normal. The constant redefinition of what constitutes the normal along with the constant push for society to accept and integrate new elements in the form of technologies, may be pushing the threshold of just how much and just how fast some of these technologies can be integrated.

If the normalization process implies a particular kind of adjustment to shock, whereby the shock of modern technologies is simply dismissed in light of their general usefulness, Carl Cassegard discusses a slightly different response to the shock of modernity through what he calls the process of naturalization. According to him, naturalization means that one has grown used to an environment that was once shocking,[25] where getting used to shock means learning how to live one's public life with shock while spending one's private life in isolation from shock. Analyzing modern shock through the prism of Marakami Haruki's novels, Cassegard argues that the way in which his characters are able to withstand shock is through a detachment of the mind and the self from relations to other people and things. The process of naturalization of shock is thus one in which the individual detaches himself/herself from the surrounding environment to a point where he/she becomes indifferent to change. If modern shock is embedded in all relationships with the outside world, then solitude becomes only a temporary escape, one that is often resisted by our dependence on the outside world:

Not only is increasing isolation characteristic of societies today, but also the vigor with which it is combated, the desperation of the search for belonging, as evinced in the resurgence of nationalism and ethnic struggles. The very same struggles reveal that the return of shock is the price for which the attempt to renew the aura in the realm of human relations is to be had [...] This much is still true in Benjamin: that in modernity external relations without shock are impossible.[26]

One of the side effects of the seeming inevitability of shock in modernity may be our attempt to control it through risk management. From menus to vacation packages, from types of schools to career choices, from clothes and fashion to technologies, from partners in life and even death choices, one's life in a shock society is dominated by a constant push to choose and to choose well. We are taught to devise criteria, to build standards and to read consumer reports in order to make the best choices. We are taught to fear risk, yet embrace it at the same time, to manage it properly, yet to take it, to resent it and cherish it at the same time. The modern lifestyle requires an incredible amount of risk-taking, from taking on tuition loans, mortgages, and car payments, to changing careers, moving from one place to another, investing into a new business or the stock market. The risks that we are willing to take in order to "succeed" in life involve the ability to manage stress much more than ever before.

As we are left to make more and more decisions on our own, we are also taught to trust the very institutions that impose risk-taking on us: banks, stock markets, exchange commissions, federal reserves, insurance companies and more. Our commitment to the validity of these institutions and our willingness to trust abstract systems seems to be in an inverse correlation to our willingness and ability to trust ourselves and people around us. Putting our retirement in a fund that could well crash in the stock market is nothing compared to the security systems that we build around our homes, our families and ourselves. Our inability to deal with risk at a much more personal level, and the rising levels of fear in society, are signs that perhaps trust in abstract systems is not as easy as one may think.

If trust—in institutions and other abstract systems as well as in people—requires time, then one should not be surprised at the low levels of trust, risk-taking and social engagement in Central and Eastern Europe. These are not necessarily characteristics of an anomic society with a weak civil society and a slow transition towards democratization. These are things to be expected in a restructuring society, in which many of the social security mechanisms have collapsed, leaving people overexposed to the shock of change and fearful of the future. The non-traditional and certainly non-linear transition to modernity and capitalism in Central and Eastern Europe, the swift change from one social and political logic to another, has perhaps left these societies not only disoriented but also a little more aware of the whimsical nature of change. The stability that much of the West enjoys has allowed change to occur within a relatively stable environment that was favorable to a quick integration of those changes. This has certainly not been the case in transitioning Central and Eastern European states, particularly when it came to changes brought about by the process of economic reform.

Shock therapy

The concept of shock has perhaps become most popular in the contemporary Central and Eastern European context through what was known as shock therapy. The therapy implied had little to do with any sense of refuge or escape, soothing or calming, curing or vindicating. Shock therapy became a term used to address the radical economic reform aimed at curbing inflation after the liberalization of prices, which marked the transition to a capitalist market economy. It had been attempted before in several other parts of the world, including China and Latin America, with Bolivia often being pointed to as the big success story before 1989. The choice of the phrase was inspired by its use in the medical field: shock therapy being designed to address a series of psychological disorders through electrical shocks administered under the direct supervision of a doctor. The shocks did eventually calm the patient down, yet only after a rather painful process.[27] While the association of the phrase shock therapy with transition economies is said to originate in op-eds that appeared during discussions of the Latin American transitions to democracy in the 1980s, the term stuck and was passed on to the analysis of other transitions.

That shock could be associated with the idea of therapy seems rather odd, since more pain is not often the solution that we prescribe to something that is already painful. Yet shock therapy or a quick transition to a capitalist economy was seen by many as a much better option than gradualism, or step-by-step reform. In the case of Eastern Europe, Jeffrey Sachs, the famous economist who helped Bolivia through its transition, took the lessons he learned in Bolivia to Poland, transforming the latter's economy into one of the most successful in Eastern Europe.[28] While Poland is still being paraded as an example to the rest of the transitioning world, many are quick to point out that its success was relative and certainly not without consequences.

Daniel Singer in his article on the Eastern European transitions argues that just like lobsters do not love to be boiled alive, the people of Eastern Europe also do not love having their living standards cut. To prove it, he rightfully points out that in the 1994 elections, the Poles were quick to vote out the coalition that supported shock therapy and went for the alternative.[29] He also points out that perhaps in Eastern Europe, life under capitalism will not necessarily turn out to be as dazzling as the US model—as portrayed in American serials such as *Dallas* or *Beverly Hills*—or as the British or Swedish model, but rather as the Bolivian model. For while shock therapy has been paraded around as the successful transitioning strategy, the success of these transitions is often measured in light of GDP increases and levels of integration into the market economy as opposed to actual levels of satisfaction at the individual and social level. Countries like Romania and Bulgaria have for years now seen their image suffer because of their choice for a more gradualist economic reform which did not follow the advice of the so-called shock therapy. Blamed on the neo-communist regimes that came to power after the 1989 revolutions, these gradualist policies eventually gave in to more radical economic reforms, despite a series of pressures that risked destabilizing the already fragile economic and social order.

Jeffrey Sachs, considered by many to be the father of shock therapy as a transition policy, argues that the fast vs. gradualist distinction comes from a misunderstanding of what shock therapy actually is. Shock therapy, according to him, can be applied in two very different situations: first, in a situation of monetary chaos—like hyperinflation or extreme shortage of goods because of massive price controls—in which a decisive economic action can end the crisis; and second, in a situation in which gradual economic reform policies and lobbying can help reform an economic and political system. Thus, he argues, Poland was a case of both quick and gradual reform, and the assumption that reform necessarily occurred at a much faster rate in Poland is in many ways wrong. That the political will was stronger, making the reforms much more efficient, was a different issue.[30]

If it is not the speed, what is it then that makes shock therapy, shocking? According to Theodore Gerber and Michael Hout, it is the human cost: the sharp decline in the standard of living, high inflation coupled with a very unstable economic environment, the widening gaps between the poor and the rich, the rise in corruption and decline in traditional values. Gerber and Hout summarize their argument with a popular Russian joke: "Everything the Communists told us about communism was a lie. Everything they told us about capitalism turns out to be true."[31] While Russia also toyed with the idea of shock therapy, its reform process followed a much slower track than its Central and Eastern European counterparts. After a less intensive shock therapy, Russia now has two-thirds of its people live in poverty, one of the shortest lifespans in Europe, greater mortality, decreasing population, an industrial production that is less than one half of what it used to be, scientific centers that have been destroyed and some of the highest rates of corruption. The human cost of privatization and shock therapy—or more shock than therapy as Gerber and Hout call it—has thus been much higher than expected in Russia.

Shock therapy thus brought about much more than economic reform. It shook the very core of many of the societies to which it was applied, bringing about irreversible social changes along with a chaotic environment. Shock therapy did more than just cure the patient: it changed and transformed the patient into something/someone that was no longer recognizable. The new Central and Eastern European societies had to learn to do more than just adjust: they had to learn to accept change as something positive and to embrace what they had become. Faced with a brand new economic and political environment and a constantly changing self, Central and Eastern European societies entered into a different kind of shock, something that some sociologists described as a collective culture shock.

Collective culture shock

The idea of a culture shock is relatively new and perhaps most often associated with groups of people that find themselves uprooted and placed into an unfamiliar environment, most often for educational, business or diplomatic purposes. In sociology, culture shock has been examined in light of a series of different phases, based on individuals experiencing a significant change in cultural environments. Presentation sessions focusing on different aspects of each of these phases have become a staple in all international student orientations in the US as well as orientations for Peace Corps volunteers and business people traveling abroad. The different stages of culture shock are generally accepted to be: the honeymoon stage, the rejection stage, the regression stage, the recovery stage and the reverse culture shock upon return to one's home country. The stages represent the time that it takes for one to adjust to a new environment and the likely reactions one is to expect.

While culture shock has for the most part been considered to be an individual phenomenon, it is only within the last ten or fifteen years that the idea of a collective culture shock has made its way through the sociological community. Interestingly enough, this idea was not associated with migrating communities or collectivities, as one would expect—such as the community of refugees or immigrants—but rather with collectives that were undergoing big transformations at home: such as societies in transition. Feichtinger and Fink argue that one may speak of such a collective culture shock in instances "where an abrupt change in the political system influences the cultural context. [...] In this case culture shock is not initiated by the geographical change of going abroad, but is caused by influences on the existing social and cultural system."[32] The stages of the collective culture shock that they identify are almost identical to the stages of individual culture shock, thus raising the question of the extent to which one's familiar environment can change to a point where it becomes shocking and unknown, thus requiring rediscovery.

The collective culture shock in a period of transition can easily be connected with what we earlier described as shock therapy: a series of economic, followed by political, reforms, aimed at radically transforming an economy into a capitalist, market-based economy. That these reforms are introduced by the very citizens/politicians of the country undergoing the reform, implies a process of desired self-change. The need for adjustment is thus to a large extent self-imposed, the choice of maintaining one's familiar environment still being there. The pain of the transition followed by the need to readjust—the collective culture shock—is something that is always done for a greater good or a higher purpose: better standard of living, more opportunities and freedoms. As in individual cultural shock however, modes of resistance continue to be developed even in instances where one is completely aware of the need to and the importance of adjusting. The shock thus is as much a result of the changes that the society is undergoing as the resistance that it is putting forward.

Defense mechanisms and symptoms of withdrawal, which are indeed highly prevalent in most transition societies and certainly so in the case of Central and Eastern Europe, are thus indicative of the extent of the change—how radical the change is—and the impacts that this change has on everyday life. The feelings of intense nostalgia, the lack of trust, the social and political apathy, can be perceived as different forms of resistance to the collective culture shock. The difference between individual culture shock and collective culture shock lies in the fact that in the first type one may always find comfort in the idea that the home one left behind will be there upon one's return, while in the second—particularly when associated with transition periods—one is giving up a certain lifestyle for good, never hoping to be able to acquire it again. The anxiety over the finality of this decision—the road of no return—creates intense pressure on the individual as well as the collective, with few reassurances to fall back on.

Extremes of poverty and wealth as shock

One of the most shocking aspects of the transition in Central and Eastern Europe, and Romania in particular, has perhaps been the appearance of extremes in both wealth and poverty. In Romania, stories of abandoned retirees frozen in their apartments because they could not afford to pay their electricity bills in winter, or stories of mothers drowning their infants because they did not have enough food to feed them, seem nightmarish and almost unreal. While Romanians have certainly been used to poverty, this new extreme seems to be out of place even in a society that suffered through years of hardship. The shock of poverty is not only felt in these extreme situations. With the transition, middle-income families see themselves forced to count every little penny to make sure all basic expenses are met, and struggle to provide their children with a future. The other extreme—that of wealth—is also becoming more and more prevalent, with people flaunting expensive Hummer SUVs, clothes and cellphones. The experience of this extreme wealth is also new and shocking, not only to those who see it, but also to those who have it. Wealth becomes something to show off in visible investments—such as opulent housing, cars, jewelry and technology—as opposed to something that is invested. The mismanagement of wealth is obvious in the tendency to first show your wealth off and only afterwards figure out what to do with it.

Perhaps most shocking of all is the visibility of the gap between the poor and the wealthy to which the middle class is suddenly exposed through street beggars, old ladies selling flowers or food from their gardens at the open markets or street corners, abandoned or runaway children, or collapsing homes in suburban villages. A simple trip from the city center to the margins of town reveals shocking differences and almost alternative realities. As the purchasing power of most middle-income families has significantly decreased, people are forced to keep up appearances by investing most of their money in clothes, jewelry and cell-phones to save face. The majority of people under thirty-five spend most of their money on cigarettes, clothes, cell-phones and going out, while only some of them enjoy the luxury of buying a home, taking a vacation or saving and investing.

Extreme poverty has already begun to touch populations that were, until now, protected either by the welfare state or by the family: the retired elderly and children. While retirement was relatively comfortable before the revolution, with many elderly going back to their villages and making a comfortable living off subsistence agriculture, with more and more elderly forced to sell their houses and move into apartment buildings in the city, we see them unable to pay for basic expenses: such as electricity bills and maintenance. With the welfare system in collapse, many of these elderly are forced to resort to extremes such as selling their train coupons—one of the benefits that they still get—in order to pay their electricity bill in winter. Children are also taking to the streets either as a result of abuse and extreme poverty in their family or as a result of the failure of the orphanage system to provide them with jobs and places to live after they turn eighteen. Many of these children are forced into prostitution and take to the streets, begging, selling and consuming cheap and harmful drugs, and stealing. That families are no longer able to provide a safe cushion for these vulnerable populations is also a sign that family ties have weakened, with children too pressured by their daily life to be able to take care of their parents and vice versa.

The idea of sharing wealth or giving back to the community is still new or close to non-existent in much of Central and Eastern Europe, or more specifically Romania. Those who are wealthy seek to maintain their wealth and often see giving it away as a threat. Wealth can be exchanged for services and only in very few instances is wealth given away for charity. The sense of responsibility to one's neighbor or community has all but disappeared and people are reluctant to help each other. With prices on the rise and the prohibitive cost of apartments, young people are finding creative ways to make a life of their own: either sharing spaces with each other, spending more time in school dorms, living with parents or moving abroad. Parents and grandparents are often pushed out of their spaces to make room for the children. Many are considering moving back to the traditional villages where prices for houses are more reasonable and a vegetable garden can save a part of one's income.

Technologies of distraction: dealing with shock

Dealing with shock, despite its modern perception as something increasingly positive, has been a skill that people have had to develop throughout time. The almost instinctive turn towards nostalgia—seeking refuge in memories from the past—or solitude—clearing of the mind from the stimuli present in everyday life—has nowadays been replaced with a series of so-called technologies of distraction, most of which are focused on visual distractions. From the theater to the circus, to the movies, amusement and theme parks, from art and TV to advertising and marketing, from fetish shows to comedy clubs, from mysticism and religion to sci-fi and reading, everyone finds their own different way of escaping shock. That these escapes are often illusory in nature, points to the power that illusions have in providing a quick and efficient way to escape the pressures of everyday life, to gain perspective, to change our mindsets and pretend we are someone else, someplace else. Putting things in the realm of the imaginary, of the hypothetical, can help us imagine different outcomes, give us hope when there is no rational reason for it, and allow us to distance ourselves from difficult settings and situations.

Paradoxically, escaping shock often involves exposing ourselves to a hypothetical world of shock, for many of these illusory escapes seek to recreate instances of shock in secure environments where one is immune to its negative effects. Amusement parks are perhaps a great example of this, where much of amusement seems to be provided by a series of different shocks: whether physical—through roller coasters and other types of thrilling rides; emotional—through exposure to different cartoon characters, for example, for children; or psychological—through the constant teasing of feelings of extreme fear and excitement. Shock has become a fetish of modern society, a thrill that, when it does not frighten us, amuses us, or sometimes both.

Distraction technologies need not however be only reliant on their ability to relax the individual by showing him/her the harmlessness of shock. In his treatment of the epic theater, Brecht argues that while the role of the theater is to distract, it is also to provide opportunities for self-reflection during that distraction.[33] The fragmentary nature of Brecht's epic theater is supposed to offer those moments of self-reflection in the middle of the theatrical experience, allowing the audience to absorb shock and not only block it out. By presenting shock through the medium of theater, one is able to create a hypothetical realm in which the experience seems real, yet it is not, in which one can identify oneself with the character yet be able to rationally separate oneself from the dilemmas faced by the character.

In this way, the hypothetical realm allows us to deal with the problem of shock by creating an instance whereby the moment of shock can be suspended in time, allowing for a rational consideration of its consequences. Shock is not as sudden in its consequences, nor does it appear as inevitable. The illusory can thus become a training ground for learning how to deal with different instances of shock, allowing for the imagination of a series of scenarios in which a positive outcome is most often possible, independent of the situation at hand.[34] With the immediate availability of this training ground, taking risks and accepting shock seems easier, with consequences often taken a little lighter. The idea that one can choose between a series of different consequences puts us at ease.

The possibility of choosing outcomes is a way of controlling the uncontrollable, of imagining that one has the power to decide what is and what will come. As Patricia Pringle argues: "We are linked to our times not only by the ability but also the desire to see in particular ways."[35] The new technologies of distraction are designed in a way that often gives us the false impression that we can control everything we see—video games, interactive TV, and even interactive theater. This often spills into an increasing need to control all representations and interpretations of the real. In her article on what she calls "the shock of the real," Beatriz Jaguaribe argues that these tendencies for control can be increasingly dangerous as "both written narrative and visual imagery [...] unleash an intense, dramatic discharge that destabilizes notions of reality itself."[36]

Using the case of Brazil, Jaguaribe argues that the media shifts a little too quickly from the extremes of disenchanted images presented by documentaries showing the poverty of favelas, the rise in crime, street children and poverty, to the re-enchantment of those same cities through fantasies of wealth, beauty and the good life. During this emerging crisis of representation, as she calls it, reality appears not only highly fragmented, but is often confused with the fantasy—both the enchanted and disenchanted one. Thus, using the example of the maid in Proust's novel, who cries when reading about poverty in a novel yet is unable to relate to similar situations in the real world, Jaguaribe argues that mediatic depictions of the "real" in Brazil's movies and documentaries oftentimes confuse the meaning of the so-called cathartic scenes:

> In many ways, the "shock of the real" unleashes a cathartic release, but contrary to the response elicited by Greek tragedies or romantic poetry, the cathartic element here does not necessarily wish to provoke the classic sentiments of compassion and pity. Rather, in many instances, the cathartic triggering is purposefully ambiguous. Such an ambiguity is not related to the subtle, veiled ploys of the narrative or image. After all, the realistic depiction of violence or strong emotional feelings is easily apprehended by readers or viewers. But what is not so easily understood is the meaning of such violence and emotion, not only because reception varies but also because there is no overarching interpretative ethos to provide solace and meaning to such cathartic representations.[37]

The lack of what Jaguaribe calls an overarching interpretative ethos, leaves everyone to their own devices of interpretation, often causing a distorted response to otherwise relatively clear situations. The reaction to media depictions of real life events such as kidnappings or crime is often confused with reactions to similar events presented in the movies: the focus lies on what happens next or properly capturing the scene, rather than on emphatically connecting to the harmed characters. Curiosity and the very process of representation take precedence over otherwise shocking events that are very real in their consequences.

Tim Armstrong argues that these instances of distraction point to a fragmentation of the self, which seeks an escape in illusory interpretations of reality in order to work out instances of trauma, consciously or unconsciously experienced previously. This fragmentation of the self causes confusion as to what the "real" self is, often creating the illusion of a single, stable and integral self that exists outside of the illusory.[38] In our constant search for pleasure, happiness and non-fragmented selves, we turn to the realm of the illusory for compensation. Freud and Marcuse have been two of the writers that focused on capturing the shortcomings of the rational realm of "reality." Using Freud's analysis of the pleasure principle vs. the reality principle, Marcuse identifies two different sets of problems that are significantly affecting the politics of modern society: 1) the question of happiness and 2) the question of liberty. He notes that much of modern happiness is directly connected to the process of production and consumption, both of which are repressive of the pleasure principle—mainly erotic in nature. The repressiveness of production and consumption thus

> lies to a high degree in its efficacy: it enhances the scope of material culture, facilitates the procurement of the necessities of life, makes comfort and luxury cheaper, draws ever-larger areas into the orbit of industry—while at the same time sustaining toil and destruction. The individual pays by sacrificing his time, his consciousness, his dreams; civilization pays by sacrificing its own promises of liberty, justice, and peace for all.[39]

Yet, if repression had become an integral part of the modern lifestyle through the process of production and consumption, that is not to say that happiness and liberty cannot exist. One of the most creative ways in which modern societies have been able to reconcile the pleasure principle with the reality principle has been through phantasy. Marcuse argues that Freud himself also identified phantasy as an escape:

> Freud singles out phantasy as one mental activity that retains a high degree of freedom from the reality principle even in the sphere of the developed consciousness. [...] Phantasy plays out a most decisive function in the total mental structure: it links the deepest layers of the unconscious with the highest products of consciousness (art), the dream with reality; it preserves the archetypes of the genus, the perpetual but repressed ideas of the collective and individual memory, the tabooed images of freedom.[40]

Phantasy, as an experience of its own, creates a world in which the individual can escape the reality principle and live out the pleasure principle outside of any social constraints and other forms of repression. Both at an individual level as well as at a social level, phantasy promises to reconcile the pleasure principle with the reality principle, in that it allows for an easy back and forth switch, where one could easily fall into a dream-like state and live the phantasy of freedom and liberty while at the same time continuing to accept the norms and repressions of progress and civilization. Yet the line between the realm of phantasy and the realm of the "real" may not be as clear as one may think. Our increasing ability to manipulate the realm of phantasy—through mere manipulation of images and experiences within this realm— also has a direct effect on the realm of the "real." As Jaguaribe suggested earlier, phantasy makes the realm of the "real" more distant in its consequences, often creating a feeling of detachment that can bring about sometimes dangerous consequences. Others have interpreted this detachment, or splitting of the self, as Armstrong calls it, from a slightly different perspective.

Philip Wexler argues that what we are dealing with is no so much a splitting of the self, but rather an emptying of the self. Similar to what Marx described as the process of alienation, or Weber as the process of "mechanical petrification," this emptying of the self is directly connected to the increased mechanization of modernity and its effects on social relations. The antidote that Wexler proposes is the counter process of "re-selfing" or what Fromm referred to as "de-alienation."[41] According to Wexler, the emptying of the self occurs in two stages: an emptying the self of its original, instinctual desires, followed by an increased domination of the self by different kind of technologies. The most powerful instinctual desires that Wexler identifies are directly connected to the need to believe in the divine or the sacred.

If progress and modernity have led to an emptying of the self through desacralization, then, Wexler argues, one needs to attempt to find new ways of sacralization. Re-conceptualizing the sacred beyond what Marx called an alienating religion, means finding a more empowering relationship with the sacred, learning to look at it beyond salvation. This relationship is what Wexler calls inner-worldly mysticism which can function as an efficient mechanism of re-selfing without appealing to the salvationist calls of religion. He mentions three distinct strategies of re-selfing that are available to the modern individual:

> The first emphasizes active self-transformation through ritual, behavioral action that is scripted by collective memory. The second is a more cognitively based alteration of meanings, definitions, categories, and collective representations which change

the self imaginatively, by mental re-figuration. The third is an emotional fusion of self and sacred, collective Other, an emotional re-energizing that is accomplished in part by the activation of historical, collectively (though esoterically) recognized visionary experiences.[42]

None of these mechanisms seem to be significantly different from previous mechanisms of engaging with the sacred, but perhaps what they do suggest is that the relationship with the sacred has been diversified without necessarily building an inherent contradiction between traditional religious forms of relating to the sacred and the new, inner-mysticism forms of relating to the sacred and of re-selfing. If Wexler is right, then perhaps the rise of different forms of mysticism—from herbalism, to miracle workers, to horoscope readers, yoga practices and kabalistic practices—is a direct result of the need to re-self and redefine one's relationship to the sacred at a time when everything else seems to challenge it.

Mysticism has certainly played an important role in helping people through difficult times. It is no coincidence that many developing and transitioning countries often experience a significant rise in religious and mystical activities, from the number of churchgoers, to the number of believers and different forms of miracles and miracle makers. Mysticism has played an important role in giving people hope by allowing them to separate themselves from the rational harshness of reality and to seek solace and support in something that can transcend that reality. In the case of transitioning Romania, there is an abundance of stories that point to the essential role that mysticism played in keeping people's spirits alive. One of these stories, published in one of Romania's leading national newspapers, is particularly illustrative of people's desperate need for dreams and miracles.

In a small village in Giurgiu county, thousands of believers came to see the crying icon of Mary, who was claimed to have cured hundreds of people. A professor from the faculty of theology in Bucharest, however, challenged the power of the icon during a televized show, arguing that the icon was merely a scam that helped the local church receive more donations. After the show, a revolt picked up in front of the church with churchgoers coming from different corners of the country to receive the miracle of the crying icon, challenging the professor and proclaiming the true ability of the icon to give them peace and calm. Perhaps the most realistic of them all was Rodica Lupu-Savei, one of the churchgoers, who, when interviewed, pointed out the real purpose of the icon:

> It is such a cruel gesture to cut someone's wings when they are still hoping. How can an icon harm anyone? I come here for some time now. I never expected miracles from the crying icon, but the mass gives me quiet and calm and makes me feel better.[43]

In this case, re-selfing meant perhaps nothing more than the ability to hope and gain some perspective, even when more rational arguments stood against it. The important support that hope provides in periods of transition is perhaps not to be neglected, and the ability to hope against hope is not only something necessary but something that we should perhaps admire.

Shock, illusions and disillusions

Through the concept of shock, this chapter has explored different ways of perceiving the process of modern social change as well as the increasingly important role that illusions, or the realm of phantasy, play in our everyday lives. The transition from a negative to a positive connotation of shock has significantly shifted the way in which we approach change, making the latter much more desirable and to a certain extent unquestionable in its means. Change is embraced as something positive, independent of its immediate consequences, while illusions play an important role in providing both a constant element of hope as well as an essential element of escape. The transition from one illusion to another, along with the inherent process of disillusionment—the death of one illusion in order to make room for another—now occurs in a phantasy realm that can also be more easily manipulated, one that is no longer clearly differentiated from the realm of the "real," and thus, one that risks carrying dangerous consequences into our everyday life.

By exploring the changes in the way in which people have historically related to the process of change and the shock associated with it, the chapter has tried to point out that more than just being associated with periods of great social change, shock has become a constant of modern life, one that people have learned to adjust to through a number of different mechanisms: from associating shock with helpful technologies, to internalizing shock as something "normal" and perhaps even "therapeutic", to seeking refuge from shock into different realms of phantasy. Despite these different attempts to adjust to shock, change, as experienced in the post-communist world, remains a traumatic experience, one that has however been silenced—thus experienced mainly in the private realm—by overly enthusiastic attempts to dismiss the post-revolutionary period as extremely painful and difficult, fraught with disappointments and economic struggles, and above all, damaging to people's sense of confidence and trust in the state.

While this chapter has attempted to add to the theoretical framework of disillusionment during transitions, by seeking to explain why the shock of transition is oftentimes labeled as positive, the following chapters seek to provide the empirical details that lend stability to this framework. By focusing on key moments of change: the 1989 Revolution and the period immediately following the revolution, the chapters build alternative approaches to otherwise classic moments of interrogating social change (revolutions and civil society) by focusing on personal testimonies that challenge the trajectory and success of the Romanian Revolution as well as the democratic nature of the political establishment that was to follow.

The following chapter explores the transition from the communist illusion to the capitalist illusion through the eyes of the 1989 Romanian revolutionaries and follows the process of illusion/disillusionment in light of their dreams, actions, motivations and their post-revolutionary experiences and reflections. Using the theoretical framework presented in Chapters 2 and 3, this new chapter seeks to understand, on the one hand, how the democratic illusion came to dominate post-revolutionary discourses despite the fact that the ethos of the Romanian revolution was based on less ambitious socialist reforms; on the other hand, it seeks to examine how sometimes random events and decisions made on the spur of the moment led to significant changes in the course of the Romanian Revolution, ultimately sealing its unexpected success. The personal disillusionment of many of the former revolutionaries is used as a metaphor for better understanding the dialectics of the process of collective and individual illusion formation and disillusionment.

Notes

1. See for example Samuel P. Huntington, *The Third Wave: Democratization in the Late Twentieth Century* (Norman: University of Oklahoma Press, 1991).
2. See Michael Burawoy and Katherine Verdery, *Uncertain Transitions: Ethnographies of Change in the Postsocialist World* (Lanham, MD: Rowman and Littlefield, 1999).
3. Sigmund Freud, *Beyond the Pleasure Principle*, trans. C.J.M. Hubback, The International Psycho-Analytical Library, ed. Ernest Jones (London and Vienna: The International Psycho-Analytical Press, 1922).
4. Charles Baudelaire, *Paris Spleen* (New York: New Directions Publishing Corporation, 1970); Charles Baudelaire, *Les Fleurs Du Mal* (Boston: David R. Godine, 1985).
5. Georg Simmel, *The Sociology of Georg Simmel*, trans. Kurt Wolff (Cambridge: Free Press, 1964).
6. Walter Benjamin, *The Arcades Project*, trans. Howard Eiland and Kevin McLaughlin, ed. Rolf Tiedemann (Cambridge, MA: Belknap Press of Harvard University Press, 1982).
7. Walter Benjamin, *Illuminations*, trans. Harry Zohn, ed. Hannah Arendt (New York: Schocken Books, 1968).
8. Benjamin, *Illuminations*.
9. Carl Cassegard, "Shock and Modernity in Walter Benjamin and Kawabata Yasunari," *Japanese Studies* 19.3 (1999), 238–9.
10. Terry Eagleton, *Walter Benjamin or Towards a Revolutionary Criticism* (London: Verso Editions and NLB, 1981).
11. Benjamin was an avid collector of books and miniature objects and believed that the art of collecting symbolized in many ways the ability to build a different relationship with the object whereby the latter carried a particular experience or memory that could trigger the memoir involuntaire allowing for a richer daily experience and way of living. By collecting miniature objects—rendered inefficient by their size—Benjamin sought to make precisely the point that objects are not only meant to be "used" but rather to be admired and appreciated for their interior life.
12. See the proliferation of TV reality shows such as *Survivor*, *Shipwrecked*, *Extreme Makeover*, to mention just a few, where surpassing a series of artificially set obstacles or difficulties becomes a goal in itself that can define one's success, abilities, and even happiness.
13. See the explosion of shows on the Travel Channel or National Geographic focusing on new culinary experiences, travel extremes and the exploration of the "exotic."
14. See Rolando Vasquez, *Poetry and Modernity: Walter Benjamin's "On Some Motifs in Baudelaire"* (2006. Working draft. For more information

contact author.); Timothy W. Luke, *Scanning Fast Capitalism: Quasipolitan Order and New Social Flowmations*, available at: www.uta.edu/huma/agger/fastcapitalism/1_1/luke.htm (accessed May 15th, 2006).

15 A type of chocolate and nut paste that was very popular among children, yet difficult to obtain because it had to be imported from West Germany.

16 Susan Sontag, "Under the Sign of Saturn," *Under the Sign of Saturn* (New York: Anchor Books, 1972), 115–16.

17 See testimonies regarding similar experiences with nostalgia throughout Central and Eastern Europe in Henri Vogt, *Between Utopia and Disillusionment: A Narrative of Political Transformation in Eastern Europe* (Oxford: Berghahn Books, 2005).

18 Cassegard, "Shock and Modernity in Walter Benjamin and Kawabata Yasunari," 242.

19 Cassegard, "Shock and Modernity in Walter Benjamin and Kawabata Yasunari," 249.

20 The concept of spleen is borrowed from Baudelaire's vision of reality as spleen—dirty, corrupt and in your face—thus suggesting that shock can act as a way to escape reality (and spleen) by opening up spaces in which the individual can seek refuge and find some form of consolation.

21 Carl Cassegard and others have called the same process, the naturalization process.

22 Tim Armstrong, *Two Types of Shock in Modernity*, available at: http://personal.rhul.ac.uk/uhle/012 (accessed May 15th, 2006).

23 Timothy W. Luke, "Technology as Metaphor: Tropes of Construction, Destruction, and Instruction in Globalization," paper presented at the International Studies Association annual conference (San Diego: 2006).

24 Timothy W. Luke, "Transnationalities: Embedded, Imagined, and Engineered Communities," paper presented at the conference "Rethinking Spaces: Transnational Representations" (McGill University: 2006).

25 Carl Cassegard, "Murakami Haruki and the Naturalization of Modernity," *International Journal of Japanese Sociology* 10 (2001).

26 Cassegard, "Murakami Haruki and the Naturalization of Modernity," 88.

27 See Leonard Roy Frank, *History of Shock Treatment* (San Francisco: Leonard Roy Frank, 1978).

28 Jeffrey Sachs, "Shock Therapy in Poland: Perspectives of Five Years," Lecture, *The Tanner Lectures on Human Values* (University of Utah: 1994).

29 Daniel Singer, "Europe's Crises," *Social Justice* 23.1-2 (1996).

30 Sachs, "Shock Therapy in Poland: Perspectives of Five Years."

31 Theodore P. Gerber and Michael Hout, "More Shock Than Therapy: Market Transition, Employment, and Income in Russia, 1991-1995," *American Journal of Sociology* 104, July (1998).

32 Claudia Feichtinger and Gerhard Fink, "The Collective Culture Shock in Transition Countries—Theoretical and Empirical Implications," *Leadership & Organization Development Journal* 19.6 (1998).

33 Bertolt Brecht, *Brecht on Theater: The Development of an Aesthetic*, trans. John Willett (New York: Hill and Wang, 1964).

34 Even tragic theater is no exception, for even when focusing on the inevitability of certain events, it suggests different possible, and positive, outcomes.
35 Patricia Pringle, "'Spatial Pleasures," *Space and Culture* 8.2 (2005), 155.
36 Beatriz Jaguaribe, "The Shock of the Real: Realist Aesthetics in the Media and the Urban Experience," *Space and Culture* 8.1 (2005), 70.
37 Jaguaribe, "The Shock of the Real: Realist Aesthetics in the Media and the Urban Experience," 70.
38 Armstrong, *Two Types of Shock in Modernity*.
39 Herbert Marcuse, *Eros and Civilization: A Philosophical Inquiry into Freud* (Boston: Beacon Press, 1966), 100–1.
40 Marcuse, *Eros and Civilization: A Philosophical Inquiry into Freud*, 140–1.
41 Philip Wexler, "'Re-Selfing' after Post-Modern Culture: Sacred Social Psychology," *Alienation: Exploring Diverse Realities*, ed. Devorah Kalekin-Fishman (Jyvaskyla: University of Jyvaskyla, 1998).
42 Wexler, "'Re-Selfing' after Post-Modern Culture: Sacred Social Psychology," 84–5.
43 Carmen Plesa and Daniela Sontica, "Icoana-Minune, Pricina De Scandal," *Adevarul* August 11th, 2005.

5

The illusions and disillusions of the Romanian Revolution: the case of the Timisoara revolutionaries

The controversies surrounding the 1989 Romanian Revolution

Using original data extracted from a series of interviews with the leaders of the Timisoara Revolution, newspaper articles dating back to the period immediately following the revolution and comments collected during the 2004 Timisoara symposium commemorating fifteen years since the revolution, this chapter seeks to understand why many of the leaders of the Romanian Revolution feel betrayed, abandoned and generally disillusioned and the extent to which their experience is reflective of the way in which other Romanians have experienced the transition. By seeking to determine at which point the transition from revolutionary enchantment to post-revolutionary disillusionment occurred and what the circumstances were that led to it, the chapter follows the historical thread of the revolution, picking out events and circumstances that have either been surrounded by controversy or have remained for the most part silent/silenced. This particular portrayal of the Romanian Revolution sheds a different light on the process of change, as a slow and confusing one, often uncontrolled and left at the whims of accidental occurrences. By focusing on the marginal and often untold stories of those who felt betrayed, left behind, or abandoned, this chapter seeks to portray and understand the lows as well as the highs of the revolution.

There are a series of images and narratives that have grown to dominate the discourse on the 1989 Eastern European revolutions and the overthrow of communism: the bulldozing of the Berlin Wall, the mass demonstrations in city squares, the trial and death sentence of Ceausescu, the rise to power of former dissents like Vaclav Havel or Lech Valessa, the first free elections, the taking down of communist statues and symbols and the victorious marches of ecstatic citizens who felt free for the first time in over forty years. The general image is one of positive relief, of radical change and movement towards democracy. And yet a series of other narratives challenge this traditional view, arguing that the initial positive relief was quickly replaced by a sense of loss and confusion, that the original expectations of radical change gave in to a relatively slow and divisive transition and that the push for democracy was not the inspiration for the revolutions but something that came afterwards along with a new set of international pressures and expectations.

Fifteen years into the transition, Nicolae Badilescu, one of the main leaders of the Romanian Revolution in Timisoara—where the first mass demonstrations occurred—confessed that if he could go back in time, he would not incite people to go out in the streets, he would not attempt to topple the Ceausescu regime and would in fact choose to wait for a more reformist communist government.[1] Another two leaders of the Timisoara Revolution, Claudiu Iordache and Lorin Fortuna have expressed similar feelings of disappointment and regret.[2] The period immediately following the revolution, including the new political regime, the transition process and the series of democratic reforms, caught many of the revolutionaries by surprise. And yet, was that not what they were out in the streets for? Surprisingly, the answer might turn out to be no. The Eastern European fight for freedom and democracy, that has served as a model for democratic transitions in other parts of the world, might turn out to be less glorious than initially portrayed, and more fraught with confusion, unrealistic expectations and a lack of understanding of what was to come.

The Romanian Revolution in particular continues to stand as a great site of contestation, with people still looking for "the truth" about what happened, heroes and criminals still to be disputed, disappearances and murders still to be elucidated. What emerges from this confusion is a series of narratives that focus on the emotional side of the revolution, people's dreams, first expectations, fears, courage, misconceptions, hesitations, dismay, ecstasy and pain. These narratives are perhaps a part of every revolution, though they are rarely used to draw any theoretical conclusions, for their sinuous path and unpredictability rends them less fertile for such pursuits. Anthropologists, sociologists and journalists are left to pick up these pieces and build an image that can draw on people's empathy and create the necessary resources and support for international aid or international interventions. These narratives could however constitute a rich and resourceful research ground for those who are willing to accept more flexible frameworks of understanding and knowing.

Revolutions are living things that often span far beyond the few key days that bring about the actual fall of a regime. Revolutionary ideals are continuously reworked and challenged even by those that built them in the first place. The collapse of a regime, the fall of a statue, the invasion of a city square, the execution of a former dictator, are the ecstatic moments of a revolution. The disinformation, the slow rate with which news and change travels from the capital to the provinces, the radical difference between the experience of the elite and that of the remainder of the population, are also important parts of a revolution. Tiziano Terzani, an Italian journalist living in China who was traveling throughout the former Soviet Union at the time of the collapse of the communist regime, portrays the latter very effectively through images of small cities and villages that even months after the collapse of communism still debated whether to remove the official communist portrait or slogan, images of people confused by the sudden inaccessibility of personal use products such as soap, toothpaste or underwear because of the sudden collapse of the market, and the sudden emergence of previously suppressed nationalist and sometimes xenophobic movements.[3]

Revolutions are often made possible by the unrealistic ideals of those who led them, by their distorted visions of democracy, and sometimes even by the "luck" of surprisingly warm weather during a politically heated winter—thus allowing more people to come out and demonstrate—a working sound station and a balcony from which the crowd can be addressed, or the existence of large avenues and industrial platforms along which people can be gathered and incited to participate.[4] These unrealistic ideals could be viewed as the positive illusions necessary for a collective to emerge from an otherwise hopeless situation, but they could also be viewed as the excessive illusions that led to the later plunge into a state of disappointment and in some cases even despair—a state that proved to be extremely detrimental for the democracy-building process and the new capitalism illusion that would come to dominate the social and political horizon of all of Central and Eastern Europe.

By focusing on the most important controversies that surround the Romanian Revolution, and applying a framework that looks at the process of illusion formation and loss—disillusionment, this chapter hopes to offer an alternative view of the process of social change in Romania. There are a number of controversial ideas that surround the Romanian Revolution, the most important of which are: 1) that the Romanian Revolution was to a large extent unexpected; 2) that the main ideal of the revolution was a liberal democratic one; 3) that there were no negotiations with the Ceausescu regime; 4) that the National Salvation Front was the first political consolidation of power that came after the fall of the Ceausescu regime; 5) that there is "a truth" about what happened during the Romanian Revolution, particularly with regards to the violence and deaths that ocurred.

Was the Romanian Revolution largely unexpected?

There were several incidents that made it obvious that Romania, like the rest of Eastern Europe, was on the verge of a big change before 1989. While most examinations in the Eastern European literature argue that the Romanian revolution was perhaps the most unexpected of them all—both in its timing as well as in its ability to completely destroy the Ceausescu regime—a closer examination of a series of incidents—such as the Valea Jiului revolt in 1977 and the Brasov demonstrations in 1987—reveals the increasing weakness of the communist regime in Romania and the erosion of one of its most powerful tools: propaganda. These two incidents marked the passing of an important threshold in the Ceausescu communist regime: the realization that the regime was not only afraid but also weak.[5] Coupled with the changes in the international and national political opportunity structure, like the fall of the Berlin Wall, the series of velvet revolutions throughout Central and Eastern Europe and the pressure from outside put on Ceausescu to adopt a series of reforms,[6] they provide an essential explanation as to why the Romanian Revolution occurred when it did. The question remains however as to why the revolution appeared as impossible to achieve as it did—perhaps even more on the inside then on the outside. The answer lies perhaps in the difficulty of even imagining a different future for the country after over forty years of dictatorship. The strength of the communist illusion lay not so much in people's agreement with it, but perhaps in the people's fear of anything significantly different. The over-reliance on routine and a certain sense of security, had made people fearful of the radically new and different.

Valea Jiului, 1977

The 1977 revolt in Valea Jiului was triggered by a series of different reasons, the most powerful of which was perhaps the extreme poverty and insecurity in which the miners and their families lived.[7] Valea Jiului is a coal-rich area of Romania, where most cities are built around the mining industry. These mining towns were as dark and bleak as one can imagine: the apartment buildings were poorly built, electricity and heating were often out, layers of soot covered everything from cars to buildings and people, food shortages were the norm rather than the exception, and social services were close to non-existent. The symbol of the strong and hard-working communist miner that was often invoked in communist propaganda in order to justify increasing work quotas was certainly challenged by the misery of miners in these towns. There was nothing glorious in their suffering and this particular communist propaganda must have seemed ludicrous to those who were sweating every day in the mines. It is thus no surprise that it was here that the first anti-communist revolts in Romania erupted.

The timing of the revolt was directly connected to Ceausescu's latest decision to extend the age at which miners could retire, thus forcing them to continue to work under conditions and circumstances that would most likely cut their life expectancy to almost their retirement age. In his attempt to repay all of Romania's foreign debt, Ceausescu pushed the entire country into one of the worst economic recessions it had ever experienced.[8] The Valea Jiului miners' demonstrations were a desperate cry for a more decent life, for food and better health care, for better schools and a little more time to rest. The demands were by no means outrageous, and while the character of the revolt was initially socio-economic in nature, it was quickly transformed into a political protest once the repression became imminent and visible.

The way in which the revolt unfolded pointed to a number of things: 1) that despite hardships and disillusionment with the Ceausescu regime, people were not yet ready to ask for radical changes but rather hoped for a mere improvement of existing conditions; 2) that Ceausescu continued to be caught up in his socialist dream and honestly believed that his policies were going to bring the country to a powerful international position; and 3) that when faced with rejection, Ceausescu was ready to respond with physical and psychological torture. In many ways, this revolt, and Ceausescu's answer to it, predicted the violent turn that the Romanian Revolution would take in 1989 and also hinted at the increasing weakness of the Ceausescu regime and Ceausescu's vulnerability as an individual.

Called to Valea Jiului to answer the demonstrators' concerns, Ceausescu was surprised to see not only that people did not have the patience to listen to him, but that the miners did not seem to be intimidated by him. In recounting the episode, Ruxandra Cesereanu notes that Ceausescu was afraid and had to be rushed out of the crowd so as not to be attacked. This was perhaps one of the first times that Ceausescu felt the rage and resentment of his own people. This was in complete contradiction to his strong personal belief that he was a loved and respected leader. The "Down with Ceausescu" slogans that could be heard from the crowd seemed inconceivable when coming from his own people, and thus Ceausescu's immediate response was to refer to this group as nothing but a minority, a band of hooligans, gypsies, impostors and criminals—all the marginalized groups of Romanian society, the "others" that did not belong to his beloved people.[9]

As hooligans, the rebel miners could be punished and tortured, while the rest of the country was for the most part oblivious to the incident, with rumors as their only source of information. Ceausescu decided to seal off the area from the rest of the country and submit the miners to an intense reeducation program that did not shy away from using physical and more importantly, psychological abuse. In the meanwhile, he revamped his propaganda campaign, increased his media exposure and continued to glorify his persona and achievements. It is not clear whether this image revamping was aimed solely at improving his popularity or whether it was an instinctive self-protective response aimed also at proving to himself that he continued to be a loved and popular leader. As things appeared to get back on track, the years to come would only get tougher, with the economy continuing to decline and the general lever of misery continuing to rise.

Brasov, 1987

Ten years after the Valea Jiului incident, and only two years before the Romanian Revolution, workers from the Steagu Rosu industrial plant in Brasov poured out into the streets to demonstrate against the proposed thirty percent salary cut after discussions with the plant authorities failed to produce an agreement. Tired of power cuts and job cuts and the general economic hardship in which the country found itself, the workers headed for the local Communist Party Council where they attacked the administrators, destroyed windows, furniture and books and tramped over a large Ceausescu photo while yelling "Down with Ceausescu" and "Down with Communism."[10]

Unlike Valea Jiului, Brasov was a more prosperous industrial town, with a historic center and an established university and intellectual elite. Located in the mountains, a few hours outside of Bucharest, with classical architecture and a rich history, Brasov was more open and informed and thus posed a much more dangerous challenge to the regime. While in Valea Jiului it was only the miners that took to the streets, in Brasov, the intellectuals and dissidents joined the workers' march demanding the removal of Ceausescu and the introduction of reforms. The level of rage seemed to be more elevated and aimed directly at Ceausescu himself. The fact that the workers were aware of some of the changes occurring throughout the rest of Central and Eastern Europe as well as in the former Soviet Union, made them even more dangerous, despite the fact that their demands remained mainly economic in nature and targeted the communist regime and Ceausescu himself only to the extent that they were seen as responsible for the general economic collapse.

While people were not yet ready to imagine a democratic future for their country, their protest clearly pointed out the general collapse of the communist/socialist illusion and the propaganda that helped support it. Ceausescu and his regime were no longer seen as viable economic alternatives for the future, although no other clear alternatives were yet on the horizon. The burning of official party symbols, books and more importantly, of Ceausescu's portrait in Brasov, sent an important signal to party officials and Ceausescu himself. The desecration of otherwise sanctified objects such as Ceausescu's portrait—present in every classroom, official building, factory floor and offices—was not only an act of disobedience but the ultimate slap in the face for a leader who adored his image and role as the absolute leader.[11] If the communist illusion was largely built on visual props, such as propaganda slogans and portraits, Brasov was the first place to clear up—while even momentarily—the visual horizon and make room for a space free of communist propaganda, free of Ceausescu images and filled with the hope for a different future. Expressing their rage and frustration out in the open made the need for and even the possibility of a change even more real.

Quoting W. I. Thomas, Goldfarb has written: "If men define situations as real, they are real in their consequences."[12] Calling the Ceausescu communist regime for what it was, and attacking the remaining of its props—this time the visual ones—constituted a direct challenge to the illusion of communism/socialism and to Ceausescu's power. The wake-up call from this particular illusion was not only hinted at through the burning of party symbols, but also called out literally through the singing of what was to later become the national anthem: "Awaken thee, Romanian!" The choice of words was no coincidence. People did feel like they had been living a nightmare for too long, and that an awakening was necessary.

The song, based on a poem written in the 1840s, symbolized a call for liberation, this time from an internal oppressor.

Sung during crucial moments, such as the Independence War (1877–1878), World War I, the moments of crisis after August 23rd, 1944 when, after the state coup, Romania turned against Hitler's Germany and then participated in the war along with the Allies, this song carried a particularly strong nationalist implication, and signified that Ceausescu and his regime were no longer viewed as representatives of this nation. The song calls out for a quick awakening, arguing that it is "now or never."[13] Although the Brasov demonstrations were met with an even harsher response from the communist regime—arrests, tortures, deportations—they also constituted a clear sign that the regime was faltering. With the precedent set, from hereon, there was no going back. It was only a question of time before new demonstrations would engulf other areas of the country.

Brasov triggered an important alarm not only for the general population, but also for the communist elite, which sensed that things were about to change. Ceausescu, once again, addressed the demonstrators as hooligans and criminals, and made perhaps one of his biggest tactical mistakes: he gave an official statement on television about what had happened in Brasov. Despite his attempt to portray the incident as hooliganism and to pre-empt any further such moves through fear of punishment, his statement only confirmed the rumors that had already been circulating throughout the country, sending a clear signal that the level of discontent was general as opposed to isolated. Instead of instilling fear, the incident only helped solidify the need for a change.[14] It did however make clear that the regime was not going to admit defeat without putting up a fight and that Ceausescu was determined to use any means possible to secure his reign. At this point, a change could only be secured through the death of the last important symbol of the regime: Ceausescu himself. Yet this was far from obvious at the time.

In retrospect, these two incidents do tend to predict, to a large extent, what was going to happen in 1989: they point to a widespread level of dissatisfaction among different strata of Romanian society, the power of the masses and more importantly the workers—thus suggesting that the next big demonstrations had to come from a strong industrial city, like Timisoara—the increasing weakness of the Ceausescu regime, and last but not least, the fact that the regime was only left with sheer military strength to fight the demonstrations and thus that a successful revolt would require that the military and the police join the demonstrators as well. This is precisely what happened during the 1989 Revolution. What made this unclear up until the very moment of the 1989 Revolution was perhaps the inability to think beyond routine, the naive belief that a communist reform was possible, the underestimation of the workers' power, the overestimation of the regime's strength, and the fear and inability to even imagine a future outside of the communist framework.

The Laslo Tokes incident and the beginning of the 1989 Revolution

That the revolution started in a town like Timisoara was no surprise. Timisoara, a large city in Western Romania that lies very close to both the Hungarian and Serbian borders, was considered to be one of the most diverse cities in Romania (with a large ethnic Hungarian, Serbian and German presence) and was also looked upon as one of the most pro-Western cities. News from abroad seeped in more easily—including news of the fall of the Berlin Wall and the velvet revolutions sweeping Eastern Europe—through Radio Free Europe and the Hungarian and Serbian TV and radio stations that could be caught along the border. In light of such news, the general atmosphere was one of expectancy. While it was unclear exactly what would happen, the probability of a change was deemed to be high.[15]

That the revolution would start as a small demonstration against the eviction of a reformed Hungarian priest was purely incidental: the spark could have potentially come from somewhere else. Yet the fact that it did happen in front of Laslo Tokes's house, which happened to be located in the center of town, at the intersection of several tramlines—which the majority of people used to commute—was essential. This gave a somewhat religious connotation to the revolt, which struck an important chord in the hearts of a deeply religious and superstitious population. The lighting of candles during the vigil in front of Tokes's house must have created a very powerful image that December 15th—the only time crowds of people could gather in large numbers to celebrate was during religious holidays when they would often light candles.[16]

The location as well as the candles drew more attention to the site. One of the future leaders of the revolution, a student by the name of Sanda Adrian, described the atmosphere as rather surprising and confusing:

> In the evening of December fifteen I was going to a party, the winter break had just began, somewhere in Fraidorf ... a far quarter of the city. In the morning of the 16th, as I was coming back, I heard rumors that people were gathering in front of Tokes' house in Maria Square. I went to see what was happening. I was a little surprised by what I saw. I recognized the faces of some other students as well as some agitators and secret police members dressed as civilians. I realized something was wrong.[17]

People were thus drawn by curiosity and by accident. From Adrian's testimony, it becomes obvious that many people came to look and left. Those who stayed however witnessed a series of interesting dynamics: 1) the arrival of several agitators—most likely hired by the local government—dressed in civilian clothes, who started throwing stones at Tokes's windows, calling for him to "Go home to his Hungarians," 2) the presence of the secret police, also dressed in civilian clothes, who could however be fairly easily identified[18] and 3) the presence of some important local party representatives that had come to negotiate.

The peaceful nature of the demonstration, that resembled more of a funeral procession than a loud violent outcry, as well as the apparent leniency with which the crowd was treated initially—the initial crowd could have easily been dispelled or arrested by the local police given that only a relatively small number of people were present—allowed the protest to gain momentum and attract the attention of those who were awaiting such an opportunity. The relatively quick appearance of anti-communist fliers and signs that complemented the shouted anti-communist and anti-Ceausescu slogans, signaled that some were ready to take this opportunity. Speculations about whether the demonstration in front of Tokes's house was planned with the hope that it would lead to a revolution are still largely unfounded, yet the ability of the population to quickly mobilize itself into a large-scale demonstration shows that the momentum was there.[19]

Fear however was also present, and Tokes himself encouraged people to go home, fearing that they would only make the situation worse for him and his pregnant wife. According to Ruxandra Cesereanu's testimony, asked whether he would have ever guessed that the gathering in front of his house would spill into a full-blown revolution, Tokes answered: definitely not. Perhaps that would have been the answer of mostly everyone present. Yet people were perhaps more ready for a change than they actually thought. The inability to expect that significant change would occur lay perhaps in the general lack of familiarity with alternative regimes and thus in the impossibility clearly formulating a new illusion or goal for which to strive.

Was the main goal of the Romanian Revolution a liberal democratic one?

Most of the evidence gathered from interviews with revolutionary leaders and participants in the Romanian Revolution, seems to suggest that the revolution had no higher goal than the removal of the communist regime and Ceausescu himself. The revolution was thus fought on no clear democratic platform—at least not the market-led democracy and democratic reforms that were to follow. One should not confuse the "We Want Democracy and Freedom" cries with cries for a capitalist economy, for most people had no idea what that was. What most people could hope for initially, was a reformed communism à la Gorbachev. Only a very small elite saw this as an opportunity to move towards a democratic system, while the majority of the people were driven to the streets out of a sheer survival instinct.[20]

Not only was the revolution not fought on a clear platform, but many of the initial participants joined in out of sheer curiosity, without knowing what was really happening. People were swept away by the crowd—or sometimes the police—while in their pajamas, on the way to the supermarket or simply chatting with neighbors about what could be happening. Some thought a prisoner had escaped, others that foreign forces had invaded Romania. The initial arrests also caught many of these people by surprise, as they genuinely had little idea about what was happening. Thus many retirees, women and children and other curious people found themselves in prison for no other reason other than just standing on the street at the wrong time. Treated as heroes upon their release, many of these people could barely make sense of what was happening around them, and were certainly not the freedom fighters that many imagined them to be.[21] In fact, as Nicolae Badilescu, one of the Timisoara Revolution leaders relates in an interview, even those who were out in the streets calling for freedom did not know what it meant. Conceptually, they had an understanding of it, but no one had ever explained to them what actions it implied and how they should enjoy it:

> We didn't know what freedom was. We believed in the notion of freedom that we had borrowed from the Greeks. From the Greeks onward, the concepts of democracy, freedom, were nothing but concepts that we read about in books. We didn't know what freedom was, we didn't know what democracy was.[22]

Fifteen years into the transition, Badilescu has grown even more skeptical of the very possibility of democracy. Seeing what the democratic reforms have brought to Romania, he is far from convinced that his initial dream of democracy is even possible:

> We were under the impression that democracy was something that actually existed in the social world. We later found that it was not the case. Democracy is not something that can actually exist. It is an invention by those who rule the world sustained by those who teach it.[23]

Claudiu Iordache, Lorin Fortuna, Sanda Adrian and many other revolutionary leaders from Timisoara all declared that their protests in Timisoara had little to do with the expectation that Romania would become the next France or Germany. In fact, to the extent that any expectations existed, they were far more pessimistic: going out into the streets, each of these leaders expected to either die or be arrested and thus started their days with final goodbyes to their families. The thought that the Ceausescu regime could fall was already ambitious, while the thought of a liberal democracy only crossed people's minds to the extent that they associated it with a series of rights, freedoms and wealth, yet certainly not with the number of painful sacrifices one had to make to get there.

Certainly no one expected the privatization of all state-owned industries and along with it the appearance of rising unemployment—something that was virtually unheard of in communist Romania—the soaring rise in inflation of up to 300 percent and prices changing from day to day, the swift decline in the purchasing power of the average family, sometimes by as much as seven to ten times from what it was before, the privatization of schools and medical services leading to significantly lower access to these services, the destruction of much of the communal property and the obvious corruption of those who made incredible fortunes overnight. In fact, if they had known this was coming, many of the workers—who were the most significantly affected by these reforms—would certainly not have been out in the streets.

This experience is by no means limited to Romania. In fact, G.M. Tamas, a famous Hungarian dissident, argues along similar lines in his article on the Hungarian Revolution and the Hungarian transition:

> we shouted on the streets of Budapest, "We Want Democracy!" not "We Want the Rule of Law," mind you, not liberty, not justice, but democracy. What people's idea of democracy was in those dizzy, exhilarating days, can be safely reconstructed from what people now consider non-democratic or anti-democratic and as such reject. [...] The East European democratic idea basically envisions a society without a state. The anti-institutional curse that seems to plague us leaves us the choice of a barbarous dictatorship or boundless chaos. In order to prevent either from happening we should understand why all the conventional expectations are being left unfulfilled.[24]

Tamas was particularly skeptical of the "democratic" regimes that were to come after the fall of communism. In the case of Hungary, he argued very strongly that the Hungarian revolution was merely the failure of socialism rather than the victory of liberal democracy. In his view, capitalism just *happened* to Eastern Europeans, and it continues to be something alien that follows an unusual logic that one must simply put up with. His warning about the moral exhaustion of the liberal regime across the world, despite the continuous push for it in the developing world, has unfortunately fallen on deaf ears. A closer examination of the workers' demonstrations in Timisoara also points to the fact that the liberal democratic dream was far from what the workers were asking for.

Workers' demonstrations in Timisoara

The Timisoara demonstrations were for the most part workers' demonstrations. Intellectuals played a minimal role in getting the crowd out into the streets, only later finding themselves as natural orators and organizers, once the mobilization had already occurred. This meant that the demonstrations were largely reactionary and did not have a clear and certainly not a unitary platform on which to stand. The demands were formulated late in the game, once it became obvious that the regime was faltering, and they continued to change throughout the upcoming weeks and months as a unitary list of demands was sought.[25]

What started as a small standout in front of Laslo Tokes's house later spilled into large-scale demonstrations once the workers from the industrial platform on the outskirts of Timisoara decided it was time to take to the streets. Between December 17th and December 20th, the workers' unions got organized and workers poured out into the streets on December 20th. During the days of the 17th to the 20th of December, the workers describe the atmosphere in their factories as one of silent revolt, where no one was doing any work, and everyone was waiting for a sign, for something to happen. Many of the workers had seen the demonstrations in front of Tokes's house and even participated in some of them. A bond of silence was formed when workers refused to report on each other and worried about those who had not showed up to work after the previous night's demonstrations—realizing that they had most likely been arrested. Their silent revolt showed deep rage against the Ceausescu regime and exhaustion with the communist demands. Yet the call to take to the streets was perhaps fired more by a desire to avenge those that had been arrested and publicly show the level of rage, rather than a desire to bring about democracy.[26]

The party's attempts to control the factories and the workers' unions by calling for a curfew and closing the gates of most factories during the day, by conducting a series of interrogations, and by sending high-level officials to factories to give a new series of propaganda speeches, backfired when the workers read this unusual behavior as a sign of weakness and fear on the part of the regime.[27] Richard Andrew Hall argues that once the myth of total control was challenged, it created a climate of over-confidence and euphoria that allowed for the workers to spill out into the streets, something that only a few days before would have been inconceivable. Misjudging the extent to which the population had tired of their propaganda, the regime mistakenly assumed that sending party officials to "explain" the situation would help calm things down. Ceausescu's public speech on radio and television on December 20th denouncing what was happening in Timisoara as a conspiracy from abroad, sent a clear signal to the rest of the country: the rumors about the Timisoara uprisings had now been confirmed, and Ceausescu appeared as nothing but a big liar. This was the signal that the rest of the country was awaiting.[28] What really helped tilt the balance however, and something that Hall does not openly address, is the open violence and repression which led not only to arrests but more importantly to the first deaths. The sudden visibility of the repression through these deaths pushed the final trigger.

Aware that some of the demonstrators had been killed—shot at—and many more arrested, starting with the 17th of December, the workers realized that things had gotten out of control. It was the first time that fire was opened against a crowd, and although the party propaganda was presenting the demonstrators as nothing but hooligans and inciters working for the Hungarian and Soviet government, seeking to reoccupy the country, to all those who had been out in the streets, this was clearly a lie. Having lost friends and family members, people poured out into the streets in even larger numbers, shouting: "We're not going home! Our dead won't let us!" The sense of duty and responsibility over the dead gave people something else to fight for: the dignity of the dead, so that their fate would not have been in vain.[29]

Did negotiations with the party elite take place?

While the Romanian Revolution is described as a violent revolution, as opposed to the velvet revolutions in the rest of

Central and Eastern Europe where peaceful negotiations allowed for a smoother transition, it would be inaccurate to say that no negotiations with the party elite were attempted in Romania. The main difference from the other negotiations occurring throughout Central and Eastern Europe was perhaps the fact that communist elites in Romania carried little power of decision without Ceausescu's approval. Ceausescu's refusal to negotiate thus put them in the position where all they could do was to grant small personal requests, in the hope that this would dissuade the revolutionary leaders enough for them to go home. It did not.

The first open negotiation occurred on the 20th of December between high-ranking party officials who were sent to Timisoara to calm the situation down, and the demonstrators outside the county council.[30] The difference between these negotiations and the velvet negotiations of other Central and Eastern European revolutions however, was that neither side came prepared to negotiate: the demonstrators did not have a well-planned committee or a planned list of demands, while the party officials were not given free rein to negotiate and were simply told to stall the situation. The delegation sent in to negotiate with the party elites was formed by an ad hoc committee of representatives and thus most members of the delegation did not know each other, and did not have a plan of action or a concrete list of demands when faced with prime-minister Dascalescu's aggressive demands. Costel Balint describes the scene as follows:

> The revolutionaries realized that they weren't ready to carry out a conversation with the leaders [...] not ready to present clear propositions, they started asking for personal items such as flats, passports, food. The discussion was ruled by fear and confusion. At a point when the discussion was inevitably drifting again towards insignificant demands, a concrete demand was uttered: the immediate resignation of Nicolae Ceausescu.[31]

This radical demand was certainly not open for negotiation at a point when the party elites were still responding directly to Ceausescu and risked their heads if anything bad were to happen. Once this clear demand was made, one could no longer speak about any possible negotiation. A series of other demands were later added to this main one: the creation of a new government; an official announcement with the total number of the dead and those who were hurt; the release of those who had been arrested; the bodies of the dead so that their families could bury them; that the events taking place in Timisoara be transmitted live on radio and TV; that a list of members of the present committee be sent over to the Serbian Consulate along with their demands to guarantee their safety.[32] Looking at these demands, it becomes obvious that while the demonstrators were clearly calling for Ceausescu to step down and for a new government to be formed, there was yet no mention of a democratic system of governance. If anything, calls for democratic elections were heard only later, when it became obvious that the old system was faltering and that a new one had to be created or at least proposed.[33]

The negotiations with the local party elite ended with no resolution. Some promises were made, out of which only one was realized: several of those who had been arrested over the previous nights were brought and released in front of the crowd that was demonstrating. This was interpreted as an important victory, with those released being treated as heroes and carried on arms across the crowd. As one of those who had been arrested, Costel Balint confesses that while in prison they had no idea what was happening outside and were even more confused when they were released into the arms of a cheering crowd.

Demonstrators—army interactions

While the official negotiations with the party elite collapsed the moment the revolutionaries asked for the resignation of Ceausescu—given Ceausescu's cult of personality, this was out of the question, party elites not having the authority to negotiate anything like that without fearing for the loss of their own lives—a different set of negotiations were conducted in the streets between the army that was sent in to put down the demonstrations and the demonstrators. Not an uncommon theme throughout other revolutionary moments, including the Tiananmen Square revolt, the demonstrators approached the army not as a united enemy but rather as individuals who had also experienced the communist regime first hand and suffered from poverty and oppression. And they were right to do so.

The atrocious conditions in which the soldiers lived, the

mandatory draft and the fact that most of the troops were not professional soldiers, conditioned to fight, all contributed to the relatively quick "turn of arms" in the Romanian Revolution. Unacquainted with urban warfare, as well as unprepared to shoot, the army was the only force large enough to withstand the hundreds of thousands of demonstrators that were at that point out in the streets. While up until then, the army was mainly used as an intimidation technique during military parades, the intimidations no longer seemed to work: the demonstrators were courageous enough to attack tanks and set them on fire as well as approach army battalions with empty hands and dare them to shoot. The shootings that did occur appeared to have been conducted from the roof-tops of buildings as opposed to face-to-face contact. Many of the killings were also a result of stray bullets shot in the air to scare the demonstrators off.[34]

Direct interactions between the soldiers and the demonstrators are described in several testimonies. Sanda Adrian recalls an incident during the morning of December 20th when the main wave of workers from the industrial platform was heading towards the city center and was met by a line of soldiers, guns pointing at them. He describes a conversation that Lorin Fortuna, one of the main leaders in the Timisoara Revolution, had with the soldiers:

> Fortuna then told them that even the buttons on their jackets and the bullets that they would use to shoot us where paid by us. He then kneeled along with the rest of the crowd and to our surprise, the soldiers were commanded to leave. They simply took their guns and left.[35]

Other testimonies talk about demonstrators confronting the soldiers directly with chants and questions such as: "Are you really going to shoot at us? Look at us, we are just like you! We are the people you are supposed to be protecting! Who are you protecting if not us?"[36] Faced with an enemy formed by mothers and workers, many of whom were their own friends and relatives, the soldiers did not take long to realize the absurdity of the situation in which they were placed. Military commanders also refused to allow for a bloodbath to occur and disobeyed Ceausescu's orders of shooting into the crowd. The "turn of arms" officially occurred on December 22nd, when it was obvious that the Ceausescu regime was about to fall. On that day, the first free newspaper appearing in

Timisoara, *Revolutia*, announced that "The Army is with us!"[37]

Despite the turn of arms, the killings continued, this time most likely conducted by the secret forces—also known as the Securitatea—which were specially trained to protect Ceausescu and the regime. Unlike the regular police and army forces, the Securitatea was probably one of the most highly indoctrinated groups, formed by a group of people who swore to protect the Ceausescu clan to their death. In the general confusion, many of the bodies of those killed and wounded disappeared from the streets as well as public hospitals, most likely in an attempt to hide the upheaval. Given these disappearances, an exact count of all those who were killed in the Timisoara Revolution seems almost impossible. The initial reports that tens of thousands of people were being killed were blown out of all proportion, the actual number of deaths rising to no more than two thousand people.[38]

While many of the deaths appear to have been accidental, and the disappearance of the bodies is clearly connected to the regime's attempt to clean up the signs of its violent repression, conspiracy theories around this issue abound. People want concrete answers and unitary enemies to point the finger at. Unfortunately, they may not be so easily identifiable: the secret structure of the Securitatea, and the broken chain of command, made certain decisions untraceable and the identification of "the guilty" difficult. The unresolved issue of the disappeared bodies continues to hang as a deep disappointment above the head of the Romanian Revolution. The fact that only a handful of people have been prosecuted for these murders has left much of the population deeply scared and with a sense that many have died in vain and unavenged. The obsession with the Securitatea and the secret archives has been a subject of deep political controversy that seems to forever reappear around election time.

While much of the literature on the Romanian Revolution focuses on the trauma experienced by the demonstrators, one often forgets the trauma experienced by those who suddenly found themselves on the wrong side of the barricades: the soldiers and particularly the secret police and some of the party elite. As the regime collapsed almost overnight, many of these people found themselves not only out of a job but also without protection and perhaps more importantly, without a justification for their former actions. They appeared as villains not only to others, but also to themselves. This trauma seeped through every level of society: from the highest officials who lost their jobs, homes and fortunes, to the low-ranking officials and store managers who suddenly found themselves on the margins of society. While most of the former communist elites are now assumed to have secured jobs in the new government or taken advantage of the privatization process by buying the industries they used to manage, it is still unclear to what extent this was a widespread practice. Informal conversations with neighbors and friends reveal that this was not the case for many of the former communist officials, whose families had to pay dearly for their past actions: lawsuits, criminal records, poverty, inability to find new jobs. The level of suicides, divorces, crime and drug use amongst these families ran high immediately after the revolution, for these were the people that often stood to lose the most from the collapse of the communist illusion.[39]

Some did indeed manage to secure positions in the newly formed post-communist government, dominated by the National Salvation Front (NSF). The presence of many members of the communist elite in the NSF led to a series of controversies in the period immediately following the revolution, shedding doubt over the possibility of a true break with the communist past and staining the pride of many of those who fought in the revolution in order to get rid of those very elites. Many however wrongly assume that the NSF was the only political alternative after the Romanian Revolution. Examining how and why the NSF came to dominate the post-revolutionary political horizon might help us better understand the process of social change and the extent to which all radical social movements inevitably rely on the past for inspiration and experience. As much as the new is wanted, when it fails to organize itself, a reformed past wins almost by default.

Was the National Salvation Front the first political formation in post-communist Romania?

While the post-communist political horizon was dominated by the emergence of the National Salvation Front (NSF) as the transition government and then the first freely elected government of Romania, the NSF cannot claim to be the first political formation in post-communist Romania. This privilege must be reserved for the Romanian Democratic Front (RDF), a political organization formed by the leaders of the Timisoara revolution that led the first negotiations with the communist part and publicly expressed the first criteria for an independent Romania.[40] With a loose structure and next to no political experience, the RDF played an important role at the local level, yet failed to make itself known nationally. With its lack of political experience and access to the real powerhouses of Bucharest, the RDF was quickly brushed aside by the NSF, with little acknowledgement for its efforts and original ideas. While the RDF only existed officially for a few months after the Romanian Revolution, being absorbed—of free will—into the NSF, the platform on which it was built was significantly different and to a large extent much more representative and democratic than that of the NSF.[41]

The Romanian Democratic Front (RDF) was formed during those intense days of demonstrating and dodging bullets in the main square in Timisoara, by the leaders of the Timisoara Revolution who found themselves stranded in the Opera House balcony having to address the crowd, keep them out in the square and give them a sense of direction for the future. The Front was not created as a political party, but rather as a political organization, a guiding force meant to ensure the success of the Romanian Revolution—defined as the removal of the Ceausescu clan from power—and use people's creative energies in order to put forward an original political platform on which a new regime could be organized. The RDF did not have the political know-how nor the political instinct to become more than an ad hoc organization and turn into an actual political party, but it did play an important role in shaping the first political ideals of post-communist Romania and giving people a sense of mass participation. Lorin Fortuna, the main leader of the RDF, describes it as such:

The Romanian Democratic Front was created in illegality, being the first political organization with mass membership with a concrete platform expressed through the Front's proclamation on the 20th of December 1989. The Front organized and led the Timisoara revolt until its final victory.[42]

The formation of the RDF represented the culmination of a series of events that led to the Timisoara revolution. Formed by workers along with some intellectuals (Nicolae Badilescu was a poet and Lorin Fortuna was a professor at the Politechnique), the RDF was the first attempt to establish a new political power in the country, to reclaim the public space and redefine it. Filling the empty shoes of the regime that had just fallen was however a more difficult job than expected. None of the members of the RDF had held positions of power before, nor were they acquainted with the necessary bureaucracy that went into administering a region, never mind a country. Sucked into politics, the RDF leaders found themselves in unexpected positions with important decisions to be made under an intense time pressure. Within a matter of days, they had been catapulted from their position of observers into a position of main political actors on a stage that was highly unfamiliar to them. The unfamiliarity of this territory stripped them in many ways of their original enthusiasm and pushed them into bickering, suspicions and infighting. As Hannah Arendt points out in her preface to *Between Past and Future*, the post-revolutionary territory can be full of surprises with ideals of freedom and representation quickly tarnished. The responsibility of holding a political position is often overburdening, causing a series of deep disappointments. Referring to the French revolutionaries, Arendt describes the aggressiveness of the public political realm and the inevitability of distancing from the population at large:

> [The collapse], to them a totally unexpected event, had emptied, from one day to the next, the political scene of their country, leaving it to the puppet-like antics of knaves or fools, and they who as a matter of course had never participated in the official business of the [Party State] were sucked into politics as though with the force of a vacuum. Thus, without premonition and probably against their conscious inclinations, they had come to constitute willy-nilly a public realm where—without the paraphernalia of officialdom ... all relevant business in the affairs of the country was transacted in deed and word. It did not last long.

> After a few short years they were liberated from what they originally had thought to be a "burden" and thrown back into what they now knew to be the weightless irrelevance of their personal affairs, once separated from the world of reality by ... the "sad opaqueness" of a private life centered about nothing but itself.[43]

Caught up in the initial thrill, sucked into local or national politics during and immediately after the revolution, many of the RDF members later abandoned their ideals and retreated into the safety of their private lives. The abandonment however was in many cases not voluntary and often triggered by a deep disappointment with the direction in which the country was going and the way in which many of the leaders of the Timisoara Revolution were quickly pushed aside when it came to the formation of the first political parties and the first government. During its short-lived existence, the RDF was however an important site for formulating the first political demands of the Timisoara Revolution and coming up with a new political formula to govern post-communist Romania.

The document that stands at the basis of the RDF was its original Proclamation, written by hand on the Opera House balcony, read out loud to the crowd standing in front of the balcony and also partially presented during the first negotiations with the party elites at the county council. Printed in the first free newspaper in Timisoara, *Victoria*, the Proclamation of the RDF reads as follows:

> As instructed by the Action Committee of the Romanian Democratic Front, we read the following proclamation:
>
> I. The Romanian Democratic Front is a political organization formed in Timisoara for the purpose of starting a dialogue with the current government in order to help democratize the country.
> II. We submit the following list of demands to the Romanian government as a basis for this dialogue:
>   1. The organization of free and democratic elections.
>   2. The freedom of speech, press, radio and TV.
>   3. The immediate opening of the Romanian borders.
>   4. Integrating Romania in the group of states that guarantee and respect fundamental human rights.
>   5. The immediate release of all political prisoners.
>   6. Economic reform, including the creation of private initiatives in industries and agriculture.
>   7. Providing the necessary food for the entire Romanian population.

8. Educational reform in the spirit of democracy.
   9. Religious freedom.
   10. Adequate health care at western standards.
   11. The closing down of all stores serving only the elite.
III. Concerning the Timisoara events:
   1. We firmly demand that all those who ordered fire against the demonstrators be put on trial.
   2. We demand a complete list of those who were found dead, hurt or disappeared.
   3. We demand that the dead be returned to their families to be buried in the local tradition.
   4. We propose that the 29th of December be declared a day of national mourning for the heroic victims of the revolution.
   5. We demand the immediate release of all those who were arrested during the demonstrations.
   6. We demand that all forces of repression against the peaceful demonstrators in Timisoara as well as the rest of the country be called back.
   7. We demand that the authorities officially acknowledge the action committee of the Romanian Democratic Front founded in Timisoara and the initiation of a dialogue with the Front.
IV. The Romanian Democratic Front calls the entire country to:
   1. Join the Romanian people in their righteous and peaceful fight for the democratization of our country.
   2. Create local committees of the Romanian Democratic Front in industries and institutions throughout the country in order to ensure the creation and development of the democratic process.
   3. Peacefully call for their constitutional rights.
   4. Join the general strike—except those sectors of the national economy that necessitate continuous efforts—starting with the 21st of December until the final victory.

We thank the people of Timisoara who heroically faced tanks, armored cars and bullets in order to bring the Romanian people out of the dictatorship.[44]

There are a series of ideas that come out of this proclamation: 1) a clear sense that there was a need for reform: economic, educational, health care, political; 2) a call for a number of freedoms: freedom of speech, freedom of press, religious freedom and freedom of movement; 3) a clear sense that the current government could not lead these reforms and give people these necessary freedoms and thus that a new government needs to be elected. While the proclamation clearly calls for a reformed communism, it does not appear to directly call for its complete removal. The ideals presented in this proclamation were however difficult to implement without any enforcement power or idea as to exactly where to begin.

The short administration of the Timis county by the RDF revealed a lack of management skills as well as the increasing lack of trust developing among the revolution leaders. The testimony of Sanda Adrian, as one of the younger members of the RDF, is particularly relevant, speaking directly to the chaotic situation that followed the collapse of the communist regime in Romania. As one of the founding members of the RDF, Adrian remembers the battle for power that started around December 23rd, when the coordinating committee of the RDF moved from the Opera House balcony to today's mayor's office and began to assign different roles to the its members. Adrian describes the situation as chaotic, with the revolutionaries taking over the old administration's offices and randomly assigning tasks to people on the basis of trust alone as opposed to necessary skill. The roles were divided among those present on the balcony, with some of the former communist elites that helped in the revolutionary effort being given a series of important positions. The level of distrust was prevalent, and Adrian found his loyalty questioned as well after leaving for only a few days to celebrate Christmas with his family and develop some photographs that were shot during the revolution.[45]

The rapidity with which new power structures were created and slowly solidified after the revolution was breathtaking. The quick turnaround in power, the sudden availability of positions that before would have seemed unattainable, the decision-making power of people that only a few days before were tied to the mechanism of the state or a particular industry or university, blurred everyone's vision, allowing for many mistakes to be made, for egos to be hurt and powerful resentments to be built. Those resentments persist today. But perhaps the deepest resentment is that carried by the average people in the street, turned heroes for a few days and then dropped right back into the sea of anonymity.[46]

While the Romanian Democratic Front was the first democratic political body in post-Ceausescu Romania, its existence was to be relatively short lived. As the RDF was struggling to keep Timisoara under control and had begun to reconstitute the city's administrative bodies following what it considered to be a democratic assignment of functions to those revolutionaries who had distinguished themselves on the Opera House balcony, a new political body was being formed in Bucharest: the National Salvation Front (NSF). Neither the RDF or the NSF were originally formed as political parties, and only one of them expressed a clear intention to play an important role in governing post-Ceausescu Romania: the RDF. As the RDF was attempting to develop innovative governing schemes, political and social committees that would draw their membership from workers' unions in Timisoara, the NSF was establishing its political presence much more broadly by spending most of its time live on the newly liberated national television. While the RDF recognized the NSF almost as its equivalent in Bucharest, sending in a delegation of revolutionaries from Timisoara to discuss some of the innovations as well as reform ideas that it was coming up with, the NSF gently dismissed the RDF delegation, agreeing though that the RDF should simply become a local branch of the NSF. The Timisoara Revolution, along with the other mini-revolutions that followed in the other major cities in Romania—Cluj, Brasov, Iasi—had an entirely different dynamic from the Bucharest Revolution, with the big cards continuing to be played in the capital.[47]

While the RDF came to power relatively smoothly with workers assigned to different working committees and with a clear mandate not to allow any of the former communist elites back into politics, the power struggle was much more intense in Bucharest, where most of the important communist elites lived. While the RDF was mainly formed of intellectuals and workers, the NSF was largely formed by dissidents, intellectuals, and many former communist elites who had now established themselves as reformists–including its main leader who was to run Romania for a total of ten years afterwards, Ion Iliescu. Bucharest was where the real fight for power was being fought and the RDF's willingness to give up its power and role was very much based on a naive acceptance of the NSF as a similar organization that would have the necessary power and credibility to continue what the RDF had started at the national level. The disappointment with how the NSF handled itself came immediately after the fall of Ceausescu through its acceptance of many of the former communist elites in its political structure and its participation in the first free elections that took place in March of 1990, despite clear promises at the beginning that the NSF was only an intermediary political body that would help with the transition process as opposed to an actual political party that would seek a more permanent political role in the elections.

Former RDF members feel they have been cheated out of their revolution, that their success was practically stolen by the NSF and Bucharest, and that their genuine, though sometimes naive and inexperienced ideas for reform, were shunned by the greed of many important political players in Bucharest who were fighting to secure their position in the new government that was about to be formed. The democratic illusion under which the RDF was still living for the first few months after the revolution was quickly shattered when it became obvious that the decision-making power had now been taken away from the population at large and put into the hands of a small elite that gained their credibility and fame while on national television, during that last week in December.[48]

While rule by an elite is how most democracies continue to function, it is obvious that people imagined that democracy would give them a sense of power similar to the one that they had felt while out in the streets, calling out their demands, sending representatives to the balcony and hearing their concerns talked about out loud in front of the crowd. The RDF was formed on a similar type of ideal, imagining that local governments would from now on be formed by representatives from local businesses and industries as well as the population at large, that communication would be much more open, that these committees would literally have the power to think up how the new government system should look, how laws should be redrafted, what kind of reforms would be most needed in each of the different parts of the country. The RDF had hoped that regional autonomy would play a much more important role in post-Ceausescu politics, and that local governments would be trusted with much of the decision-making process. Although the RDF proved to be fairly creative in its organizational structure—at least the way in which it initially imagined this new organization structure—its lack of consideration for outside as well as strong inside interests, its lack of contact with many of the country's elites from Bucharest, as well as its lack of experience with politics, made it fairly easy for it to be pushed aside. Naively accepting the NSF's rise to power as more legitimate, the RDF was quickly dismantled and simply vanished within a matter of weeks.[49]

It would be unfair to claim that the RDF did not have its own problems. The way in which many of the committee heads were named under the new local administrative structure created by the RDF was certainly questionable, as Sanda Adrian also points out.[50] The main leader of the RDF, Lorin Fortuna, quickly lost much of his credibility in Timisoara, being questioned because of his northern Romanian roots. Residents of Timisoara and the Banat region have always been very proud of their origin and often consider themselves superior to the rest of the country: more hardworking, more exposed to Western influences and thus more experienced, more nationalistic. Pride and nationalist feelings played a very important role in the Romanian Revolution, this being one of the few occasions in which regions could openly express resentment, in a way, towards other regions/parts of the country.[51]

The view that the Romanian Revolution was a united effort is in many ways mistaken. The revolutionary ethos was different in the different regions of the country, often following a different set of interests and visions. That the revolution started in Timisoara added to the already inflated ego of this region, where people tend to think of themselves as superior to the rest of the country. That the Timisoara revolutionaries were later pushed aside from national politics was treated as a direct affront, one that re-emphasized the ruptures between Bucharest and the rest of the country and the continuous "dictatorial" style with which the capital decided to continue to conduct business.

The first free elections and the end of the Romanian Revolution

While some argue that the Romanian Revolution was never completed, that it was hijacked or stolen,[52] most people will agree that the revolutionary fervor ended with the death of the Ceausescus. The shock of the unrest that was to come afterwards was only matched by the initial enthusiasm that people felt right after the revolution. Although the international press warned against some of the difficulties that were about to come, the country continued to be engulfed in a combination of euphoria and disappointment. The fight for power in the weeks and months immediately following the death of the Ceausescus was probably one of the most well documented in history, since a large part of it occurred live on TV. The fascination with free speech, the plethora of newspapers that appeared, the fact that the average person was now reading three to four newspapers a day and watching TV for hours every day, the parade of new political characters that were emerging, the constant reiteration of ideas such as freedom, democracy, election, capitalism and reform, were all overwhelming. The quick formation of a transition government by the National Salvation Front and the coagulation of new political parties occurred with unbelievable speed. Everyone was discussing the fate of the country, and yet few truly understood what it meant to introduce reform, transition towards capitalism and a democratic system. Many expected help from the West and hoped that the country would be able to join Western Europe's standards of living within a few years. What happened instead was a completely different story.

The first year following the Romanian Revolution was marked by two main scandals: 1) the decision of the National Salvation Front to become a political party and run for elections—which they naturally won given the constant exposure they had received through the media and 2) the so-called "mineriada," where the newly elected government was blamed for calling in the miners from the north of the country to suppress a month-long demonstration that was contesting the results of the first free elections. The two scandals are closely related and reflect the first interventions of intellectuals in politics. While the revolution was for the most part started and led by workers, intellectuals did start to play a more important role in the coagulation of the first political parties and in the first political debates. Many of the intellectuals began to challenge the National Salvation Front on the basis of its connection to former communist elites: its main leadership was formed by former members of the communist elite—Iliescu and Roman—and its principal members counted a large number of former members of the communist elite.

The fear that the revolution would be turned into a coup d'état, with a portion of the former communist elite taking over again, was real, yet mainly perceived by a small intellectual elite formed by writers, professors and students. Their open protests following the first free elections reflected two different levels of awareness in the country: 1) the intellectuals' understanding that the freedom that they had fought for was quietly being taken over by the "reformist" branch of the communist elite and that their orientation continued to be socialist, despite the democratic rhetoric and 2) that of the population at large who were for the most part unaware of the dangerous path on which they were about to embark and who saw the intellectuals' demonstrations—which at some point did get violent—as a threat to the stability of the country and thus a threat to the success of the revolution.[53]

The post-revolutionary fight for power can also be interpreted as a fight of several new illusions/ideologies attempting to replace the old communist one: while all of the new illusions were backed by a democratic rhetoric, their visions were significantly different: the National Salvation Front was for the most part headed in the direction dictated by Iliescu: slow reform with the maintenance of a clear socialist focus, while the traditional parties—nationalist and liberal parties—supported mainly by intellectuals, were headed in the direction of what they interpreted to be Western capitalism and democratization. While the RDF's vision was never fully explored, it might have contributed to the formation of a real "third way" an alternative path that would follow neither that of communist reform, nor that of "shock therapy." The death of RDF's voice after the revolution marks the death of any ideals of representation and people's democracy. The failure to accept that their sacrifice would so easily be abused by incoming politicians, left many of the participants in the Romanian Revolution feeling like they had been served a lie and that the "truth" about that revolution is yet to be unearthed.

Is there "a single truth" about what happened during the Romanian Revolution?[54]

Many are still looking for "the truth" about what happened during the Romanian Revolution: whether they are looking to identify those who shot the demonstrators, or those who called the shots, or whether the revolution was truly a grassroots movement or more of a coup d'état, the search for "a truth" continues. The idea that there may not be a unified vision of what happened during the revolution seems unacceptable, and rumors and speculations are preferred to any attempts to embrace the revolution as a more complex process, in which the sides are not so clearly defined. The search for truth is ultimately a search for someone to blame. While the failures of the communist regime could be blamed on Ceausescu, the pains of the transition could not so easily be attributed to a single person or group.

The death of Ceausescu provided people with an important sense of relief but also gave them the confidence that justice had been done and that the evil was pushed aside. And yet the communist regime was not upheld by force alone but also by high levels of participation in the illusion that Ceausescu was selling, whether it be the illusion of progress or the illusion of strength and fear. The death of Ceausescu was highly unexpected. While the majority of the population shouted "Down with Ceausescu," it is unclear to what extent death was necessarily desired. The surprise of the execution lay on both sides: Ceausescu, who was in complete disbelief up until the very moment of his death, and the population at large, who saw this as largely unexpected and for a while even questioned the extent to which his death was real.

Ceausescu's execution was a political move secured by a new political regime that needed to consolidate its power, gain the trust of its citizens, ensure calm on the streets and stop the sporadic shootings by the secret police that were still causing a large number of deaths. Ceausescu's capture and trial were as surprising as the rest of the events that engulfed the country. Left by himself, deserted by all his close friends including the helicopter pilot who saved him from the crowd invading the government building from which he attempted to address the crowd in order to bring about order, Ceausescu was quickly captured and put to trial. Whisked away from the balcony by one of his ministers, still in complete shock and disbelief after hearing himself booed by the crowd, Ceausescu attempted to flee, only to find himself abandoned by a roadside and having to catch a ride that would drop him right at the military base in Targoviste where he was eventual tried and shot. The trial was a show trial, and although captured on tape and broadcast internationally, it consisted mainly of a series of accusations led by the judge himself, Ceausescu's refusal to accept the trial as legitimate and insistent demand to only speak in front of the people, and the handing down of a decision that was in fact already taken hours before: the death sentence by execution. The actual execution occurred only hours after the trial, and although meant to be caught on tape, Ceausescu and Elena's death occurred unexpectedly when one of the soldiers started shooting without command and was followed by the rest of the platoon.[55]

The execution was cruel, occurring on Christmas Eve, an important religious celebration for a majority of Romanians. The tens of bullets shot into the couple tore their bodies apart, their brains splattered onto the wall and skull fragments on the ground. Those who were present recall that soldiers took some bone fragments and soaked their handkerchiefs in Ceausescu's blood as memorabilia. After their death, there was more concern about the lack of a tape to prove the execution than the cruelty of the act itself. The bodies disappeared for a few hours, having been thrown out of sight by mistake, causing an uproar by those who feared that now they no longer had proof of their deaths. The tragic-comic aspects of the execution make it seem almost unreal. In fact, many speculations still circulate as to the circumstances of the Ceausescus' death.[56] After their parents' death, Ceausescu's children continued to grapple with the guilt assigned to their family—and invariably to them. Zoe Ceausescu, his daughter, died alone, being refused the right to continue her career as a scientist, while Valentin Ceausescu is still struggling to regain some sense of historical and personal esteem. Talking about his father, he portrays him as a victim of his own ideals and illusions:

> [My father] was a very devoted man. Whatever one says about him, he truly believed in a Communist Romania ... You may find this strange, but I believe that my father headed towards death truly believing that the workers were supporting him ...

and even loved him. This is what happens with this kind of personality cult, you see, it works both ways. You build something and soon you're convinced that it's real.⁵⁷

Ceausescu's children, just like the Romanian people, were all victims of their parents' unguarded illusions. Their lives have been ruined by their parents' demands and controlling character, and after their parents' death, by the continued resentment of the Romanian people. In the end, everyone was a victim of the same illusion: not just those who died working or in jail during Ceausescu's regime, or those who died on the streets in Timisoara and the rest of the country, but also the Ceausescu family itself.

The truth, the lies, the disillusionment

While many, including people like Lorin Fortuna, claim that the Romanian Revolution was never completed, most textbooks, articles and journals consider that the Revolution ended with the death of Ceausescu and the first free elections. The ideals of the revolution, while seemingly true, have not necessarily led the country to where it was hoping to go. Disappointment continues to reign, and Romania is not the only one that experiences it.

During a symposium in Timisoara, celebrating fifteen years since the Romanian Revolution, about forty different participants in the Romanian Revolution, many of whom were some of the main leaders of the demonstrators, were airing their frustrations. Discussions covered reflections on how the revolution was manipulated by the Bucharest fight for power; the need to find the "truth" about what happened during the revolution, particularly with regards to the killings; the need to prosecute those who were directly involved in the killings; the frustration over who was receiving benefits from the government program that established special pensions for victims and leaders of the revolution; and the need to document and bring together all the materials recorded during and immediately after the Romanian Revolution.⁵⁸

Claudiu Iordache, one of the main leaders of the Timisoara Revolution, and also one of the few Timisoara revolutionaries to be included in the first free government in Bucharest, has written several books expressing his disappointment with the way in which the revolutionary ideals were manipulated and gave way to greed and lies. The moral decline of the Romanian political elite seems even more dangerous in a society that celebrates freedom yet is too exhausted to carry yet another fight for justice and anti-corruption. He argues that Romania after the revolution clearly shows the dangers of giving up the fight after the fall of the Ceausescu dictatorship. Iordache puts his finger on an interesting phenomenon: the lingering post-revolutionary disappointment that no one is willing to fight any more, the deep sense of political and social apathy and the complete and willing return of most people to the private sphere of their personal lives. Iordache concludes his book *Romania Lost* with an interesting meditation on the nature of today's social and political reality: "Nothing is more fragile than the real."[59] Even illusions seem to be more secure than what actually lies in front of us.

The post-communist period seems to be lacking a sense of justice, thus leaving many to feel betrayed, and kept away from the "truth." Even the compensation packages for the victims of the revolution and their families have caused disputes over misallocation and misuse of funds. The attempts to obtain these benefits and to appropriate certain symbols and actions that became particularly visible during the revolution reflect an interesting combination of despair, greed and the need for a sense of accomplishment on the side of those who participated in the revolution.

During the above-mentioned symposium, a mother was arguing that her son should receive special recognition and a series of benefits for having been the one to create the famous sign of Ceausescu with a Hitler-like mustache that appeared in countless photographs and films of the Timisoara Revolution. This attempt to appropriate certain symbols of the revolution as belonging to the specific people who created them, despite the fact that the meaning was acquired as the sign was passed around in the crowd, is an interesting example of the extent to which many of the former revolutionaries are looking for a sense of recognition and public acknowledgement of what they did.

This acknowledgement becomes even more important in situations where many of these initial heroes of the revolution quickly slipped back into an anonymous status, often one of abject poverty (since many of the demonstrators were workers in state factories that were later privatized in the first round of reforms, and thus lost their jobs and only source of income). The cries of these people are often heard during the commemorative month of December during small gatherings of former revolutionaries, symposiums and articles that appear in the local press. For the most part they are ignored, most heroes of the revolution being invisible to the population at large. Conversations with Timisoara revolutionaries revealed a clear feeling that they have been forgotten, that their efforts were left unappreciated, and beyond all, that the feeling of unity and solidarity that they once felt in the crowd of hundreds of thousands of people that came out to demonstrate during the days of 20th and 21st of December, was wasted and would never come back again.

The invisibility of most of the heroes of the revolution versus the visibility of a few—those who appeared on national television—created an interesting rift between the population at large and the new political elite. Access to television, the power of visibility, allowed some to create a fame that most others lacked and created a situation where power—the power of being visible—could be easily abused given that access to the television station was relatively unrestricted during those first few days after the television tower was taken over. A similar kind of rift, also based on this idea of recognition and visibility, emerged in Timisoara as well, with those present on the balcony of the Opera House versus those sitting outside in the crowd. The relatively random self-selection mechanism that allowed for some to play a key role in terms of shaping the main demands of the Timisoara Revolution—the so-called Timisoara Proclamation—as well as the first independent political body after the fall of communism—the RDF—allowed for some to become much more visible than others.

When one of the main leaders of the Timisoara Revolution, Nicolae Badilescu, openly states that if he had the choice he would not only not have encouraged the revolution, but would have defended the former system, one knows that somewhere, somehow, something has gone wrong. Struggling to make ends meet and living under the constant threat of being thrown out of his nationalized apartment that is being claimed by its former owners more than forty years after being home to an entirely new family, Badilescu faces the criticism of his own family and friends who often approach him with regrets.[60] As radical as this may sound, anyone familiar with the diversity of the Central and Eastern European post-communist environment, knows that the success of the 1989 Revolutions is relative and that many are still nostalgically recalling the bygone days of communism when they all had a job, were given an apartment, there was enough food to put on the table, the kids did not have access to drugs, there was no crime and prices were reasonable enough for an average family to afford a decent lifestyle. Those who invoke the bygone days are often those who lost their jobs during the privatization process, those who are retired and living off a monthly pension that will not even pay their electricity bill, those who cannot afford a place to live—the price of an apartment being around €40,000 when most people have a salary of about €250 /month[61]—those who see their children being victims of crime, human and organ trafficking and drugs, those who are thrown out of their formerly nationalized houses, or those who find themselves unable to pay for basic healthcare.

Lorin Fortuna, the main leader of the Romanian Democratic Front, also describes a similar feeling of helplessness. He blames the current state of affairs, though, not on the naivety of the revolutionaries, but rather on the greed of those who could not wait to get their hands on power and goods. Fortuna blames the recklessness with which the new capitalist model was enforced for the current state of poverty and corruption, yet he would not go as far as Badilescu to say that he would not do it again. In fact, he argues that it is our duty to continue our revolution, to pick it up from where we left it in 1989 and take it to where we were hoping it would go, now that we have learned a few lessons and have a better idea of what we want.

While Fortuna's conspiracy theory about the country being taken over by the Masons[62] has not gained much credibility among the majority of the population, who unfortunately treat this revolutionary hero with contempt and indignation, he does have some interesting arguments to make about where and why things went wrong. In a private interview Fortuna declares that:

During the Romanian Revolution, we didn't have time to prepare ourselves, to think about what we would like to put in place of Ceausescu's communist system. The desire to simply overturn this system was so overwhelming and everything that happened, happened so fast, within a week, that it took us completely by surprise.[63]

Asked whether there were other alternatives to the capitalist model, Fortuna answered:

I think there would have been if we had had enough time to think them up. But we didn't have time... So, because of this we fell from bad to worse, from an overly centralized state, to an overly decentralized state.[64]

Fortuna describes the current situation as one in which people are blinded in a different way: while during communism the blinding was done in an obvious, forceful manner, now people are forced into a different level of subsistence, one where they can see, imagine and sometimes even reach out to all that they dream of having, yet are kept in a constant state of economic struggle due to the disparities between prices and salaries. Always concerned by how to meet the next economic struggle—buying tiles for the bathroom or kitchen, new windows, new refrigerator, TV or oven—there is very little time left to consider the political, economic or social alternatives to the current situation. Forced into a new state of submissiveness, Romanians have found that even heroic revolutions will not change things enough to actually satisfy everyone.

The Romanian Revolution left not only some of the revolutionaries feeling disillusioned, but also many of the intellectuals. Irina Culic argues that those intellectuals who were able to adapt quickly to the new system of opportunities either by entering politics or associating themselves with the newly created non-governmental organizations and research institutions, were able to better capitalize on the changes brought about by the revolution. Those who continued to do the same thing as before: teach or publish in obscure publishing houses, quickly found themselves marginalized.[65] Alina Mungiu-Pippidi however talks about the disillusionment of intellectuals more in terms of their participation in the Romanian Revolution. She claims that their disillusionment is to a large extent their own fault, because they failed to create the structures that would allow them to come to power after the revolution—many of the intellectuals who initially joined the first free government later resigned, appalled by the infighting for power and greed that they were faced with—and because of their anti-capitalist mentality, their lack of a political message, their lack of pragmatism and expertise as well as their lack of public authority.

Addressing the much controversial question of the anti-FSN demonstrations after the first free elections and the "mineriada," where many students and intellectuals were attacked and beaten up by miners, Mungiu-Pippidi argues that those intellectuals' pro-Western and anti-socialist stance did not stand on a clearly defined platform, thus allowing the powers that be to paint their demonstrations as a direct attack to the stability of the country.[66] The chants heard during these demonstrations of: "Death to intellectuals!" just like a few months before, one heard the chants of "Death to Ceausescu!" expressed the degree to which intellectuals were separated from the masses and the extent to which they were not trusted. Not knowing how to appeal to the masses, the intellectuals were too quick to unveil the new socialist illusion that the FSN was building and the threat that this posed to the country's democratic transition. Unable to assess the extent to which people wanted to believe the promises that they were being handed, the intellectuals assumed that their vision was clear to everyone else, that the threat the they perceived to the newfound freedoms was obvious. Yet, as Mungiu-Pippidi clearly points out in her article, by quoting the Romanian philosopher Constantin Noica in a letter to his friend Cioran,

> Now it seems to us that it is not liberty which is proper to man, but necessity; that man does not revolt against whoever takes his liberty, but against whoever takes his necessity, his necessary sense of living, or, as you would have it, his necessary "nonsense" of living.[67]

As we see from testimonies of the leaders of the revolution, other participants and intellectuals, the revolution was after all not only the glorious moment that we often like to depict but also the site of many shattered illusions and disappointments. And perhaps this disillusionment was not so much directly connected to a series of unrealistic expectations but rather to the lack of expectations, or put another way, not knowing what one should expect. The high levels of surprise and shock diminished people's ability to absorb it and pushed them into a position where simply dreaming of a glorious end was more convenient.

What was left untold

There are many stories surrounding the Romanian Revolution that for the most part have been left untold or lying at the margins of the larger discourse on revolutions. These stories are often treated as side stories or unexplainable events, of little relevance to the more important unfolding of events, not fitting into many of the theoretical frameworks of explanation that we have already created. And yet these stories are just as much a part of the revolutionary experience, if not closer to it, for they point to the truly chaotic character of events: the overwhelming shock, the puzzling reactions of the regime and the way in which the revolution was lived by those who did not have high aspirations, who were not necessarily out in the streets or leading the demonstrations, who were simply living through the revolutionary experience like characters trapped in an unfamiliar environment that they were forced to maneuver.

Unusual incidents such as the military parade that Ceausescu ordered on the day of the 17th of December in Timisoara, or the hot water and heating that kept running all night long in Timisoara during the night of the 16th to the 17th of December,[68] the destruction of store windows and party symbols and their quick replacement the following day, left the majority of the population that was still indoors at the time, highly shocked and intrigued. These are the incidents that were part of the everyday experience during the 1989 Revolution, much more so than the calls for reforms and demonstrations in the streets during those first few days of revolt. These are the events that left people bewildered, that created the first rumors and myths with regards to the Romanian Revolution.[69]

A highly traditional society, where most generations can still trace their direct ancestors—grandparents and sometimes parents—to the villages of Romania, many of those living in Timisoara chose to deal with this high level of confusion by attributing the events to some higher force. Much of the conversation surrounding the Romanian Revolution focused either on the question of mysticism—the higher force here being in many ways almost Godly—or on a series of different conspiracies—the higher force being a series of obscure international interests in our region and our people, whether it be the Masons, Jews, Americans, Russians or Hungarians.[70]

The mystical elements that are often mentioned as surrounding the beginning of the Romanian revolution in Timisoara are things like: the weather—it was unusually warm for December, which allowed people to stay out in the streets longer and later—a sign that God was watching over them; the skies that had a strange reddish color, a sign that something big/bad is about to happen; the candles in front of Tokes's house; the blessings offered by a local priest to the first demonstrators as they walked towards the city center; the call for the priests to start ringing the church bells in recognition of what was happening and in order to call more people out into the streets; the crowd praying: one of the first gestures when the workers' demonstrations began was that the entire crowd kneeled and started praying—and when approaching the army forces that were there to break away the demonstrators, one of the first gestures was again to kneel down as in prayer.[71]

The religious connotations of the Romanian Revolution were very powerful not only in those initial images but also in later testimonies. Many of those who were out in the streets speak of an unprecedented feeling of almost religious grace in the crowd, of purity and unity like they had never felt before: people were good to one another, they were hugging each other, sharing the little food they had, taking care of each other in case someone was hurt, offering shelter to those who could not go home. There was this never before experienced sense of goodness that gave them strength to keep going. Many say they miss that feeling and that they would give anything to get that back. The idea of Romania as a chosen nation appears again and again in many of these testimonies, focusing on the uniqueness of the Romanian people and of their God-chosen status.[72]

Nicolae Badilescu, in his interview, points out that the purity and uniqueness of the Romanian Revolution went unobserved in the West, where the regular conceptual frameworks for analyzing revolutions did not look at details such as the fact that the demonstrators, while destroying party symbols and burning Ceausescu's portrait, were careful enough not to step on the flowers in the main square in Timisoara. Lorin Fortuna, in his interview, also speaks of Romania as a chosen nation, one that is bound to play a key role in the international context. As amusing and naive as some of these ideas may seem to a Western public, they played an essential role in gathering the support of more people, in motivating the crowd to stay out in the streets, in giving people a powerful sense of belonging and being.

While religion and mysticism proved to be essential elements in gaining the support of the population at large as well as in making sense of the shocking changes occurring at the time, a series of other elements also played an important role: the creative use of space of the Timisoara revolutionaries as well as the emergence of informal channels of communication that proved essential for maintaining a sense of calm and confidence. The organization and use of space proved to be just as important as the chants or the political platform of those out in the streets. Without some luck and creative use of space, the Timisoara Revolution might never have turned into the life-changing event that it became.

While it was pure luck that the initial spark of the revolution occurred in a central part of town, through which many commuters had to pass, making the initial demonstrations much more visible, many of the later choices regarding the use of space seemed to be largely intentional. The workers who organized the massive demonstrations in Timisoara were fully aware of the trajectory that their march should take in order to gather more people: starting at the far end of the industrial platform, the workers marched past all factories on the platform, picking up delegations from each and every one of them. They then marched down some of the main avenues in town, past the student dorms and the university, past churches and the Serbian consulate—making sure that the Serbian consul could see them and transmit information about the demonstration to the outside—and towards the city council and the main city square—strategically located between the Opera House, an imposing building with a large balcony, and the local cathedral.[73]

The strategic use of the Opera House and its balcony as the main site for the revolutionary leaders and a perfect place from which to address the crowd, proved to be essential to keeping the demonstrators out in the street and inciting more people to come out. The balcony was the power position par excellence, the panopticon of the Timisoara leaders, the place from which they could control the crowd. The Opera House offered a large space for meetings and yet also a secure space for the leaders to consolidate their demands and speak out to the crowd. This was the site where the committee formed by several demonstrators, including Nicolae Badilescu, Lorin Fortuna, Claudiu Iordache, Chis Ioan and Traistarul Marinela, first formed the Romanian Democratic Front.[74] The balcony came to signify political power, and coined the expression of "Lumea Buna a Balconului" (the High Society of the Balcony)—also the name of a book written by Titus Suciu, a Timisoara revolutionary. While the Opera House balcony in Timisoara was the space that helped create and bring together the leadership of the Timisoara Revolution, for Bucharest, that space was the television tower and the studio from which live images reached the rest of the country with news of what was happening. Space, and access to a particular space, thus played a vital role in deciding who were going to be the future leaders of the Romania.

Symbols and signs also played a key role in the Timisoara Revolution. The placards carried by the demonstrators were an important visual call to action and carried the initial set of demands of the demonstrators. The defamation of party symbols and transformation of a Ceausescu portrait into a visual slogan by drawing a Hitler-like mustache on his face, were essential mechanisms for relieving tension and channeling energies towards one main goal: the removal of Ceausescu and his regime. Turning the regime's propaganda tools into weapons to be used against them was a strategic choice meant to once and for all unveil the communist illusion as an illusion. The flag with the gaping hole in the middle—the place where communist symbols once lay—was a great symbolic image of what people were feeling and thinking: an integral part of themselves had been removed, one that was at once celebrated and to a certain extent grieved.

Balint's own reaction to being handed a flag with a hole in the middle upon his release from prison, speaks to this:

unaware of the symbolism of the flag, Balint asked that he be given a "whole" flag as opposed to a torn one. Expressing his surprise when seeing a series of symbols and signs, Balint also mentions seeing a puzzling image of a man hanging pears on a tree in front of the city council during the demonstrations. The scene seemed to him inexplicable at the time, transforming the demonstration into a surreal experience. The message however may have been fairly straightforward, given the Romanian saying that the impossible will only happen "when the poplars start making pears." Well, the poplar in front of the city council was now making pears, thus the impossible had just occurred.[75]

The level of creativity in the Timisoara Revolution is obvious not only through symbolic scenes such as this one, but also through the way in which people organized themselves in different situations. The improvised system of communication, while very simplistic, was also very efficient. Given that all telephone lines had been cut off and that there was no way to communicate with the outside or even among themselves other than through direct, person-to-person communication, the revolutionaries came up with a system of small notes, that could be passed around in the crowd, from person to person, until they reached their destination.[76] This is how those on the balcony of the Opera House could be updated on what was going on in the negotiations with the city council, or how the crowd could send in suggestions or messages to those on the balcony, and it is how the first news of demonstrations in other small towns across the county came in and was communicated to the crowd from the Opera House balcony.

Other examples of this creative spirit are the attempts to provide some sense of security as well as to ensure that the outside world was informed about what was happening in Timisoara by sending messages to the local Serbian consulate; the way in which demonstrators approached soldiers, shaming them into dropping their guns and running; the way in which the revolutionaries dissuaded the "people's army"—miners sent in from Oltenia to beat up the demonstrators with sticks—from carrying out their task, by sending representatives to meet them at the train station with food and explain to them what the real situation was, arranging for them to sleep in local gyms for the night and arranging for them to go back the following day; the way in which everyone came together to ensure that the crowd stayed in the main city square until their demands were met—the bread factory delivered bread, the meat processing plant delivered salami, water was also made available, etc; and last but not least, the way in which, under such pressure and with such little time to prepare, a revolutionary committee could be formed, clearer sets of demands could be expressed and the first political body could be formed.[77]

This high level of creativity was key to the success of the Romanian Revolution, and space, symbolism and creative communication played a particularly important role in the ultimate success of the revolution, where success was initially defined by the fall of the Ceausescu regime. What was to follow was a different question. This sense of grassroots creativity was quickly lost as the decision-making was taken over by a controversial new governing group and as the initial revolutionary illusions were twisted and transformed into a new set of promises that helped legitimize a particular view of democracy and capitalism, one not necessarily supported by the population at large.

This chapter has sought to show that many of the actions and decisions that are usually interpreted as legitimizers of the democratic turn in Romania and throughout Central and Eastern Europe, are not so clear cut, and that in fact the democratic foundation on which the new capitalist illusion was supposedly being built was much more feeble than one may suspect. This challenges many of the discourses on the failed reform process, governmental corruption and weak civil society as the main causes of the slow democratic consolidation in Romania. If anything, this chapter suggests that one needs to look more carefully at the origin of the democratic turn in Romania, to understand the extent to which the new capitalist illusion was built almost in direct contradiction to people's initial expectations and desires. The Romanian and Central and Eastern European revolutionary enthusiasm, that was so inspirational for many international reform leaders, was thus wrongly interpreted as an enthusiasm for building a market-economy or even being more like the West. This has created a particularly tense relationship between the state and society whereby social cohesion occurs under an illusion that is regarded as both illegitimate and yet in many ways, necessary. To further legitimize this particular capitalist illusion, the Romanian state together with a series of international institutions such as the IMF and the World Bank, used the revolutionary ethos as the basis for setting up a new discourse on civil society and the key role that the latter will play in the process of democratic consolidation. The new capitalist illusion thus had at least two main pillars to support it: first, the twisting of the initial demands of the revolutionary leaders and demonstrators to mean a call for a market-democracy; and second, the new discourse on civil society. As we will see in the next chapter, this particular discourse on civil society managed to deepen the rift between society and the state, by creating a series of civil society institutions that acted more as an official political opposition than a representative of the population at large, as well as by further alienating the few elites that did manage to gain the trust of the population at large during those tense months following the Romanian Revolution.

Notes

1 Nicolae Badilescu, interview by author (tape recording, Timisoara: December 13th, 2004).
2 Claudiu Iordache, interview by author (tape recording, Bucharest: January 15th, 2005); Lorin Fortuna, interview by author (tape recording, Timisoara: December 14th, 2004).
3 Tiziano Terzani, *Goodnight, Mister Lenin: A Journey through the End of the Soviet Empire*, trans. Joan Krakover Hall (London: Picador, 1994).
4 See testimonies in Costel Balint, *1989: Timisoara in Decembrie* (Timisoara: Editura Helicon, 1993).
5 Jeffrey C. Goldfarb, "1989 and the Creativity of the Political," *Social Research* 68.4 (2001).
6 Richard Andrew Hall, "Theories of Collective Action and Revolution: Evidence from the Romanian Transition of December 1989," *Europe-Asia Studies* 52.6 (2000).
7 The events described under this particular section come from testimonies available in Balint, *1989: Timisoara in Decembrie*; Ruxandra Cesereanu, *Decembrie '89: Deconstructia Unei Revolutii* (Bucharest: Editura Polirom, 2004); Vladimir Tismaneanu, *Condamnati La Fericire: Experimentul Comunist in Romania* (Sibiu and Brasov: Fundatia Exo, 1991); Vladimir Tismaneanu, *Comisia Prezidentiala Pentru Analiza Dictaturii Comuniste Din Romania: Raport Final* (Bucharest: Romanian Presidency, 2006).

8 Ceausescu was successful in making Romania virtually debt free at the cost of one of the worst economic crises the country ever experienced. Ironically, after 1989, most other Eastern European states were forgiven their large debts by the international community. Twenty years of near starvation had been in vain.
9 Cesereanu, *Decembrie '89: Deconstructia Unei Revolutii.*
10 The events described under this particular section come from testimonies available in Balint, *1989: Timisoara in Decembrie;* Cesereanu, *Decembrie '89: Deconstructia Unei Revolutii;* Tismaneanu, *Condamnati La Fericire: Experimentul Comunist in Romania;* Tismaneanu, *Comisia Prezidentiala Pentru Analiza Dictaturii Comuniste Din Romania: Raport Final.*
11 Both Cesereanu and Balint address this question.
12 Thomas, quoted in Goldfarb, "1989 and the Creativity of the Political," 994.
13 *Desteapta-Te Romane (Awaken Thee, Romanian): Romania's National Anthem,* available at: www.national-anthems.org/anthems/country /ROMANIA+ (accessed March 29th, 2007).
14 This is directly reflected in testimonies presented in Balint, *1989: Timisoara in Decembrie:* Cesereanu, *Decembrie '89: Deconstructia Unei Revolutii.*
15 The description of what happened around Laslo Tokes's house come from testimonies available in: Balint, *1989: Timisoara in Decembrie;* Cesereanu, *Decembrie '89: Deconstructia Unei Revolutii;* Badilescu interview; Fortuna interview; Iordache interview; Sanda Adrian, interview by author (tape recording, Timisoara: December 20th, 2004). To ensure a more natural flow of the narrative, I will not provide these citations unless the reference only appears in a particular citation. Instead, I will simply note "see initial list of citations" when there is a general consensus in the literature as to how the events occurred.
16 The gathering occurred only a couple of weeks before the Christmas celebrations in Romania when vigils and lit candles are a common sight. That this would happen in the center of town, in front of a private house, is highly uncommon.
17 Adrian interview.
18 It is unclear to me what allowed for this identification: whether it was their attitude, the fact that they were armed or simply the fact that some people were able to recognize them from previous events in town where they were in police uniforms.
19 See initial list of citations.
20 See Adrian interview; Badilescu interview; Fortuna interview; Iordache interview.
21 Balint, *1989: Timisoara in Decembrie.*
22 Badilescu interview.
23 Badilescu interview.
24 G.M. Tamas, "The Legacy of Dissent," *The Revolutions of 1989*, ed. Vladimir Tismaneanu (London: Routledge, 1999), 195.
25 Testimonies regarding the workers' demonstrations come from: Badilescu interview; Balint, *1989: Timisoara in Decembrie;* Cesereanu, *Decembrie '89: Deconstructia Unei Revolutii;* Fortuna interview, Adrian

interview. To ensure a more natural flow of the narrative, I will not provide these citations unless the reference only appears in a particular citation. Instead, I will simply note "see initial list of citations" when there is a general consensus in the literature as to how the events occurred.

26 See initial list of citations.
27 Balint, *1989: Timisoara in Decembrie*.
28 Hall, "Theories of Collective Action and Revolution: Evidence from the Romanian Transition of December 1989."
29 See initial list of citations.
30 Balint, *1989: Timisoara in Decembrie*.
31 Balint, *1989: Timisoara in Decembrie*, 90.
32 Balint, *1989: Timisoara in Decembrie*.
33 Balint, *1989: Timisoara in Decembrie*.
34 This is reflected in a series of different testimonies by: Badilescu; Adrian; Balint, *1989: Timisoara in Decembrie*; Fortuna.
35 Adrian interview.
36 Balint, *1989: Timisoara in Decembrie*.
37 "Proclamatia Frontului Democratic Roman Constituit La Timisoara," *Victoria* Anul I, Issue I 1989.
38 Cesereanu, *Decembrie '89: Deconstructia Unei Revolutii*; Balint, *1989: Timisoara in Decembrie*.
39 These are commonly held opinions in Romania although mainly based on testimonies of friends and friends of friends. To my knowledge, there is yet no official document tracking what happened to members of the former nomenklatura except in cases where the latter managed to keep their jobs or became the subject of a public investigation.
40 See "Proclamatia Frontului Democratic Roman Constituit La Timisoara"; Gheorghe Crisan, "Interviu Cu Domnul Ioan Lorin Fortuna, Liderul Frontului Democrat Roman Din Timisoara," *Victoria* Anul I, Issue I 1989.
41 This results from interviews with the founding members of the NSF: Adrian interview; Badilescu interview; Fortuna interview; Iordache interview.
42 Crisan, Gheorghe, "Interview with Mr. Ioan Lorin Fortuna—the leader of the Romanian Democratic Front in Timisoara" (published in Romanian), *Victoria*, Anul I, Issue I: 3.
43 Quoted in Goldfarb, "1989 and the Creativity of the Political," 1007.
44 "Proclamatia Frontului Democratic Roman Constituit La Timisoara."
45 Adrian interview.
46 Many of these resentments were expressed during the Fifteen Years since the Timisoara Revolution Symposium that took place in Timisoara, Romania in December 2004.
47 See the testimonies of Sanda Adrian, Lorin Fortuna and Nicolae Badilescu.
48 Again see testimonies of Sanda Adrian, Nicolae Badilescu and Lorin Fortuna.
49 Original members of the NSF also experienced a similar disillusionment

THE ILLUSIONS AND DISILLUSIONS OF THE 1989 REVOLUTION 135

when its local and enterprise committees were suppressed along with the move to become a political party. For more details see: Vladimir Pasti, *Romania in Tranzitie: Caderea in Viitor* (Bucharest: Nemira, 1995).

50 Adrian interview.

51 These are commonly held beliefs within Romania.

52 See Fortuna interview, Claudiu Iordache, *Romania Pierduta* (Bucharest: Editura Irini, 1995); Claudiu Iordache, *Clasa Nevrednica* (Bucharest: Editura Irini, 1997); Claudiu Iordache, *Polul De Putere* (Bucharest: Editura Irini, 2002).

53 See Cristian Badilita, "Visez Un Singur Gest De Razbunare—Ca Peste Douazeci De Ani Piata Universitatii Sa Se Numeasca Piata Ion Iliescu," *Adevarul* June 15th, 2005; Cesereanu, *Decembrie '89: Deconstructia Unei Revolutii*; Andrei Cornea, interview by author (tape recording, Bucharest: January 20th, 2005); Radu Filipescu, interview by author (tape recording, Bucharest: January 19th, 2005).

54 While the answer to this question will seem evident to most Western academics, the almost obsessive focus on finding out the "truth" about the Romanian Revolution as well as the communist dictatorship of Romania (thus the controversy surrounding the Secret Security Archives discussed earlier) continues to dominate many of the discussions on the subject. The sense that they have been "duped" is pervasive not only amongst the revolutionaries, but also among the average citizens who are for the most part convinced that "a truth" exists yet is kept hidden from them. This has emerged as perhaps one of the most powerful myths of the Romanian Revolution.

55 Many of these events were caught on tape and aired live on Romanian TV as well as international stations such as CNN. The events are recalled as they have been watched by the author.

56 These events are described in Balint, *1989: Timisoara in Decembrie*.

57 George Galloway and Bob Wylie, *Prabusirea*, trans. Constantin Sfeatcu (Bucharest: Editura Irini, 1991), 57–8.

58 I attended this symposium during the winter of 2004, as a special guest, and presented a paper on the way in which the Romanian Revolution was presented in the international press.

59 Iordache, *Romania Pierduta*, 149.

60 Badilescu interview.

61 These figures are based on average costs and wages in some of the major towns of Romania, including Bucharest and Timisoara, as of 2004.

62 This conspiracy theory, while well researched from a historical point of view, has made many distrustful of Lorin Fortuna, whom they often choose to classify as a slight "loony." Whether they are right or not, Fortuna remains an important leader of the Romanian revolution with insightful information about this historical event.

63 Fortuna interview.

64 Fortuna interview.

65 Irina Culic in Andras Bozoki (ed.), *Intellectuals and Politics in Central Europe* (Budapest: Central European University Press, 1999).

66 Alina Mungiu-Pippidi, *Politica Dupa Comunism* (Bucharest: Humanitas, 2002).

67 Alina Mungiu-Pippidi in Bozoki (ed.), *Intellectuals and Politics in Central Europe*, 76.

68 This was highly unusual, since hot water was well rationed, particularly during winter.

69 These events are described in Balint, *1989: Timisoara in Decembrie*.

70 Balint, *1989: Timisoara in Decembrie*.

71 See Balint, *1989: Timisoara in Decembrie*; Adrian interview.

72 This comes out of most conversations with former participants in the Romanian Revolution that the author had during the Timisoara Symposium celebrating fifteen years since the Timisoara Revolution.

73 This also comes out of testimonies of former participators in the Timisoara Revolution. See above footnote.

74 Balint, *1989: Timisoara in Decembrie*.

75 Balint, *1989: Timisoara in Decembrie*.

76 Anyone living in Timisoara at the time experienced this, including my own family.

77 See testimonies of Balint, *1989: Timisoara in Decembrie*; Adrian interview; Badilescu interview; Fortuna interview.

6

The illusions and disillusions of civil society: the case of the Group for Social Dialogue

Based on a series of interviews with the founding members of the Group for Social Dialogue—the first civil society organization in post-revolutionary Romania—clippings from the group's magazine entitled 22—one of the most popular political magazines in the months immediately following the revolution—as well as a rich secondary literature on the larger concept of civil society, as viewed and interpreted by a number of leading Central and Eastern European writers and philosophers, this chapter seeks to reveal how the civil society illusion was particularly built in Romania in order to fit and support the larger capitalist illusion. This chapter also seeks to underline the striking discrepancies between initial imaginings of the role of civil society by different Central and Eastern European writers and later use of the concept mainly in conjunction with a series of national and international NGOs. These discrepancies become particularly evident in the evolution of the Group for Social Dialogue, from a group intending to give voice to the general grievances of the people, to a political institution that played the role of an unofficial opposition party, and later to an outsider both to the political game as well as the larger NGO community.

Given that civil society discourses have played an essential role in justifying and consolidating the democratic turn throughout Central and Eastern Europe,[1] it will be interesting to see the extent to which attaching such high hopes to this concept was justified, both from the perspective of the international community, but more importantly, from the perspective of the so-called civil society institutions in Romania. Once again, this chapter seeks to show that the initial revolutionary ethos had little to do with this particular understanding of civil society, which was by no means representative of the population at large, nor was it true to its initial commitment to bridge the gap between society and the state. If anything, the civil society democratic illusion was for the most part ignored by the population at large, who saw both national and international NGOs as nothing but better-paid job opportunities or at the most, generous institutions able to pick up the slack from the dying welfare state. Perhaps the most damage was done to the elites who put their faith in the civil society democratic illusion, only to later realize that its impact would be far lower than the one initially expected.

By focusing on the emergence of a particular East European understanding of civil society as anti-statist, a rather artificial connection between civil society and democratization practices and assumptions that the strengths and weaknesses of civil society can be similarly measured across different contexts, this chapter seeks to challenge common misconceptions about the nature of Romanian civil society, and more importantly, provide an alternative understanding of the role of civil society through the particular trajectory of the Group for Social Dialogue. Focusing particularly on the oftentimes arbitrary distinctions between the realm of civil society and that of the political, the chapter seeks to show that, at least in the case of the Romanian transition, the two were intrinsically connected.

The emergence of the Eastern European concept of civil society as anti-statist

Communist Central and Eastern Europe had little if any understanding of the concept of civil society as we know it today. The average person was most likely not familiar with the term, while the elite was familiar with its meaning from classical texts. The international press was perhaps the first to associate Central and Eastern European dissidents with the birth of an underground civil society movement whose aim was to reform/destroy the communist state. Civil society was thus far from being the protector of certain civil rights guaranteed by the state (as it is considered to be in liberal democratic states) for the communist state guaranteed no such rights. If anything—to the extent that it was first equated with dissident movements—it was considered to be the realm that would help formulate what those rights should be. The notion of rights that was formulated by the dissident groups in Central and Eastern Europe was one based on a common sense of morality and respect developed outside of a state, for the state in general was deeply distrusted.[2]

The democratic order imagined by the Central and Eastern European dissidents was one that was based on a morality of truth—what Havel called "living in truth," calling the lie a lie[3]—as well as on rejecting all forms of oppressive authority that seek to monopolize truth—often translated as a rejection of politics and political leadership in general.[4] This particular vision of democracy thus rejects the state and the structures on which the liberal state is built. Despite a general acceptance of the liberal state after the 1989 Revolutions, the fundamental distrust of the state remains an important characteristic of most Central and Eastern European societies, undermining many of the attempts to present the state under a more positive light and encourage more trust in state institutions.

The anti-statist and more importantly the anti-political attitude of the underground society formed by Central and Eastern European dissidents, is particularly challenging of the "civil" vision of civil society, for the rejection of politics and solidified power structures in general—such as the state—can easily be viewed as anarchic and certainly not conducive to a civil attitude in society. The vision of civil society that the Central and Eastern European dissidents had in mind, if any, was a combative one that would constantly resist the oppressions of the state—in their case, a totalitarian state.

The collapse of the totalitarian state has demanded a redefinition of civil society, one that would not be combative of the state, but rather supportive of it. Tamas argues that we are still struggling to make that transition and that in many ways we continue to dream of a society without the state—which serves to justify the centrality of the myth of civil society since 1989: "The flight from politics is a profound need: it is one of the most important historic versions of the desire for freedom."[5] Defining freedom as the flight from politics is however something that could potentially turn out to be quite dangerous, particularly in a context where democratization is directly connected to the state-building effort.

The myth of post-communist civil society is built along two main principles, according to Tamas—a noncoercive political order and a nonhierarchical structure. These principles are dangerously close to the theoretical principles of communism, and Tamas is afraid that the new myth of civil society is nothing but a way to reinvent communism: "the way civil society is thought today, it seems to confirm that communism is right and liberalism wrong."[6] More importantly though, what Tamas is pointing out is that in post-revolutionary Eastern Europe, one needs to stay away from any new salvationist promises, whether they come from civil society or the state. The myth of noncoerciveness and nonhierarchy is after all just a myth, because the post-revolutionary world is precisely a world of aggressiveness, rising inequalities and power infighting. Yet one can easily see how a post-revolutionary situation can be particularly prone to accept and hope for such myths.

Standing on fresh ground with lingering excitement from the never before felt sense of social solidarity that brought millions of people onto the streets, one gains a new sense of hope, of goodness, unity and courage, a similar sense of morality that could potentially be expanded and maintained. Yet the immediate fight for power, the corruption, the rising inequalities that slap everyone in the face, the economic hardships, provide a quick wake-up call and perhaps a push over towards the other extreme: apathy and hopelessness. Tamas need not worry that the civil society illusion has found too many followers in Eastern Europe. In fact, the illusion may be stronger on the side of the international funders, for on the ground, a new sense of pragmatism is using this illusion to secure political positions, form strong oppositions, create new education programs and replace the welfare state that is crumbling.

Legitimizing the civil society—democratization connection

The legitimation of a particular connection between civil society and democratization in the Central and Eastern

European context was made possible by a particular combination of: 1) the post-revolutionary euphoria under which many of the former dissidents entered politics; 2) the aid coming from the West immediately after the fall of communism—aid that was often attached to a very specific set of democratic reforms and institution-building as well as the private investment of a series of important foundations and civic associations that prided themselves on being the guardians of democracy in other parts of the world; 3) the introduction of a discourse of rights through human rights activism that appealed in particular to certain minorities and the dissident elite.

The original Eastern European ideal of civil society as a society that escaped politics and the state was thus co-opted under a new ideal: that of civil society as key to developing new democratic institutions and governing systems. The transition was made possible by the initial post-revolutionary euphoria, in which many of the former dissidents and intellectuals suddenly entered the realm of politics promising to create a new kind of state, a state that could be trusted. With Vaclav Havel becoming the president of Czechoslovakia and later the Czech Republic, the ideal of the philosopher king was closer to reality then ever. Many of the other Eastern European countries followed his example with much of the dissident elite forming new political parties or running for political appointments. The legitimacy of the newly formed governments in Eastern Europe was thus to a large extent measured in terms of their ability to co-opt former dissidents with a clear anti-communist stance and reject former communist elites, that did, however, find their way back into many of the newly formed governments.[7]

Western financial support focused both on the creation of strong liberal state institutions as well as the creation of civic associations and foundations that would help develop "civil society" in Eastern Europe. Civil society was thus understood to be a series of NGOs and other voluntary associations that would help engage citizens in the democratization process by raising their awareness concerning the necessary democratic reforms, the respect of minority rights and necessity to engage actively in their society. These NGOs were taught how to measure levels of reform and protest any tendencies that ran against the established set of reforms; they were taught to engage the local governments and teach them management skills as well as force them to adopt mechanisms that would engage their constituencies; they were given financial support for citizen education, study abroad, minority and environmental protection programs.[8]

Democracy-building was however focused both on institution-building—the strengthening of state institutions—and civil society-building. While these efforts were supposed to work in tandem, they often ended up undermining each other and creating confusion with regards to the role of the state vs. the role of civil society. Actors kept stepping back and forth between their political role and their civic activism role while many NGOs adopted a similar mandate to that of state institutions, sometimes even turning into political parties.[9]

While many of these NGOs that came to represent civil society were viewed and described as grassroots movements, a majority of them were far from that. Much of their legitimacy came from a handful of people, many of whom were former dissidents or members of the intellectual elite, and all of them were dependent on outside funding and programs that saw little voluntary support, engaging mainly people that could directly benefit (financially in many instances) from them. This is not to say that these programs were not needed or beneficial. In fact, they played an essential role in addressing a series of important social needs that the state could no longer support: everything from special education and training, to medical support and environmental protection. The civic and voluntary character of many of these programs however need not be overstated, as it most often has been, for volunteerism and the culture of giving is yet to be developed in much of post-communist Central and Eastern Europe.[10]

The idea that civil society was the easy solution to just about every bump in the road to democratization caused all creative efforts to go into figuring out how this could be achieved. The idealization of civil society and the role that it can play in bringing about harmony in society conveniently helped to simplify and legitimize a series of international and national practices, including important economic and political reforms as well as international interventions in transitioning states. This idealization however was not without consequence.

Holding NGOs to higher standards than they can withstand and using them to uphold an unrealistic ideal of a society is a straight road to disillusionment. The alternative might be to disconnect the concept of civil society from the democratization debate and allow for a more localized understanding of both its structure and process. As David Blaney and M.K. Pasha argue, doing this might open the road for a series of other important interpretations of phenomena related to social change, particularly in societies in transition. Taking the example of Pakistan, Pasha argues that if one looks past common assumptions that the lack of efficiency of democratic states is necessarily a sign of an evolving rift between state and society, one might be able to see the historical possibility of a different kind of state creation and evolution and connection between state and society.[11] Opening one's eyes to these possibilities is essential for understanding social change beyond the increasingly restrictive discourse of civil society.

Weak or strong civil society: how do we measure?

If civil society lies at the intersection of society and the state, the post-revolutionary Central and Eastern European civil society is certainly facing the state more than society, with a majority of people involved in civil society interested more in the political game and how it affects social change and development. Social services and volunteerism are secondary to the strengthening of state institutions and the influencing of political and economic reform. Civil society in most of Central and Eastern Europe has not seen the grassroots support that characterizes it in places like the United States, not has it seen a similar kind of commitment to community values and working together towards common goals. Whether this necessarily signifies a weakness of civil society is however questionable.

While many writers, such as Marc Morje Howard,[12] Gabriel Badescu, Paul Sum and Eric Uslaner,[13] equate the weakness of Central and Eastern European civil society with the low level of participation in its institutions—which has direct effects on the democratization and reform process—

alternative views of civil society might interpret the same weakness as nothing but a sign of a different forms of engagement. That civil society does not enjoy the same levels of popular participation need not necessarily mean that it is weak, but simply that it is expressing its goals in a different manner. Given that the family unit—which also includes the extended family—has been traditionally stronger in Central and Eastern Europe than in a place like the United States, civil society may be constrained to a more family-oriented approach than a community-oriented one. If civil society is often associated with a series of institutions and NGOs in the Western world, perhaps it might be more appropriate to associate it with different kinds of associations in the Central and Eastern European context, which has been traditionally distrustful of institutions in general.

Civic skills can hardly ever be taught outside of a context that naturally encourages them and finds them beneficial. Without clear and direct benefits, people will not choose to invest their energies into something that might prove to be wasteful or simply not likely to bring about any real effects. Convincing people that community work or volunteering is not something to shy away from and that a personal investment in the affairs of the local and national administration is not only healthy but beneficial for them in the long term, will take more than a few seminars on leadership and civic skills. The pervasive cynicism and pragmatism (materialistic, "What do I get out of this?" type pragmatism) that dominates much of Eastern Europe is not unfounded, for this is how one survives in these new democratic regimes. Only when survival will no longer be dependent on distrust, cheating and stepping ahead at every cost will a sense of community become important and visible.

In a place that has always rejected institutions and has sought to create alternative mechanisms of survival, it is hardly any surprise that the use of an institutionalized definition of civil society will result in finding it to be weak. It is doubtful that Eastern Europeans will be more trustful of institutions—whether state or private and civil society institutions—any time soon. Yet, with more and more countries in transition, the desperate need for a democratization model seems to trump all fears that such a model might now apply universally. Idealized visions of the democratic state—as well as civil society—appease the otherwise grim and hopeless horizons that many of these societies are facing. Dahrendorf sees the role of the state as "... a vision of hope which lifts people's spirits above the routine of normalcy"[14] while Havel sees it as:

> a product of society, an expression of it, an image of it. It is a structure that a society creates for itself as an instrument of its own self-realization. If we wish to create a good and humane society, capable of making a contribution to humanity's coming to its senses, we must create a good and humane state. That means a state that will no longer suppress, humiliate, and deny the free human being, but will serve all the dimensions of that being. That means a state that will not shift our hearts and minds into a special little niche labeled "superstructure," tolerated and developed for decorative purposes only.[15]

The modern Central and Eastern European states however could not be further from this image. The disconnect between state and society seems to be larger than ever despite modern communication technologies, a more or less free press and more access to state institutions. If anything, the new communication technologies have managed to open people's eyes even wider when it came to government corruption and infighting, rigged elections and false promises. One can only hope that these states are not an image of their societies, for if they are, then we may be in deeper trouble than we know. How this rift was created has been the topic of many conversations, both within academia and outside of it. Contemporary political scientists have tried to explain it in light of modern phenomena of political apathy or disenchantment with politics, yet quick fixes to the problem have yet to be found. That this rift exists even in societies where governmental corruption and infighting is not so much of a problem, might suggest that we are looking for solutions in the wrong places.

Alina Mungiu-Pippidi, a Romanian sociologist and political scientist, argues that the disconnect between society and the state, at least in the case of post-communist Romania, is due to the lack of vision of political parties, one of the main mechanisms of representation in a liberal democracy. Because Eastern Europe has very little experience with political party organization, and because politicians have been, for the most part, unable to offer clear alternatives and visions for the future of the country, most people feel like the moment of elections is really a moment of non-choice. Mungui-Pippidi notes an interesting phenomenon that arises as a result of this: the feeling that civil society needs to somehow take over politics, because civil society institutions are the only ones that can be trusted and are more connected to society at large. She goes on to explain:

> A political scientist looking at this phenomenon [...] sees something entirely different: that the historical political parties fail, even after ten years, to produce candidates for the presidential elections and to in fact produce quality candidates; that civil society, by itself or through its leaders, continues to be a form of doing politics of a group of people that believe it is OK to do politics without political parties, and they have nothing to lose because of this, and that in the end, it is still the old communist party that is providing the day-to-day functionaries of the government.[16]

According to Mungiu-Pippidi thus, the source of the problem is: 1) the failure of the state to organize itself in the prescribed institutional structure; 2) the failure of civil society to take over its role as representative of society as opposed to yet another political player; and 3) the failure of the masses to identify with either one of these institutions: the state or civil society, for it is unclear which does what and where their allegiance lies. The result of all this seems to be that neither politics nor the private realm are working according to the liberal framework, thus leaving the population at large with no alternative, hope or vision, but to seek refuge in their job, their family, and oftentimes foreign countries (leading to a large brain drain problem). Mungiu-Pippidi calls this the lack of hope capital, a play-off on what Putnam called social capital.[17]

The solution that Mungiu-Pippidi offers, that of "intelligent politics," suggests that there is a model of what constitutes "intelligent politics" and that this model can be replicated. Unfortunately, the rules do not seem to be that simple, and the negative hope capital that Mungiu-Pippidi describes might be a necessary protection mechanism in a transitioning society that is constantly faced with new promises, an increasing set of economic and social challenges and constant changes. Keeping a pragmatic approach to everyday politics—sometimes called being cynical—gives one enough distance to manage the contradictions of transitions through the stability of smaller units such as family and friends. While this may not be an ideal situation, it does help people manage.

Although this brief overview of the civil society literature, particularly in the Central and Eastern European as well as Romanian contexts, does not do justice to the wealth of material on this subject, it has consciously sought to focus on a small number of issues—anti-statism, the civil society—democratization connection, measuring civil society as a way of determining success in the reform process—as a way to introduce a more empirically grounded discussion on the particular way in which civil society developed in Romania and the extent to which it was influential in a number of important political decisions following the 1989 Revolution.

The Group for Social Dialogue—the first civil society organization in Romania

If "hope capital" now seems to be depleted, hope resources ran high immediately following the 1989 Revolutions, particularly in Romania, where the radical transformations following December 1989 would have been inconceivable even a few months before they unfolded. As everyone's energies went into creating a new government and investing in people and personalities that could be trusted, one particular group managed to capture the attention and enthusiasm of a large part of the Romanian population: the Group for Social Dialogue (GSD). The GSD was formed in the days immediately following the fall of the Ceausescu regime in Romania by a series of Romanian intellectuals and dissidents who came together under the impulse to create a space for discussion that would facilitate the democratization process. Given its elite membership of intellectuals and dissidents, many of whom came back from exile from Western Europe or the US, the group gained immediate national and international attention and quickly became the compass that would help orient anyone trying to navigate the Romanian Revolution and the immediate post-revolutionary period. The group was consolidated almost instantaneously and gathered momentum after its first press conference at the famous Hotel

Intercontinental in Bucharest and more importantly, after it managed to secure a home in the center of Bucharest on 120 Victory Street.

For the next two years the group played an essential role in national politics, helping to shape the new political arena, bring together different parts of society and consolidate a path for the Romanian transition. The group's magazine was one of the most well-read magazines in the country, helping to increase the group's visibility and attract the attention of all different layers of society. The group brought hope and the promise that all concerns would be addressed equally and fairly. Although playing an essential role in national politics, the group also became the symbol of civil society in Romania, self-naming itself a civil society organization aimed at guarding the rights of the Romanian people—including minorities in Romania—and watching for any abuses of the newly formed government. The GSD was considered to be the birthplace of Romanian civil society, the site where many of the new-coming foundations and associations were formed, where interest groups were consolidated and new social and political agendas were written.

The GSD thus emerged as a natural case study for anyone studying civil society in the Romanian context, being the first self-proclaimed civil society organization in the country as well as the birthplace of essentially all civil society organizations that were to be formed afterwards. Judging from the experience of the GSD, the definition of civil society, at least in the Romanian case, has to be very flexible, particularly given the important role that the GSD played in the formation of the new government, its direct implication in the formation of an unofficial and later official political opposition party and in the formation of other NGOs. The GSD's experience underlines the fact that neither Havel nor Konrad's illusion of civil society as apolitical, nor the Western democratic illusion of civil society as a grassroots organization, were founded in the actual experience on the ground. If anything, both of these illusions helped set up unrealistic expectations that ended up disappointing both the Eastern European, and in this particular case the Romanian, elites, as well as the international donors who sought to measure participation in civil society as proof of democratic consolidation.

This is not to say that the money poured into different civil society institutions went to waste, but simply to show that under these particular discourses it is hard to see the actual role that civil society organizations, such as the GSD, did play in transitioning Romania. It is clear that the GSD, as well as other institutions that would be labeled as civil society organizations, did play an essential role in helping people better understand the institutional framework of the new market-democratic system and their role within this system, as well as in providing support to those who could no longer be helped by the crumbling welfare state as well as to discriminated minorities. When talking about the Central and Eastern European transitions, it is however essential to point out the different ways in which civil society institutions evolved and how they were affected by an all too rigid expectation of what their role should be.

The remainder of this chapter is based largely on interviews with several of the GSD founding members and information collected in the GSD archives, focusing mainly on the original ideals of the group, the first years of the GSD, the first disappointments and how the role of the group has changed in the meanwhile. The information was consolidated with certain questions in mind: 1) how the definition/understanding of civil society was first formulated and later evolved in post-communist Romania and the extent to which this definition fit the more common Western model of associational life; 2) the role that civil society—in this case the group—played in the relationship between state and society; 3) the expectations—coming both from the national as well as the international arena—that were attached to these newly created civil society groups, like the GSD, throughout Eastern Europe, and the extent to which those expectations were met; and 4) how the role of the group has changed more than fifteen years down the road and the lessons that were learned, if any.

The historical evolution of the GSD as the first civil society group in post-revolutionary Romania reveals the extent to which, in practice, the birth of civil society was much more influenced by things such as location and visibility, membership and appeal to a particular set of well-connected elites, political aspirations, the upholding of a particular set of moral standards and the return to power of minority groups that had until then been discriminated against, as opposed to obtaining grassroots membership and support, creating representational mechanisms for the population at large, or addressing common concerns such as increasing poverty, unemployment or restitution. The GSD is emblematic of many other civil society organizations throughout Central and Eastern Europe, to the extent that it questions its democratic base and role in addressing the concerns of the many, as opposed to the minority or the elite.

Identifying the group's founding members

While the group now lists over fifty members, the founding and perhaps most active members of the group number around twenty-five. Each member of the group could be considered an intellectual of some kind, some more public than others, yet each with their own voice. The group is impressive not only in the wide range of interests that its members exhibit: from architecture to literature and philosophy, to journalism and political science, to public advocacy and representative politics, but also in its ability to engage all these different interests towards a common cause: that of ensuring a transparent transition towards a more democratic state. The contributions of each of the group's founding members became visible not only through the weekly magazine that the group publishes, 22, but also through their individual public careers: TV interviews and campaigns, book presentations and talkshow discussions, exhibitions and public speeches, panel discussions at conferences and plenary meetings and presentations within the Romanian parliament and senate.

While tracking the individual achievements of each of the founding members would necessitate a separate book in itself, the following briefly focuses on the intellectual and political interventions of a few, selected on the basis of their various interests, level of public visibility and the author's accessibility to their persona. They are: Gabriela Adamesteanu, Mariana Celac, Andrei Cornea, Radu Filipescu, Thomas Kleininger, Gabriel Liiceanu, Horia-Roman Patapievici, Alin Teodorescu and Rodica Palade.

Gabriela Adamesteanu, for a long time the editor-in-chief

of the group's magazine, 22, recently returned to her career as a literature writer and essayist while also continuing to pursue her journalistic interests as editor-in-chief of the "Cultural Bucharest" supplement. As a writer and translator, Adamesteanu has published over five novels—the first of which established her as one of the best young Romanian writers—and two political essays, and has translated important writers such as Guy de Maupassant and Hector Bianciotti. She plunged into the public arena, shortly after the 1989 Revolution, when she started writing for 22, establishing a new journalistic style: one that combined reporting with the sensibilities of a novelist, thus being able to capture not only the important events and controversies that marked Romania's transition, but also the emotions surrounding those events and oftentimes, the nonsensical nature of policies and shifting political positioning of different actors and parties.

With a straightforward writing style and an incredible power of analysis and perspective writing, Adamesteanu wrote articles on everything from the mineriada episode, to pension reform and the transformations in the Secret Security mechanisms; she also wrote critical film and book reviews, as well as editorials on the state of the Romanian transition, defending a number of important public intellectuals as well as discussing and tracking the often acrobatic maneuvering on the Romanian political scene. Like many of the group's members, Adamesteanu became an official scribe of the Romanian transition, using her personal sensibilities to tackle issues and problems that she would have probably otherwise never have written about.

Mariana Celac, although an important founding member of the group, kept a much lower profile than Adamesteanu. An architect by training, Celac was a known dissident, speaking often to Radio Free Europe against the Ceausescu regime and its destructive policies, particularly in rural areas. After 1989, while keeping the role of an advisor and fellow intellectual within the group, Celac continued to pursue her career as an architect and urban planner, initiating a number of interesting projects both within Romania and abroad that sought to investigate the way in which the communist ideology used and abused space as well as some of the ways in which these abuses could be rectified through increased awareness and reattribution of roles to significant buildings such as the famous Palace of the People.[18]

Celac has served as a much-needed inspiration to a number of up and coming Romanian architects, focusing her attention on a spatial investigation of the Romanian transition: from the old communist flats to the emerging suburbia—both rich and poor, from the idyllic Romanian villages, to the oftentimes deserted and impoverished rural areas. One of the most interesting projects that Celac has been working on, together with two other young architects and photographers—Iosif Kiraly and Marius Marcu-Lepadat—has been the Tinseltown project, investigating the Roma palaces in a number of different places across Romania, as a sign of a newly established identity based both on newfound wealth as well as on the ability to publicly display that wealth.

Another important founding member of the group, Andrei Cornea—one of the leading Romanian public intellectuals—is a classically trained art historian and philologist who has written extensively on topics as varied as Romanian art antics, the Roman and Byzantine cultural and artistic mentalities, writing and rhetoric in ancient culture, Plato, Socrates, and the Paltinis school. Currently a professor of philosophy at the University of Bucharest, Andrei Cornea has also written a number of important articles on Romania's democratic transition, entry into the EU and NATO, its orthodox legacy, prosecution of former communists and the emergence of new class divisions. Just like Adamesteanu and Celac, Cornea has managed to turn his intellectual interests and abilities towards a deeper examination of Romania's transition, thus contributing to a critical assessment of a number of important events and legacies.

Radu Filipescu, currently the president of the GSD's administration council and also one of the founding members of the group, was a well-known dissident at the time of the Romanian Revolution, having been arrested on a number of different occasions for instigating demonstrations and publishing and distributing manifests against the Ceausescu regime. As an engineer, Filipescu holds several important patents for a number of different inventions, yet is most publicly known for his role within the GSD as well as for his work with the Association Defending Human Rights within Romania and the Association of Romanian Revolutionaries Without Privileges. He has been a key person in helping to organize the initial group's initiatives, and has also become one of the founding members of the Civic Alliance, an opposition group later turned political party that sought to consolidate the interests of civil society and represent them on the political scene. As one of the more active members within the group, Filipescu has had a chance to watch the group grow and evolve, while also participating at a number of key events and discussions that helped set up the Romanian political system as it exists today, thus being a key witness to the transition process from the inside.

Thomas Kleininger, another founding member of the group, is a well-known philologist, translator of Heidegger and Kant, yet more recently known for his involvement with the liberal movement in post-communist Romania, as the director of the Friedrich Naumann Foundation Romania, the director of the Romanian National Liberal Party research office and the director of the Romanian Commerce and Industry Office. Kleininger has also written extensively on issues concerning the role of civil society in politics, the issue of poverty and authority. More active in the group's activities in the years immediately after the founding of the GSD, Kleininger now focuses on pursuing his career as a liberal activist and forming a new liberal elite in Romania.

Gabriel Liiceanu is yet another founding member of the group, currently a professor in the Faculty of Philosophy at the University of Bucharest as well as a very well-established writer and essayist, perhaps one of the most present on the shelves of Romania's bookstores. He was written over seven major books, translated the work of Plato and Heidegger, written countless articles published in Romanian, French, English, German and Hungarian and has created a number of documentary films on the work of Eugen Ionescu and Emil Cioran. As the head of one of the biggest publishing houses in Romania, Humanitas, Liiceanu has helped promote the work of important Romanian and foreign writers and reinvigorated the literary culture in post-communist Romania. As a prominent intellectual, Liiceanu often speaks on a number of political and cultural TV shows in Romania and gives public lectures at different universities.

A good friend of Liiceanu and also a founding member of

the GSD, Horia-Roman Patapievici is perhaps the most prolific young philosopher that Romania has produced in the last twenty years. Having initially studied physics, Patapievici then moved on to study philosophy, having served as the head of the Center for German Studies at the Philosophy Department within the University of Bucharest since 1996. He has published over seven books, contributed to countless volumes and helped translate the work of David Bohm. He has also distinguished himself as a very visible public intellectual, through his presence on a number of different cultural and political TV shows as well as through his deep interest in promoting a strong cultural movement within Romania: he initiated the publication of a number of different cultural magazines and became the director of the Romanian Cultural Institute in 2005. Patapievici has also expressed an interest in the study of Romania's communist past, becoming a leading member of the so-called CNSAS—the National Council for the Study of the Former Security Archives. This position has put him in the middle of a number of different controversies surrounding important Romanian personalities accused of having collaborated with the former Romanian Secret Security.

Last, but not least, Alin Teodorescu has followed a slightly different trajectory from the other founding group members, having established himself as a prominent politician after serving as the head of the Soros Foundation Romania[19] from 1990 to 1996, as well as a researcher within the Sociology Institute at the Romanian Academy and the Institute of Marketing and Polling in Romania (IMAS). Formerly a member of the Romanian Communist Party, Teodorescu joined the Romanian Social Democratic Party in 2004, serving as personal counselor to the prime minister on issues surrounding public administration and later as the head of the prime minister's counseling office. He currently serves as a deputy of the Social Democratic Party and is a member of the Committee for Economic Policies, Reform and Privatization.

While this is only a short selection of the group's founding members and their past and current status within Romania's political, economic, social and intellectual circles, it serves to point out both the diversity of the group as well as the different sets of interests that it has helped represent and serve.

Although the personalities presented above chose different trajectories as well as different levels of involvement with the group, they each contributed significantly to the group's establishment on political and civil society arena. More importantly though, this helps to point out the elite status of the group and its crucial influence on the post-communist political formation and later on political criticism within transitioning Romania.

Location and visibility

What allowed the group to gain such visibility and influence immediately after the fall of the communist regime was not only the presence of important dissidents and the public attention throughout the media and TV, but also its ability to secure a location in the center of Bucharest, close to the seat of government and easily accessible for anyone who wanted to reach out to it. Having a central space, as well as a space that allowed for both public and private discussions, was essential in creating a setting that was conducive to dialogue. The house on 120 Victory Street was a newly renovated two-story classical building in the very center of Bucharest that was designed for Nicu Ceausescu—one of Ceausescu's sons—to use as a meeting place for the Young Communists' Union. The house was fully furnished and had several conference rooms, meeting rooms, a bar, and offices: the perfect site for negotiating how Romanian society should look in the future.

Securing the house gave the group a different presence, a place to meet regularly, a place to interact with others, give interviews and organize debates. The process of securing the house speaks of the influence that certain group members had immediately after the revolution. Less than a week after the group was formed, with a signature from Silviu Brucan,[20] the house was given to the group under special lease. Registering the house and the group itself as an association proved to be a difficult process, since there was no legislation at the time that allowed for the creation of independent associations. The group was finally registered, along with the house, under a 1930s law that allowed for the creation of independent associations.[21] While the government lease appeared to be a blessing at first, it later became a tool that incoming governments could use to intimidate the group—by threatening to end their lease and evacuate them from that location—whenever the group was perceived to be too threatening to their position. This did not stop the group from continuing its activities as before and in spite of all the threats, to remain up to this day at 120 Victory Street.

It was at this location, during those fervent days following the Romanian Revolution, that the debates leading to the formation of the new government, the new legislation and political reform were held. The GSD essentially became the interim Romanian parliament, a forum for discussion and meeting place for anyone who wanted to play a role in the new consolidation of power and social organization of the country. The GSD was compared to the "Gare de Nord," the main train station of Romania, where journalists, ambassadors, politicians, donors, dissidents, union leaders and average people, came together to discuss the future of Romania. As described in those early days of January 1990, the place was constantly swarming with people coming in and out, sleeping on the couches, talking and eating at the bar, holding conferences and meetings, writing statutes for newly formed organizations and associations, debating what the next steps should be, receiving advice from other revolutionary leaders from Eastern Europe, giving interviews, receiving guests from outside, managing donations—such as the recording studio that was donated by George Soros and that allowed many of these meetings and debates to be recorded—and putting together the group's magazine.[22]

Mariana Celac, one of the founding members of the group, compares the space with that of the Smolnii Institute in St Petersburg, a space where similar meetings were held years ago—meetings that allowed for the formation of the leadership of the Bolshevik revolution.[23] She talks about the evolution of the group in terms of the pre-Smolnii period—the first consolidation of the group in small apartments under the leadership of several dissidents where the first discussions and ideas about the group were discussed—and the Smolnii period—the period after a location was secured and there was room for the group to engage in actual social dialogue. The post-Smolnii period however, that Celac does not talk about, is perhaps the period where the group started to lose much of its initial power and influence and shifted its role from a political powerhouse to a political advisor and sometimes, a political opponent.

A sign of that loss of power is probably also signaled by the fact that there have already been several attempts to reclaim the space that the group currently occupies (which legally belongs with the state yet, in 2005, has been officially given to the GDS for use over the next ten years). These challenges come from those who perhaps see this particular moment of vulnerability in the group's power as a perfect time to do away with it, for the group, while less powerful, still constitutes a threat to all those who are afraid of their critical spirit and clarity of vision.

Debating the group's goals and ideals

The GSD became a civil society organization simply by calling itself one. Although the group initially did not have a clear understanding of what civil society was, its agenda focused on defending a number of rights and ideals: human rights, minority rights, the ideal of an independent voice—independent from the voice of any other political party or political group, and the ideal of social communication and dialogue where all social concerns could be voiced. Despite its civil society status, the GSD had strong political aspirations, suggesting that its definition of civil society was certainly not exclusive of a political role—whether in a direct leadership or an advisory position. The unity of the group was provided by a series of friendships as well as a genuine commitment to reform and democratization.

Even among the founding group members, however, there were clear disagreements when it came to more specific questions as to whether the group should turn into a political party or support a certain political party versus another, whether the group should focus more on questions regarding the state and state transformations or society at large, or whether the group should play a more active role in the reform process—forming focus and research groups that could come up with a set of clear solutions, or whether they should stand back and maintain an observer and critic position—one that was more familiar to the intellectuals who formed the group. The answer to each of these questions marked a significant step in the self-definition process of the group as well as the role that it continued to play in the newly freed Romanian society.

The name of the group—The Group for Social Dialogue—clearly appealed to the need for free and open discussions under a Habermasian ideal of speech. The symbolism of the name marked an important focus of the group: that of ensuring a voice for minorities in the newly formed Romanian society. The dialogue was not only a dialogue between the state and society, but also a dialogue between the Romanian majority and a number of different minorities, including the Hungarian, German and Roma minorities. In an interview featured in the group's magazine's 10th anniversary special edition, Alin Teodorescu, one of the founding members of the group who was later to become an important player in national politics, recalls the way in which the name for the group was chosen. During a discussion with Sorin Vieru—another founding member of the group—Teodorescu suggested the name of "Group for Social Self-Defense" after the Polish model of the KOR founded by Jacek Kuron, Michnick and Walesa. Yet, as Vieru correctly noticed, this name was more appropriate for a group that was openly going to be engaging in a fight with the political regime. Suggesting that such an aggressive name might not be conducive to the dialogue that the group was hoping to start, Vieru proposed the current name of the group—the Group for Social Dialogue—so that it could be more inclusive of minorities, particularly given the fact that some of the group's members were of Jewish, Hungarian or German descent.[24] The name stuck and came to symbolize the birth of the first civil society organization in post-communist Romania. Choosing this particular name for the group set the tone for the role that the group was going to play. The initial declaration of the group, put together immediately after the fall of the communist regime, established the boundaries and role of the group. The declaration reads as follows:

> The Group for Social Dialogue is founded as an independent legal group starting today, December 31 1989. The group aspires to represent the true consciousness of this society that has been humiliated and torn apart. We would like to contribute to exiting the current social disaster and restructuring.

The Group for Social Dialogue is an independent, strictly informal group that is not subordinated to any political party and that refuses any collaboration with those who supported the former regime. Every member of the group has the right to his/her own opinions and political orientation that do not speak to the status and orientation of the group as a whole.

The Group for Social Dialogue is a space for critical reflection on the fundamental problems that the civil society of Romania is faced with today and on its inclusion in the European context: civilization—culture—politics—civil society—ecology. The group is a debate club between intellectuals of different professions that has set its goal on exploring different avenues of development and organization of this society with respect for human values and human rights. The Group for Social Dialogue hopes to become a laboratory in which economists, sociologists, politicians, historians, philosophers, urban planners, writers, theology writers and more find (and search) together the strategies and solutions that the Romanian society will need in the near future.

The Group for Social Dialogue will organize public debates among the different social classes: students, workers, army, intellectuals, that were until recently under the ideological veil of communism. The topics of discussion will be: pluralism, free unions, parliament, political parties, civil freedoms, human rights, the division of powers, culture and its values, ecology, urban studies and more. These meetings will be organized starting January 15, 1990.

The Group for Social Dialogue is gathering testimonies on the December Revolution and of the moments that led to it (photographs, depositions, video recordings and more).

The Group for Social Dialogue proposes to put together a weekly magazine that will act as the mirror of a new Romanian civil society in all of its aspects.[25]

There are a series of themes that emerge out of this declaration: 1) that the group would be representative of Romanian society; 2) that the group would clearly separate itself from the former communist leadership and adopt an anti-communist stance; 3) that the group would create a critical space for reflection through meetings, open dialogue and debates, research and gathering of testimonies as well as the publication of the group's magazine; 4) that the group would uphold human values and human rights; and 5) that the group would act as a laboratory in which different solutions would be discussed and tested before implementation. The extent to which the group was able to meet these initial goals becomes evident in the evolution of the group. While initially envisioned outside of a political structure, the group was forced to enter politics by naturally organizing itself into an efficient opposition to the increasing nationalist and neo-communist tendencies of the newly formed government. The group's lack of political experience—most members were members of an intellectual elite and not politicians—had a big say in how the group was going to react to the power infighting that dominated the years following the revolution.

The GSD and the "true consciousness" of Romania

Going through some of the group's original ideals will reveal the extent to which the group developed according to its original expectations and the series of challenges that it faced in fulfilling those expectations. The group's ideal of representing the true consciousness of Romanian society—in its very own formulation—suggests that one such consciousness actually existed. How exactly the group was going to tap into this consciousness and represent it, is unclear beyond the invitation for dialogue. Yet it was clear from the very beginning that not everyone would be able to participate in this dialogue. While some of the GSD members were indeed sociologists, the GSD itself did not have the means to tap into in-depth sociological research that could attempt to reveal this consciousness, nor did it have the intent to do so. While aimed at representing society as a whole and identifying and addressing larger social problems, the GSD was and remained an elite group, focusing mainly on the intellectual community and the political leadership.

During the interviews, it became clear that the group saw a direct connection between the idea of consciousness and that of a common sense morality. The word conscience—"constiinta" in Romanian—has clear religious connotations and reflects the idea of an almost pre-existing set of morals that already exist within us and simply need to be uncovered. Rodica Palade, Andrei Cornea and Thomas Kleinegger—three of the founding members of the group that I interviewed—all talk about the moral criteria of the group as being the foremost important element of their unity. Kleinegger describes morality in terms of some commonly agreed-upon basics—such as no lying or stealing. He attributes the group's particular sense of morality to a series of important philosophical influences that dominated intellectual life at the time: 1) the Havelian influence and his idea of "living in truth" as an essential form of resistance to communism, and 2) the Noica[26] influence and his particular vision of intellectuals as aloof, separated from the pettiness of everyday concerns.

If the Scottish Enlightenment saw civil society as an attempt to escape the morality of the church and the state, the GSD's vision of the latter—along with probably most dissident groups in Central and Eastern Europe—was quite the opposite: an attempt to recreate a moral realm, one that could better help guide society both in its social and political decisions. The morality that the new civil society and groups like the GSD were trying to rebuild, was a morality based on a sense of tradition and history that had to a large extent been either destroyed or rejected by communism. Kleinegger admits that there was a certain level of naivety in the group's particular approach to morality as a guiding element, but it was this naivety and the sense of purity that came along with it, that constituted the true post-revolutionary ideal of many of the dissidents, intellectuals as well as some of the revolutionary leaders.

The GSD took its role as a moral compass seriously and when faced with shady political and economic deals as well as the clear anti-minority and anti-tolerance stance of the National Salvation Front, the GSD started raising a warning by drawing people's attention to the diversions from democratic reform and violations of rights and political promises. Under the banner of "no to perestroika" and "no to corruption," the group set out to unveil the non-democratic nature of many of the reforms introduced at the time, many of which sought to create a reformed socialist state à la Gorbachev. They also set about unveiling a series of corrupt deals that secured the comfortable transition of many of the former communist elite members into positions of power—whether in the public or the private realm. Realizing that their fight was limited by their non-party status, many members of the group started to wonder whether a political position would not be better suited, particularly given the fact that the group's popularity would easily ensure them a place at the political table.

After all, this was the model followed by most other Eastern European dissident groups, which were able to secure important political positions after the fall of their respective communist regimes. One of these dissidents, the Polish revolutionary leader Adam Michnik, visited the group in February 1990, urging its members to take a political position, win the elections as a pro-European anti-nationalist coalition, use their anti-communist stance as their main form of legitimacy and push for the formation of national and international structures and mechanisms that would help democratize the country.[27] The group's hesitations were based largely on a moral ground and belief that they should not go back on their initial promise: that they would be an independent group, outside of the official political framework, focusing mainly on larger social concerns and ensuring a social dialogue. The thought of placing themselves on an equal footing with the National Salvation Front—that had broken its initial promise of not entering politics and came to run the country—was persuasive enough to convince the group to stick to its civil society status.

The debate on whether the group should enter the political arena or not, did however create new divisions within the group and amongst its supporters. The push to create a political party was realized only later with the creation of the Civic Alliance[28]—a non-governmental group later to become a political party that spun off from the Group for Social Dialogue. The GSD however maintained its independent status at the risk of losing many of its supporters and much of its legitimacy. The group decision not to enter politics caused a series of friendships to be broken, ideals to be ruined and disappointments to emerge. Those who believed that solutions could only be found and implemented in the public, political arena, left the group to pursue separate political careers, while those who believed in maintaining the group's civil society agenda continued to play an unofficial opposition role from the side.

Given the high levels of distrust of the state and state institutions in general, that made all incoming Romanian governments since the revolution particularly disliked, the group's decision to maintain its independence may not have been the worst one. The GSD members that did enter politics found that it was far from what they expected it to be and that their ability to influence change was minimal. Many of them left within the first year and went back to their teaching or research jobs. Those who stayed in politics were sometimes viewed as accomplices to a post-communist regime that was stalling the democratization process by attempting to revive a socialist system that was not economically feasible. Those who supported their original decision to remain an independent civil society group continued to justify their position in light of the actions that they were able to engage in from the margins.

The group's decision not to enter politics also played out to its advantage in terms of the standards to which it was held, for as a civil society organization, its mere critical position was enough to secure it a respectable place in society without the need to put into practice its suggestions and solutions. As the government was being blamed for a difficult transition, a decline in the economy, the loss of jobs and a chaotic privatization process that led to clear discrepancies among the population, the group could maintain its respectable position and even draw more support as an unofficial political opposition group and as an alternative to the governance that seemed to be failing. This did however have an important drawback: without the ability to enforce suggested changes and reforms, the group failed to provide an actual alternative to the bleak reality of the transition that everyone was facing. While reading the group's magazine did provide an outlet for a series of frustrations that kept gathering, and offer some consolation, it could do little more than that.

The importance of maintaining moral integrity, something that the group continued to advocate, meant little when that implied losing your job, your savings, your apartment, your benefits and ultimately your ability to survive. Surviving the transition meant that you had to compromise your morality, so people lied, and stole, and paid bribes, and begged, and backstabbed in order to survive. Yet, unlike under the communist regime, this time there was no one clear person to blame. Lines became blurred, corruption became rampant, and one could not point fingers at others without getting caught in the same net. Corruption became measured in terms of how much rather than who did what, for everyone stole. Those who stole more were somehow guiltier than those who stole less. But the ones who were the most guilty were perhaps the ones who promised that things would get better when they did not, the ones who painted a rosy picture when they should not have, the ones who played with people's hopes and expectations making them believe that the transition would be much easier than it actually was.

The GSD's anti-communist and pro-democratization stance

The GSD emerged as a clear anti-communist organization: anti-communist in that it rejected communist ideals, accepted the liberal market-based state as the only positive alternative for Romania, rejected the former communist elite and strongly believed that this elite should not be a part of the new government construction. Rejecting the old communist ideals meant that the GSD was not going to support any form of socialist reform à la Gorbachev, as was attempted by the Ion Iliescu and Petre Roman government immediately after the revolution. Speaking against attempts to stall the liberalization and privatization process, the group gained more and more support from the West, yet lost some of its support on the national level, for privatization, along with its immediate painful consequence, inflation, were not exactly desirable side effects of an already painful transition. The GSD's vision of pluripartidism and protection of rights, change in leadership and overhaul of the economy did not come easy. Changes in legislation and leadership were not enough. A true commitment to these ideals existed only in principle, without a full understanding of the consequences and pains that these changes would bring along with them.

To be a pro-democratic group, while in principle a good thing, also meant being an advocate of high unemployment due to streamlining, privatization and efficiency credits, an advocate of high inflation rates, an advocate of the destruction of nationalized farms and the loss of land for many of the small agricultural producers. It meant throwing people out of the nationalized houses that they had lived in for years in order to give them back to their previous owners, it meant increasing taxes and cutting back on state services, closing down inefficient schools and hospitals and firing many of the personnel working in the former state institutions. To be pro-democratic thus meant to support radical changes that although they promised a higher good in the end, threatened to disrupt the already shaky balance of the post-revolutionary economy.

Pro-democracy meant more than calling for democracy in the streets; it meant sacrifice and the ability to absorb more shock and change. And while moral criteria sound nice and democratic practices—when joined with an image of the West—look good, the process itself was certainly not desirable and to a large extent not associated with what people originally imagined a democracy to be. The costs of democratic leadership and economic management remained unclear to much of the Romanian population, who assumed that the Western images that they could now see on TV required little to no sacrifice and were simply possible as a result of an efficient management of natural resources and a good leadership. While people supported the idea of democracy in general and were still willing to go out in the streets to ask for it, they were certainly not ready to face the consequences of their demands.

The slow shift in the GSD's support base from the population at large in the months immediately following the 1989 Revolution, to a more elite group of intellectuals and students in the years that followed, showed an increased level of exhaustion within the population at large, pointing to their decreased willingness to openly engage with and fight unwanted tendencies in the ruling party and governance system. The general fatigue allowed people to go with the flow independent of whether they thought the direction was wrong or not. As Beata Barbara Czajkowska argues in the case of the Polish revolution, the post-communist democratic movement was in many ways a democratization by fatigue process in which many lost their belief in miracle-like solutions yet went along with anything that promised a smoother transition.[29]

The willingness and desire for people to change was thus largely overestimated. The moment hope was lost, the level of energy that was essential for supporting change went down with it. If the revolution rode on the hope that social change was after all possible, as Vladimir Tismaneanu argues was the case in the 70s and 80s—"people became convinced that the rules of the game were not eternal, that it was worth fighting for human dignity, and that success in fighting such a fight had a real chance"[30]—the post-revolutionary period was one where people lost hope, where they started to wonder if the rules of the game were in fact eternal and if the moral compass that traditional values were calling for was simply inadequate during the transition process. Success and survival were only possible in the pragmatist camp and that meant, for the most part, giving up the moral compass and forging ahead at any cost. If civil society was indeed based on the categorical rejection of the official lie, the post-communist civil society public rejection of this lie, at least in the first few years after the revolution, did little more than console.

Thus, pro-democratic civil society groups like the GSD were left to fight by themselves, without the widespread support that they had originally envisioned, without the energy that they saw pouring out onto the streets during the revolution and without important input from the population at large which preferred instead to sit back and try to bandage the bleeding wounds that the painful transition kept inflicting. Promises, whether coming from the pro-democratic civil society camp, or from the reformed communist political camp, sounded all too similar at a time when reality looked nothing like people had hoped, and thus political choice, when made, reflected just that: a sense of confusion, exhaustion, and in many cases, a constant switch from one camp to the next in the hope that one of these camps would finally bring about more visible solutions.

Critical space for reflection and protection of minority rights

Just as its name stated, the GSD was first and foremost a space for discussion where different actors could come together and work to consolidate the creation of a new social and political sphere in independent Romania. While the name might suggest a Habermasian-like role of communication, the group in fact favored certain discourses, taking very clear positions on the political scale. In the first few years immediately following the 1989 Revolution, the group played an essential role in organizing meetings and debates that led to the consolidation of the first political parties and the first free unions, as well as minority groups, different types of associations and foundations—including the Soros Foundation that was founded at the GSD and was led by one of the GSD founding members, Alin Teodorescu. The group also gave free juridical consultations, subsidized access to the internet, and published one of the most well-read magazine in post-communist Romania—22.

Named after the 22nd of December—the day when Ceausescu was captured and Romania officially began its post-communist era—the magazine played an important role in educating public opinion and exposing the average person to issues, people and debates that would have otherwise been obscured by the traditional political process. In the months immediately following the fall of the communist regime, the magazine played an important role in redirecting public opinion towards the importance of democratization and integration into the structures of the European Union and the larger international community. Although the group took a very critical position when it came to the newly elected National Salvation Front, accusing them of being too tightly connected to the communist nomenklatura, the group did maintain its criticism also when it came to other political parties and the new government elected in 1996, thus proving that although it took sides, it preferred to maintain its critical, opposition, stance.

Selling over 200,000 copies per week in its first year, *22* became the most popular weekly magazine in the country immediately after the Romanian revolution. The stories run by the magazine had a strong popular appeal in a confused Romania that was thirsty for information and new ideas. While the magazine was hoping that by educating the public about the difficult choices that they were going to have to make, people would start behaving more democratically, most were disappointed to realize that democracy did not come that easy. Political criticism was thus only appealing to the extent that it reflected a continued distrust of the state as opposed to a significant change in the democratic behavior of society at large. The post-revolutionary masses loved controversy, yet did not truly believe in diversity and were certainly not ready to trust all minorities as their equal. As Alina Mungiu-Pippidi confesses: "our naive presumption [...] was that education makes people turn towards democracy, even become better human beings, and more capable of discerning their self-interests."[31] As they were to later find out, people started displaying what she calls "anti-social" behavior that led to the rebirth of nationalism, religious fanaticism, cultural provincialism and other "non-modern" tendencies. Access to information and dialogue, something that the GSD prided itself in being able to provide, was not enough to convince the public that democracy required a change in attitude and behavior and not just a change in demands and governments.

While 22 may not have convinced everyone to act democratically, it did introduce a series of important debates and questions and put them on the political agenda, the most important of which included questions concerning human rights, environmental protection, and minority protection. Without the group's influence, it is unclear to what extent these questions would have been addressed at all, and that in itself is an important achievement. What made it clear to the group that these questions were going to need to be placed on the political agenda was the Targu Mures incident in particular.[32]

If there was one goal that the group was very successful in achieving, it was their ability to create an important space for critical reflection. Bringing together a very diverse group of people, the group's first year of existence was perhaps one of the most exciting and productive years, with lots of energy and support, many people investing in what the group stood for, incredibly dedicated members who came to work every day—despite the lack of financial compensation—with constant media attention and a high level of political influence. Although a civil society organization, the group maintained a strong influence in the political arena, regularly engaging the president, vice-president and other important political actors in their debates. The group managed not only to a open up a space for critical discussion, but to draw a more diverse group into the discussion. Although this initial level of energy and excitement could not have been maintained years into the transition, the group managed to continue to engage people, mainly through its magazine which continues to be published today, as well as its historical role: the group remains a place where people gather any time a political or social controversy arises. The group's role will remain that of a critic from the side, a little more removed from the political powerhouse then it once was, yet still influential and relevant.

The GSD as a laboratory of solutions
While the group may not have played an important role in actually looking for solutions in the political, social and economic reform process, it did play an important role in bringing important issues to the table, forming a series of important research institutions, foundations and other types of associations and keeping the government somewhat in line. Perhaps the original idea of having the group play a more important political advising role was a little too ambitious given the strict political restructuring that the country was undergoing. The group's desire to remain neutral and outside of the political powerhouse could not be matched by the desire for actual decision-making power, which was however reserved to the state legislature and executive. The ideal of becoming a laboratory of solutions was thus not necessarily met, however many of the associations and even the political party that spun off from the GSD played an essential role in future research and lobbying.

Conclusion

The assumption that civil society is one of the most important tools on the road to democratization, or that civil society is necessarily civil, representative and conducive to positive dialogue may turn out to be more questionable than expected. The extent to which this assumption can take a dangerous turn or, quite the opposite, provide people with an essential sense of hope in the midst of a difficult transition, is perhaps most dependent on circumstance, making civil society something other than the static term we often think it is. Envisioning different kinds of civil societies in light of different kinds of relationships between society and the state will thus not only allow for an essential flexibility in the term, but will also make the concept more useful for analyzing other transitioning economies by forcing us to look beyond the narrow and overly simplistic view of civil society as equalling NGOs and the teaching of civic skills, anti-corruption seminars and trust-building.

Attempts to impose the Western liberal understanding of civil society on transitioning societies such as Romania will often result in a series of confusing and often dangerous conclusions that are unfortunately used to guide many of the financial political incentives given by the West. Attempts to measure civil society according to a preconceived standard and assess the level of positive social change in light of the ability to absorb economic and political reforms at a particular speed, offer an often negative view of societies that are doing nothing but trying hard to cope with significant change. Understanding that social distrust of the state and institutions in general, or political apathy and sometimes even corruption, may be nothing but natural responses to change as opposed to abnormal behaviors that need to be quickly weeded out, might allow us to approach the reform process slightly differently and treat our citizens with a little more respect and empathy. Transitions take more time than we are willing to allow them and change does not happen according to schedule. As much as we would like to find an ideal tool, such as civil society, that can magically transform a previous totalitarian society into a democratic state within a few years, that is not likely to happen, and the consequences of forcing it to happen may end up being more dangerous than letting it be.

Forming a particular illusion of what civil society should be—as was done by both people like Havel and Konrad as well as by international institutions supporting the civil society- democracy-building connection—carries deep consequences not only when it comes to evaluating the "performance" of civil society, but more importantly when it comes to understanding the significantly different roles that civil society can play: from supporter of minorities, to political opposition, to formation of and supporter of elites, to job creation and sustainer of particular moral standards. While some of these roles may be perceived as direct supporters of a democratic state, some of them can threaten the state, divide the population and further widen the gap between society and the state. As one of the main pillars on which the democratic capitalist illusion was built in Central and Eastern Europe and Romania in particular, the (to be expected) failure of the democratic illusion of civil society to keep its promises has in many ways been ignored or blamed on corruption, a slow reform process or institutional failures. Recognizing the extent to which this illusion serves mainly as a legitimating tool for a series of practices—such as international aid, financial and political reform, and so-called grassroots actions, might save us a lot of trouble when it comes to employing similar illusions in other transitioning countries or still to be reformed failed states.

The next chapter takes us towards a different terrain, exploring ways in which visual narratives capture social change and the experience of post-revolutionary transition in Romania. Focusing on a number of different studies on visuality as well as the particular experience of a group of Romanian social photographers—the 7 Days Group—this chapter seeks to offer an alternative mechanism for understanding processes of transition. Unlike the more classical studies on revolution and civil society, this particular approach hopes to better capture and explain a series of paradoxes related to the transition from the communist to the capitalist illusion as well as explore the extent to which the new illusion of capitalism has been mainly built using visual techniques like media, advertising or branding.

Notes

1 See Ernest Gellner, *Conditions of Liberty: Civil Society and Its Rivals* (New York: The Penguin Press, 1994); Samuel Gregg, "Markets, Morality and Civil Society," *The Intercollegiate Review* Fall 2003/Spring 2004; John Glenn, *Framing Democracy: Civil Society and Civic Movements in Eastern Europe* (Stanford: Stanford University Press, 2001); Marc Morje Howard, *The Weakness of Civil Society in Post-Communist Europe* (Cambridge: Cambridge University Press, 2003).
2 See Havel, *The Power of the Powerless: Citizens against the State in Central and Eastern Europe*; Konrad, *Antipolitics*.
3 Havel, *The Power of the Powerless: Citizens against the State in Central and Eastern Europe*.
4 Konrad, *Antipolitics*.
5 G.M. Tamas, "A Disquisition on Civil Society," *Social Research* 61.2 (1994).
6 Tamas, "A Disquisition on Civil Society," 219.
7 The fight for power that emerged in this context led many dissidents to resign their political posts within the first few years after the revolution and return to the "private realm" under the comfortable protection of the newly founded research institutes and civil society foundations.
8 Vera Dakova, Bianca Dreossi, Jenny Hyatt and Anca Socolovschi,

Review of the Romanian NGO Sector: Strengthening Donor Strategies, September 2000 (2004) available at: www.donorsforum.ro/download /RomNGOreview_En.doc (accessed March 1st, 2007); William F. Fisher, "Doing Good? The Politics and Antipolitics of NGO Practices," *Annual Review of Anthropology* 26 (1997).

9 See the particular experience of the Group for Social Dialogue, who helped build one of the major opposition parties in Romania: the Civic Alliance Party. Also see the experience of the Open Society Institute in Romania, whose executive directors have moved back and forth between the public and the private realm.

10 See Dakova, Dreossi, Hyatt and Socolovschi, *Review of the Romanian NGO Sector: Strengthening Donor Strategies*, September 2000.

11 David Blaney and Mustapha Pasha, "Civil Society and Democracy in the Third World: Ambiguities and Historical Possibilities," *Studies in Comparative International Development* 28.1 (1993).

12 See Howard, *The Weakness of Civil Society in Post-Communist Europe*.

13 See Gabriel Badescu, Paul Sum and Eric Uslaner, "Civil Society Development and Democratic Values in Romania and Moldova," *East European Politics and Society* 18.2 (2004).

14 Ralf Dahrendorf, *After 1989: Morals, Revolution and Civil Society* (New York and Oxford: St. Martin's Press and St. Antony's College, 1997).

15 Vaclav Havel, *Summer Meditations* (New York: Alfred A. Knoff, 1992), 121.

16 Mungiu-Pippidi, *Politica Dupa Comunism*, 24. Translation of citation from Romanian into English by the author.

17 Mungiu-Pippidi, *Politica Dupa Comunism*, 212.

18 The Palace of the People, a project initiated and completed by Ceausescu, is the second largest building in the world after the Pentagon, and was built to house the Romanian communist regime. Controversial both in terms of its location—which required the destruction of an old monastery and removal of an old church—as well as in terms of its imposing scale, the Palace became the symbol of Ceausescu's egotism and grando-mania.

19 The Soros Foundation was amongst the first international foundations to set up offices in post-communist Romania, helping to establish and fund the most important civil society initiatives within Romania.

20 A famous communist politician who was Romania's ambassador to the US and the United Nations in the late 1950s, only to later join the dissident group as Ceausescu started to consolidate his power around his cult of personality. He was one of the signatories of the famous "Letter of the Six" that was broadcast on Radio Free Europe in 1989. He continued to play an important role in post-revolutionary Romanian politics, although he was accused on several different occasions of maintaining a communist mindframe.

21 The law must have somehow been forgotten since it appears never to have been abrogated.

22 See testimonies of: Gabriel Andreescu, interview by author (tape recording, Bucharest: January 20th, 2005); Cornea, interview by author; Filipescu, interview by author; Thomas Kleinegger, interview by author (tape recording, Bucharest: January 21st, 2005); Rodica Palade, interview by author (tape recording, Bucharest: January 20th, 2005); Alin

Teodorescu, interview by author (tape recording, Bucharest: January 23rd, 2005).

23 Mariana Celac, "An Elite That Did Not Take This Country for What It Really Was," *22* January 25th-31st, 2000.

24 Madalina Schiopu, "Interviu Cu Alin Teodorescu: Triumful Diversitatii," *22* January 25th-31st, 2000.

25 Founding Members Group for Social Dialogue, "Founding Declaration of the Group for Social Dialogue," *22* January 25th-31st, 2000.

26 A famous Romanian philosopher and moralist who left an important mark on Romanian contemporary writers. Among other things he wrote on the particularities of Romanian identity and sense of being.

27 Stelian Tanase, "22 Was from the Beginning in the Opposition," *22* January 25th-31st, 2000.

28 The Civic Alliance played a much more active role in the political arena, helping to support a number of different candidates to the Romanian parliament and presidency, including Emil Constantinescu, who, while losing the 1992 elections, managed to win the 1996 elections. The disappointment that followed his rather weak presidency weakened the support for the Civic Alliance and put the GDS in the awkward position of having to criticize the people and policies that many had hoped would bring about a much-needed change in Romania's politics. The re-election of Ion Iliescu as president in 2000 (after two previous mandates) served to further emphasize the disappointment among the population at large.

29 Beata Barbara Czajkowska, "From Tribunes to Citizens: Polish Intelligentsia During and after Communism."

30 Vladimir Tismaneanu, *Reinventing Politics* (New York: Free Press, 1992), 115.

31 Alina Mungiu-Pippidi, "10 Years of Illusions," *22* January 25th-31st, 2000.

32 March 19th-20th, 1989 marked the clear recognition of a looming conflict between Romanians and the Hungarian minority inhabiting parts of Transylvania. A series of clashes, triggered by the March 15th celebration of Hungary's independence from the Habsburg domination in Targu Mures—a Romanian city with a majority Hungarian population—left six people dead and over 300 injured. The clashes marked the first open, and largely mediated, confrontation between the Hungarian minority and local Romanians, stirring a strong anti-Hungarian sentiment throughout the country that would continue to show its ugly teeth with each request for more ethnic rights and independence from the Hungarian camp.

7
Representing illusions and disillusions: a visual narrative of the Romanian transition to capitalism

Why visual narratives?

Transitions are periods that are difficult to describe to anyone who is not experiencing them first hand. As much as we talk about high inflation, unemployment, poverty, as well as rising wealth in certain parts of society, new buildings and fashion trends, it is hard to imagine a transition using written narratives alone. The visual plays an essential role in defining the experience of people who are actually undergoing it, as change is often reflected in the immediate landscape. Change however is visible only through the juxtaposition of elements thought of as belonging to the past and those belonging to the future: the visual is thus able to capture both what is in the process of being erased as well as what is about to be built—even if for now much of the actual building remains in the planning stage. This chapter seeks to understand this process of change and to immortalize—using an imaginary camera—what Mirjana Lozanovska calls this "gap of history"—this time between destruction and reconstruction.[1] It is within this gap that new illusions are built and old ones forgotten, all visible on a new stage of performance decorated by commercials, platforms, posters, luminous signs, graffiti and architectural projects for the future. The visual enchantment of a transition impregnates all of the surrounding landscape, leaving marks that we are left to decipher.

Unlike written narratives, visual narratives follow a different logic, one where delimitations of positive and negative aspects of change are not so easily made, where hesitations are accepted, where negotiations between past and future can be reflected in something as simple as an outfit or odd mismatch of age and profession. Visual narratives appeal to a multitude of senses, transmitting different messages at the same time, underlining interesting juxtapositions and contradictions that would be otherwise difficult to express. Exploring the visual as more than just a prop for the written narrative reveals a different apprehension of change and historical moments such as transitions, whereby the apparent disharmony of elements of the past mixing with those of the future is negotiated both at an individual level—through immediate individual perception—as well as a collective one—through the manipulation of the visual by different mechanisms of the state or the economy.

Photography as a visual narrative

Photography, as one of the most popular visual narratives of the present, captures more than just a moment in time: it captures a photographer's choice of subject/object, his/her creative spirit and the spirit of the place/object under a particular light as well as the voice of the interpreter, who chooses the photograph for a gallery, album or newspaper column. But more than anything photographs are able to capture both space and time, a slice of the world that can be frozen and kept for future reflection and examination. A photograph is able to go beyond what Robert Bond calls the "spectator's fleeting, self-erasing interaction with historical moments":[2] it can slow the world down and allow us to take in and savor different stimuli beyond the initial shock, it can be used to creatively construct and deconstruct different illusions and realities, it can manipulate as well as be used as a tool to decipher manipulation.

The photographs selected for this particular chapter focus on a series of juxtapositions: 1) the everyday vs. wish images;[3] 2) rejecting the past vs. accepting it through nostalgia; 3) embracing the wish images vs. rejecting them through cynicism. Each of the juxtapositions seeks to explore the contradictions inherent in periods of transition; the difficulties of breaking with the past and embracing the present as well as imagining the future. They point to the confusing swing, from overwhelming euphoria to deep disillusionment, from an almost naive hopefulness to deep cynicism and pragmatism, that so often characterizes periods of transition.

The first juxtaposition seeks to understand the interaction between the everyday life and wish images in order to better portray the role that wish images play in giving people hope and keeping them on a particular track despite the difficulties they encounter on the way. The second juxtaposition seeks to understand how people approach the past and the extent to which both nostalgia and rejection of the past can coexist despite the seeming contradiction between the two attitudes—for change seems to demand both a separation from the past, as well as a sense of continuation, a sense of going forward that is based on a path set sometime in the past. The last juxtaposition seeks to uncover the extent to which people openly accept wish images or are apathetic and cynical towards them, depending on their particular position and status in society. The manipulation of wish images in order to secure a particular kind of transition often blurs the line between what people want and what they are told to want, making their attitude towards the transition seemingly contradictory and inconsistent.

These visual juxtapositions will help us better understand the different ways in which illusions are built, accepted or rejected, as well as the ways in which disillusions are expressed, sometimes openly, sometimes hesitantly and sometimes unconsciously. This visual examination of the Romanian transition is not an attempt to quantify the visual presence of disillusionment in Romania, but simply an attempt to better understand how certain illusions can coexist with certain disillusions, how one continues to maintain hope in something that oftentimes seems hopeless. For if transitions are times when a society negotiates the road on which it is about to embark or has already embarked on, then the daily hesitations, however small, will be essential in determining not only the route but the extent to which the destination is ever likely to be found as imagined. Following Benjamin's dictum that "history decays in images," this chapter sets out to explore the visual horizon of transitioning Romania and point to a series of important elements that have come to dominate it.

The flaneur vs. the spectator: different mechanisms of perception

There are different ways in which one experiences a transition even while in the middle of it. The experience of the flaneur versus that of the spectator is separated by two different visual techniques: one in which changes in the visual horizon become a trigger for a meditation on the nature of these changes and a potential future intervention, and the other in which the same changes are simply perceived as happening on a stage over which one has little influence beyond booing or applauding. While the flaneur sees change as inherent in the evolution of society and thus as natural, the spectator sees change as maneuvered by a series of "directors" and "screen writers" that seek to trigger a particular kind of response to it. How one chooses to experience change—whether as a flaneur or a spectator—makes a big difference in terms of how change itself occurs.

The concept of a flaneur was perhaps first used by Charles Baudelaire. The flaneur was the wanderer, the one who strolled the streets and absorbed their contrasts and intensity. Fascinated by Baudelaire's writings, Walter Benjamin picked up his concept of the flaneur and used it to describe the streets of nineteenth-century Paris, the transformations in the industrial cityscape and the influence that these transformations had on everything from fashion to the way in which people related to their environment and each other. As a modern anthropologist, philosopher and poet at the same time, Benjamin was fascinated by how change was absorbed by society and the often subtle traces that it left behind. Setting out to unearth these subtle traces, Benjamin sought to decipher the struggle with change as reflected in antiques, buildings and architecture, fashion and collectibles. As a flaneur himself, Benjamin wandered the cityscape of Paris in search of signs, memories and visions of the future, for it was these things that allowed him to understand the choices that societies made and how they went about implementing them.

The term spectator is borrowed from Guy Debord's book on *Society of the Spectacle*, a powerful critique of the transformation of reality into spectacles and lived experience into representation. The transformation of reality into an object of contemplation, the idea that one can separate themselves from "the real" and watch from the outside, is something that Debord argues is intrinsically modern. The spectacle, according to him, is not just a collection of images, but rather a particular kind of social relationship between people—dominated by a capitalist mode of production—that is mediated by images. The spectacle is not just something that one experiences but something that also acts as a legitimator for the particular conditions and aims of the capitalist system: "The Spectacle is capital accumulated to the point where it becomes image."[4]

His analysis poses reality before the spectacle into direct juxtaposition with reality after the spectacle, arguing that modern society has reached a point where reality cannot exist without the spectacle, where the two enter a process of reciprocal alienation. If the spectacle is an imposition with a particular agenda, then the spectacle does not invite dialogue. The spectator is simply forced to absorb the images and messages that come along with them, without any force of interpretation and minimal force of resistance: closing one's eyes or falling asleep. The spectacle is the "dreamworld" or the "wish-image" of capitalism, yet the spectator, in Debord's eyes, resembles more of an automaton than an enchanted flaneur that wanders through the cityscape savoring the illusion that is presented to him. The images presented to the spectator are manipulated and beg for a particular response and reaction: they force the spectator to act a certain way, make certain choices, and want certain things. By fooling the spectator that life beyond the scene resembles or is identical to the scene, the spectacle redefines what reality is and directs the spectators just like one would direct actors in a play. The spectacle is however not easily undone, for its vision and ability to control "reality" is certainly appealing, particularly at times where one is dealing with great change.

The illusion of control is thus often essential for societies in transition, offering both a sense of calm as well as a sense of purpose. The illusion of the spectacle is what often keeps transitioning societies from unraveling, from losing their sense of direction and more importantly, their sense of purpose. Debord's question of "How can the poor be made to work once their illusions have been shattered and once force has been defeated?"[5] needs to be turned on its head and reformulated into: How can any group/society function once its illusions have been shattered? The call for a world without illusions, without the spectacle, assumes that this world must have at one time existed. Yet one can hardly ever recall a time when the world was not imbued with illusions, when the world was not a spectacle of some kind.

Debord does however point to a significant change in the type of spectacle that modern capitalist societies are experiencing: a spectacle that has elevated the sense of sight to unprecedented heights, and more importantly, that has learned to manipulate this sense of sight. What is new in modern capitalist societies is the rise of the spectacle to the status of science and more importantly, a particular market niche: publicity. Learning how to best use and manipulate images in order to transmit particular messages has become an art that one can experience both on the street and in galleries. Publicity has taken over not just the billboard on the side of the street, but our entire horizon: from the logos and tags on our clothing, to the color we dye our hair with, to the perfumes we put on, to the architecture we look at. Everything has a tag, a firm, a brand, a name to be associated with and thus a message to send. The nature of the modern illusion is that it is both necessary as well as suffocating at the same time. The addiction, however, makes it almost impossible to get rid of, and more importantly, the cure, like with any addiction, involves a painful process of withdrawal and the quick replacement of the old illusion with a new one. Post-communist Central and Eastern Europe may lie precisely at this point of withdrawal and re-enchantment. Precisely how this re-enchantment occurs—through the construction of particular dreamworlds or wish images—is essential for understanding the important role that the visual plays in the Romanian transition, and most modern transitions in general.

Urban vs. rural spectacles

Industrial transformations, just like capitalist transformations, are intrinsically linked to the urban as the ultimate expression of modernity. The spectacle of capitalism in urban areas is thus different from the one in rural areas, both in the way in which it is perceived as well as the way in which it is implemented. This creates different forms of individual and collective—urban collectives vs. rural collectives—adjustments to change/existence as well as perception. As Benjamin explains:

> During long periods of history, the mode of human sense perception changes with humanity's entire mode of existence. The manner in which the human sense of perception is organized, the medium in which it is accomplished, is determined not only by nature but by historical circumstances as well [...] The adjustment of reality to the masses and of the masses to reality is a process of unlimited scope, as much for thinking as for perception.[6]

Learning to adjust our perception is an important element of adjusting to structural change in society. Relearning how to interpret and absorb what we see and experience is thus a skill required of all those who want to adjust to the new reality surrounding them. Yet this learning process is dependent on our awareness of the nature of the spectacle surrounding us. The urban spectacle of the Romanian transition is dominated by a series of important transformations: radical changes in building and design—a transition from the efficiency of bland high-rise apartments to the shining new business offices and duplex houses and apartments; an overwhelming amount of new goods reaching the Romanian market and significantly changing the sense of fashion and the street experience in general—everything is more colorful and seemingly plentiful: there's a sense that anything can be bought; the rising number of stores and the publicity that comes along with that—the parterre of every building has been turned into a store, a brand, a place to publicize something; the rise of the marketing industry and most importantly the rise of the media and communications sectors—commercials have been taken to a new level: they are no longer used to advertise a particular brand, object or place, they are used to set trends, behaviors and reactions to policy, such as entering the EU.

The Romanian street experience reflects a series of important changes and contradictions: modern architectural designs that house the upscale shopping malls, banks, insurance and advertising firms, reflect in their windows the classic architecture of older buildings that survived the grand and bland architectural designs of communism, hiding behind them rows of apartment buildings now beautified by colorful advertisements and banners that lure you towards your next trip to France, your new cell-phone or kitchen design. The parterres of every building, whether in the center of town or in the suburbs have now transformed themselves into colorful stores, salons, restaurants, bars and pharmacies; the city squares have been taken over by fancy restaurant patios; city parks have become the paradise of the homeless, where lonely statues lie covered in dust and new rollerblading and skateboarding ramps provide the only lively element of the picture. People no longer stand in lines to buy bread, milk and pigs' feet,[7] but rather to pay their cell-phone bills or buy lottery tickets.

Hummer SUVs, BMWs and Mercedes cars parade the streets like the new kings of the old "Dacias"—a Romanian-produced car—which continue to cough their way through the crowd. The latest fashions mingle with the little old ladies who continue to carry plastic bags with them at all times[8] and roam the streets appalled at the length of skirts, the crowd coming out of the new casino, or the price of a piece of cake in the old bakery where they used to enjoy a good bite years ago. The new supermarkets and malls compete with open markets that dominate the suburbs, where the kitsch attracts both sellers and buyers with goods that remind one of the "good old days" and prices that seem a little less threatening. From logos and advertisements to announcements and graffiti, to mannequins and speechless beggars, to posters about summer jobs in US resorts and the latest comedy show, the street screams at you like no time before.

Prohibitive prices in bakeries, restaurants and bars, deserted and sometimes dangerous and run-down parks and promenades, keep a large part of the population at home, where they prefer to experience the world through the security of their TV sets, leaving the streets to be dominated by the two extremes: the very rich and the very poor. It is precisely this contradiction that has fascinated many foreign photojournalists who often depict the streets of Romania as dominated by homeless orphans turned drug addicts sniffing glue, gypsies in colorful dresses roaming the city in their horse-drawn carts, or poor old ladies selling flowers at street corners to make ends meet.

A recent article in the *Washington Post* entitled "Out of the Darkness" pictured several horse-drawn carriages in a frozen Romanian village and a weeping, poorly dressed gypsy woman in an open market. The pictures took up more than three-quarters of the page and spoke for themselves. The article itself pictured Romania a poor yet eager country, where the dream of joining the EU was reflected not only in the unusually high rate of support for the EU accession but also in public spaces, with stores taking up names such as Eurovet or Eurofarma, with EU flags hanging in the most remote corners of the country and a digital clock in the main square of Bucharest counting down the days until January 2007, when Romania was scheduled to join the EU. The article then quickly moved to talk about the latest corruption scandals and the problem with discrimination against the Roma population, two of the big issues that will determine when Romania will actually join the EU.[9]

These portrayals of Romania are very common, allowing many foreigners to imagine the country as mostly backward with a few oases of wealth and modern developments. The horse-drawn carriages and the remote villages however can either be seen as backward, poor and underdeveloped or as cozy and almost romantic islands of peacefulness, tradition and nature-friendly settings. It is precisely this latter image that the Romanian government and business elite are trying to push forward through their new advertisement campaigns that are selling both the idyllic image of Romanian villages and countryside, as well as the fashionable, rich cityscape of Bucharest and the beautiful resorts and casinos lining the Black Sea coast. Caught between these contrasting visual narratives, whether coming from the outside or the inside, the average Romanian is left to defend an image that he wishes were true and cynically reject the other as yet another romanticized vision of the poor Easterners that need help.

Maneuvering in this visual horizon full of contradictions, opposing messages and appeals, requires an important set of skills that can silence negative narratives and encourage positive ones, that can ignore unpleasant views and teach you how to walk past pain, humility and suffering unaffected while focusing on everything that pleases and scintillates your senses. A new individual is born in this environment, one who learns to adapt to shock by developing a thick skin, by leaving behind potentially dangerous sensibilities and by adopting an attitude that constantly keeps its eyes on the prize. The un-adapted, the old, the romantics, the nostalgic, are left behind to build their own dreamworlds in libraries, in front of TVs or simply in their heads.

If the cityscape of Romania has been deeply marked by the spatial expressions of the communist and capitalist dreamworlds, the rural areas, which for the most part are still considered to be the main gatekeepers of traditional lifestyle and values, have also changed significantly. Although the rural continues to bear the stigma of the backward, the place to be developed, as well as the charming, the naive and the idylic, it is in many ways in these communities that the effects of the transition can become even more visible. A visual subject that is often restricted to idylic postcards and photo albums, or not so charming development reports, the rural is rarely examined for what it is: a place where tradition and change coexist, a place where modernity is still being negotiated and certainly not taken for granted.

The 7 Days Group: photographing the rural spectacle of Romania

The 7 Days Group is a group of photographers that has been traveling throughout the rural areas of northern Romania—the area is called Maramures—for the past eight years tracing both traditional habits and lifestyle changes, seeking to express more honestly some of the major transformations that Romania is undergoing, in an artistic, subtle way, yet with the eyes of a long-term observer, an observer who interacts with his subjects, who joins them for dinner and seeks to understand their lives, who plays cards with them and shares stories with them. One may easily consider the members of the 7 Days Group as visual anthropologists, expressing their findings through images as opposed to written or spoken narratives.

The group is unique in its approach to photography as well as in its composition, bringing together members with a very diverse set of skills and sensibilities, many of them having been trained in the field of humanities as opposed to photography. Among the group members, Voicu Bojan graduated from the Faculty of Letters; Cosmin Bumbut from the Academy of Theater and Film; Petrut Calinescu studied journalism and mass media and now works as a photojournalist; Bogdan Croitoru, Vasile Dorolti, Gicu Serban and Alexandru Paul are professional photographers; Silviu Ghetie was trained as a miner and now works as a professional photographer. The four foreigners in the group, Fred Rohde, Bernhard Seidel, Oleg Tishkovets and Rene Triebl now work as professional photographers but come from diverse backgrounds, one of them having been trained as an architect. Several of the group members are natives of Maramures with a vested emotional interest and connection to this particular land.

What makes the group particularly interesting for a study of this kind is both their strong connection to the place that they are photographing, and the different sensibilities that they bring into their photographs. The message is more than artistic: it is imbued with a particular vision of the changes that the photographers themselves have lived through and continue to live through, as well as their ability to interpret these changes in a sophisticated, yet simple and direct way. The way in which the shooting of the photographs takes place is also particularly interesting, insulating the photographers into a particular corner of the country and forcing them to integrate into the environment that they are portraying, so that the subjects are not simply imbued with preconceived notions and expectations of that particular area, but rather reflect a lifestyle and emotion that the photographers themselves have become familiar with in time. The photo camps are divided into seven days—thus the name of the group. The group spends six days in a particular village or area, learning about the families, people and places that they interact with and trying to capture some of the puzzles of their everyday existence. The seventh day, which in many ways carries an almost religious connotation, is the day when the photographs are put together in a local exhibition, where the villagers are invited to attend and offered some of the photographs to take home with them. Since 2000, the group has participated in nine different camps throughout the country. The group has returned to the same spot on several occasions, their photographs offering an interesting view of subtle or sometimes more abrupt changes in that particular area.

Their mission has been to travel together to a chosen spot and tell the story of that particular place as they experienced it through photography. Here is how they describe themselves:

> The 7 Days Association is about the passion of telling significant stories about us and our world through photography. 7 Days was born in 1999 in the northern Transylvanian town of Baia Mare, Romania. Once a year a few friends would spend seven days photographing in one location and choose the best works for an exhibit. 7 Days has now developed into a larger, international group. New members are selected on the basis of their already proven photographic abilities.
> The strengths of this association are: the relationships forged through friendship and respect between the members; the freedom of each member to express himself or herself in a personal photographic style; the passion of telling significant stories about us and our world through photography.[10]

Their passion for storytelling and idea to use their photographic skills to tell stories visually is particularly interesting in the Romanian context, especially given the sites of their choice. Fascinated by life in small town and rural Romania, the group has chosen to spend most of its time photographing places like Negresti, Sighet, Maguri, Poienile Izei, Orasul Victoria, Breb and Ocna Sugatag. Each of these different photo camps carries its own story traced through photographs depicting the place as well as the photographers' experience while there. Through these camps, the photographers become ethnographers who carry with them both the visual memories captured on camera as well as the ones that remain within them.

What is special about Maramures is that it is perhaps the only part of the country that maintains the old village lifestyle and traditions, from the architecture of the houses with detailed woodwork and traditional gates, to the people who still wear traditional clothing as they are out working the land. Religious holidays, weddings and burials are spectacles not to be missed, where songs and verses, traditions and dances that are hundreds of years old come alive, where the past impregnates the present and space turns into a time trap. But like most Romanian villages, the lifestyle is not easy: most work is intense physical work that brings little monetary reward. In an interview for *Photo Magazine*, Gicu Serban declared that what he was most impressed with was "people's strength, which ironically comes out of their naivety and almost unconscious desire to remain open, warm and friendly." Since the Romanian transition to capitalism, perhaps some of the most appreciated personal qualities have become that of being cunning, selfish and calculated about everything. It is these qualities that make one strong, and their opposites turn one into a weak, un-adapted individual. It is because of this that Gicu is surprised to find that these peasants' strength comes precisely from the qualities that would generally turn you into someone weak and vulnerable.

It is because of these qualities that Maramures and its people, as a subject, open up to reveal more than an urban subject would. The familiarity, the ability to approach and learn more about your subject, is what turns it into something that is perhaps easier to understand and capture. Voicu Bojan describes the experience of their trips beautifully:

> A simple walk in a Maramures village on a normal day can be like opening a box of wonders. Life flows from every corner. A man is shaving in a broken mirror; a woman is trying to lull an infant to sleep. A pretty girl is resting her arms on her garden fence, a dog is silhouetted on the brow of a hill against a cotton wool cloud, somebody is carrying a sack of milled corn on his bicycle crossbar; an old lady is shooing her chicken into a courtyard. On holidays and on Sundays people usually go to church; afterwards, you can see that everyone feels free to let their hair down. Kerchiefed women on red plastic chairs share an ice cream on the terrace, girls stroll around slowly just to catch the eye, children—all trussed up in traditional costumes like haggises—run about, in the pub there's no room to swing a cat, everyone's drinking as if his life depended on it and playing Nine Men's Morris with frenzied absorption. Gestures are baroque, the costumes are spectacular, the music is full of passion and rhythm, the food and drink are straight and rough, there is always something quite violent floating in the air, but there is also a great deal of love and acceptance. As a photographer, you feel that at any moment you could be either stabbed or hugged.[11]

And yet this romantic picture is full of elements that might seem foreign and out of place. Voicu has a sharp eye for change as well as a poetic description of how the transition is slowly being felt even in these traditional corners of the country. He goes on to write:

> These days, Maramures is a fast-changing space. Frozen in time by the immutability of 50 years of communism, it is suddenly facing the challenges of freedom—Western values are slowly

replacing the old traditions and customs, people who work the land in the same unchanged medieval style stop to drink a Coca-Cola in the secret belief it's a gift coming straight from Above, the cars have Italian or French plates, the youngsters wear fake Nike shoes and Diesel T-shirts. The deep Christian faith and traditions of a conservative population are being challenged by countless TV channels, Brazilian soaps, cheap Oriental music called manele, and the constant fights for the restitution of land confiscated long ago by the commies. Add to all this the massive migration of the population to every corner of Europe in search of a better life, add the mobile phones and internet coffee shops and you get a new species that will change the face of this land forever.

The face of this land has already been changed, as we will see in the photographs taken by the group. And along with these changes, that may seem natural and to be expected by many, what has also changed is an entire imagination, an entire way in which a society or group of people thought of themselves, or to use Katherine Verdery's phrase, an entire re-ordering of people's meaningful worlds has occurred. In this re-ordering, one can find compromises meant to help people cope, one can find the excitement of new things and the painful reminders of the past, the cohabitation of elements that would seem contradictory and the ease as well as difficulty with which the traditional and the modern are mixed. This is a space that neither the dreamworld of communism nor the dreamworld of capitalism have managed to conquer completely, a place where the past has not been erased, where remembering is allowed and in fact, a necessary part of daily life, where the modern eases into old frameworks and finds little nooks where it can lie. The rural forms its own separate dreamworld, one that has been truly asleep for hundreds of years, that has preserved much of its space and look through its people. Representing this dreamworld as an idyllic land—for tourism—is however yet another way of appropriating it: if the dreamworld of capitalism has not left its modern architectural imprint on this place, it has however appropriated it as the safe nostalgic element that can allow the past to be remembered, recreated and relived in an idyllic way, separated from the hardships of village life and true commitment to traditional values.

As tradition, along with the village, becomes something to be experienced, almost as one experiences a painting in a museum, the rural dreamworld is sucked out of its own meaning and refilled with that provided by the new dreamworld of capitalism. The villagers will soon be treated as mere actors that perform an antiquated dance for our amusement, that live in funny houses and follow strange traditions. Already, the rural development plans and the booming industry of rural and agricultural tourism are transforming this space into a mere representation of what it once was: keep the look, yet rebuild the infrastructure according to modern necessities. Following the model of the modern French country charm, the EU is seeking to turn much of rural Eastern Europe into comfortable areas where the urbanites can go retire, where one can go buy organic food and handcrafted goods, eat a traditional meal or watch how the cows are milked.[12] Many of the peasants, desperate to ensure a future for themselves and their children, welcome these changes with an optimism and naivety that is often difficult to observe. The choice between being able to enjoy the comforts of modernity and continuing a lifestyle that no longer seems rewarding and is often treated with disdain or as a mere source of amusement, has left many of the villagers with no real choice.

How these changes are negotiated, how people deal with them or internalize them, how people celebrate or resent them, is something that is often difficult to express in writing to an audience that it not familiar with the subject, that has never seen or experienced life in a traditional village. The photographs taken by the 7 Days Group are photographs taken by modern flaneurs with strong sensibilities and a very good understanding of their subject. They are taken by people who are personally invested in this transition, people who carry a strong nostalgia for the past and empathize with the pain and poverty that is unfortunately more and more visible in this area. Each photograph tells a story about this transition and how it has affected not only space but also the human spirit.

Let images speak

What follows is a slide show of photographs taken by the 7 Days Group at different historical points in the Romanian transition. Each of the photographs is accompanied by a short explanatory text written by myself as a guide to the symbolism of the photograph.

ILLUSIONS AND DISILLUSIONS: A VISUAL NARRATIVE 189

Figure 7.1 A young child on a bike in Negresti: Fred Rohde (2000)

Symbolism: A young child in the village of Negresti, wearing second-hand clothes and a fake Boss hat. The boy is riding an old bike that many villagers use to get around, carrying a traditional type of bread often baked in village bakery from grain that you provide yourself. Since he was hungry, it looks like he already enjoyed a bite.

Source (for all images): www.7zile.ro

Figure 7.2 Selling embroideries on a colorful street: Voicu Bojan (2006)

Symbolism: The traditional village bike becomes an unconventional display for traditional embroideries. Another attempt to make ends meet, selling objects that until recently were passed down from generation to generation as part of a dowry or gifts. Foreign tourists are particularly enchanted by these hand-embroideries that sell for a good price.

Figure 7.3 Two men at the "Targul de la Negreni" (Negreni Fair): Gicu Serban (2003)

Symbolism: Two middle-aged, unemployed men have found a new entrepreneurial way of getting rid of old paintings and furniture, probably an inheritance from an older and richer aunt or family member. They both look bored, enjoying their cigarettes while waiting for customers. Dressed in a mixture of different styles, most likely second-hand clothes: a combination of jeans, sweaters and suit jackets, one of them is sitting on an old paint bucket, the other on a classic chair, looking like they have come from a different world next to the pretty young ladies in the back painting and the Jesus painting down below that seems to be resting on one of their legs.

Figure 7.4 Poster for the International Film Festival, Transylvania—Romania: Cosmin Bumbut (2004)

Symbolism: The Marilyn Monroe pose mixed with the traditional Transylvanian outfit, the headscarf, a view of the old city of Cluj and the logos and advertisements on the bottom make for quite an effect.

The spectacle of communism vs. the spectacle of capitalism

In her book, *Dreamworld and Catastrophe*, Susan Buck-Morss argues that communism and capitalism were much more than two modern ideologies: they were two dreamworlds, or spectacles of modernity. Carefully modeled and implemented in a way that would arouse a particular kind of desire and expectation, these spectacles turned entire societies into the slaves of their own imagining. As different as the two ideologies or dreamworlds may appear to be, Buck-Morss argues that at the base of each lies a very similar desire for material power that can transform the natural environment: "the dream was itself an immense material power that transformed the natural world, investing industrially produced objects and built environments with collective, political desire."[13] The dreamworld was thus not just a world of material desires, but one of political desires that had to be carefully crafted, mastered, delivered and embodied.

The political dreamworld of communism was massive, strong, industrial, and embodied by dominant individuals like Stalin or Ceausescu. Its spectacle was carefully choreographed to take over the cityscape through statues, portraits, slogans and other constant reminders of the grandeur of the communist dream and the political ideology that was going to deliver it. The dreamworld of capitalism is not much different: its grandeur however relies less on the massive and the industrial and more on the appeal of the creative chic and the multi-colored service industry. The spectacle is not dominated by one individual but many, and presents itself as a constantly shifting montage of messages, images and appeals that thrill, confuse and please all at the same time.

The two spectacles, of communism and capitalism, both have the power to dominate the entire spatial imagination of a society, and while their means may be different, the goal is more or less similar: the creation of signs and symbols that would serve as a constant reminder of the path we are on and the leadership that is leading us on it. Despite this, the transition from one spectacle to another is by no means smooth, for all attempts at erasure and destruction of the old symbols are met with both enthusiasm and nostalgia. The new spectacle is never built on a clear site. Memories serve as constant reminders of what used to be even after the objects and times they were attached to are long gone. The act of erasure, although aimed at providing the opportunity for a fresh start, often ends up having the opposite effect, allowing imaginations to run free both ways: both to imagine a better future, as well as to idealize a past that was nowhere close to the glory that is now attached to it.

Attempts to reconstitute the past through selective portrayals, re-embodiment of places and events, and the passing of judgments based on the experience of the present, lead not only to controversy but also confusion. Attempts to legitimize or de-legitimize groups, individuals or even places and events, while often justified by an appeal to justice and revealing the "truth", support the idea that the past could have only been experienced in a particular way and thus all other experiences from the one portrayed are simply wrong or irrelevant. By building one "politically correct" version of the past one often discredits the memories that kept so many alive and in some instances, happy.

The clearing of space for a new spectacle is often literal, not just metaphorical: new statues are built while old ones are removed, old squares and streets are renamed, new museums are built, new artifacts are brought in while others are removed. Beverly James argues that this attempt to rewrite the past may not always be as simple as one may think, for old names, museums and artifacts are imbued with more than the objects they were attached to: they are imbued with people's individual memories, old habits and significant life events. The act of physical erasure is thus not necessarily followed by a mental erasure.[14]

Yet how we remember, and how the new spectacle of capitalism affects our predilection towards rebuilding the past through a particular set of memories, is very telling of the nature of modern transformations and modern living. Andreas Huyssen argues that our obsession with the past, memories and what he calls the tendency to "musealize" the world is nothing but a natural defensive reaction meant to "counter our deep anxiety about the speed of change and the ever shrinking horizons of time and space."[15] If the spectacle of capitalism is characterized by an increasing speed and constant bombardment with information, then it is only natural that this would affect not only what we remember but also how we remember. Huyssen goes on to argue that we may have reached a point where the act of memorization itself becomes obsolete given that memories can no longer be used to assess change—given the sheer speed at which everything happens, there is no time left for reflection. Thus, he says:

> the more we are asked to remember in the wake of the information explosion and the marketing of memory, the more we seem to be in danger of forgetting and the stronger the need to forget. At issue is the distinction between usable pasts and disposable data. My hypothesis here is that we try to counteract this fear and danger of forgetting with survival strategies of public and private memorialization. The turn towards memory is subliminally energized by the desire to anchor ourselves in a world characterized by an increasing instability of time and the fracturing of lived space. At the same time, we know that such strategies of memorialization may in the end themselves be transitory and incomplete.[16]

Huyssen however dismisses too easily other strategies of memorialization that are not necessarily intended to legitimize or de-legitimize particular aspects of our past, but rather meant to simply reconnect us to a past feeling, event or person in our lives. One such strategy is what is known as nostalgia. The feeling of collective nostalgia can play an essential role during periods of great change, for it can be used to selectively recollect positive aspects of the past that can serve as much needed escapes from an otherwise difficult present. Along these lines, Jonathan Bach argues that East German nostalgia for old "Eastern" products—that are now advertised and successfully bought on the East German market—is directly connected to the need to recall an old sense of identity, one that is not imbued with the inferiority that many East Germans are condemned to by their fellow West German citizens.[17]

The attempt to scrap the communist dreamworld and replace it with the capitalist one is thus not as simple as one may initially expect. Memories are not so quickly erased, nostalgia for the past serves as a necessary escape from an overwhelming present, and attempts to re-write or reconstruct the past often have unexpected results, leading to more controversy than settlement. Starting all over again with a clean slate is unfortunately no longer possible. The communist past is here to stay and as much as a quick erasure would make things easier, one needs to remember that the past is imbued in much more than buildings, old speeches and history books. Building upon the past requires an acceptance of both the good and the bad about the past, as well as an attempt to organically integrate its ruins into the buildings of the future.

This almost necessary interdependence of the old and the new, of the communist dreamworld and the capitalist one, is clearly marked on the Romanian landscape. The new wish image of Romania is painted on many of its walls, from shopping malls to new industries, from banners lining the newly built highways to EU flags in remote villages. And yet behind the freshly painted name of a new foreign company that just bought the old factory, lies the mark of the old communist slogan that wished Ceausescu and his people a long life; behind the new stylish name for the shopping mall, lies the old sign, that everyone remembers, the one that hints at old communist ideals such as the burning flame (Flacara) or the union (Unirea).

In recognizing the mutual relationship between space and social and political imaginaries, where space is both a reflection of a dreamworld as well as constitutive of that dreamworld, one opens up room for new kinds of narratives: how the production of particular public spaces can either open up room for political participation or close it,[18] how architecture symbolizes and carries out the political, how certain ideal (visual) narratives often repress troubling historical narratives,[19] how logos appropriate the site in which they are placed and imbue it with a new set of meanings, how space changes language.[20]

Understanding the powerful impact that visual narratives have on how we organize society and how we lead our lives, requires a careful examination of how modern political dreamworlds use space as their scene in order to mesmerize and awe the spectators. As participants in two of the most popular shows in town, Central and Eastern Europeans might find it hard to suspend their disbelief yet another time, after the promised cathartic moment of the old play never arrived. And yet the hope is there, that the new show will be better and that the ride will be a little smoother. Watching the old decorum being ripped apart and a fresh one put in is however not easy. Building on top of fresh ruins can be painful and any scraps of the old scene will serve as reminders of an old dream gone wrong. The glamour and flash with which the new dreamworld capitalism has made its presence known, the commercials, the media, the PR, will mesmerize for a while, yet any new rude awakening from yet another dream might prove to be a little too much for a place that has already been shaken enough.

As Romania is experiencing its new facelift, its new decorum being put in, its cityscape has become a tragic-comic combination of glamour and despair. Between flashy stores and signs, between sassy commercials and appealing new ads, one can spot flyers of anti-corruption campaigns, a couple of homeless children and perhaps the old lady begging for electricity money. In one of the main Bucharest metrostops, between the beggars, the fake Prada and Gucci bags and sunglasses, the walls are covered in advertisements and announcements. A large one, about two meters above ground—someone must have climbed up a ladder to make sure it would not be easily torn down—reads: "We like the end of the Ceausescu era ... We just don't like how the new era started ..." Right underneath it, someone handwrote: "Very, very true!"[21] And this probably best describes the mixture of excitement and disappointment that one walks through every day, from home to work, from work to home and then again. The dreamworld is constantly called into question, it is both desired and welcomed, rejected or cynically applauded, it is accepted with a sigh and yet it has to be, because there is no other. For a society that has already lost a big dream, the loss of another is inconceivable, so the building of the new dream is met both with unprecedented excitement as well as an overwhelming sense of caution.

Recognizing the dreamworld as dream

Susan Buck-Morss warns that dreamworlds are not harmless. In fact, modern dreamworlds turned into social projects can be the most dangerous of all. She argues that:

> The term acknowledges the inherent transience of modern life, the constantly changing conditions which imperil traditional culture in a positive sense, because constant change allows hope

that the future can be better. Whereas myths in premodern culture enforced tradition by justifying the necessity of social constraints, the dreamworlds of modernity—political, cultural and economic—are expressions of a utopian desire for social arrangements that transcend existing forms. But dreamworlds become dangerous when their enormous energy is used instrumentally by structures of power, mobilized as an instrument of force that turns against the very masses who were supposed to benefit. If the dreamed-of potential for social transformation remains unrealized, it can teach future generations that history has betrayed them.[22]

If the dreamworlds of modernity, like communism and capitalism, are indeed dangerous social projects, then why are we so intent in pursuing them? Perhaps awakening and accepting the dream as a dream is not as easy as one may think, for once the dream has seeped into every aspect of our lives, from the food we eat, to the clothes we wear, to the places we live and work in, awakening means more than giving up an ideal: it means giving up our entire mode of being. Awakening is thus more than a shake that will bring us back to the "real" world: it is the destruction of a dream that we have grown completely dependent on. Walter Benjamin argues that this destruction is only possible when the perspective of a new dream is already present, and that in fact, in our transition from one dreamworld to another we never truly awaken but rather pass through different stages of awareness:

> Every epoch, in fact, not only dreams the one to follow but, in dreaming, precipitates its awakening. It bears its end within itself and unfolds it—as Hegel already noticed—by cunning [...] It is one of the tacit suppositions of psychoanalysis that a clear-cut distinction between sleeping and waking has no value for the human being or for the empirical impressions of consciousness in general, but yields before an unending variety of conscious states determined, in each case, by the level of wakefulness of all psychic and corporeal centers.[23]

Even within these different states of wakefulness, the dream remains enchanting. Patricia Pringle argues that modernity finds spatial manipulation thrilling. She suggests that the observer of modern space is not just an agent but also an outcome, a part of the picture, someone who identifies themselves with the thing being observed:

to give attention to something aligns us physically and mentally with that thing, inciting sympathetic movements within us and unlocking deeper levels of perception. The syntactical inconsistency of the words hints at synesthesia within the process. We are both agent and outcome, both singular and plural, our sight, breath, motion, resonance, and insight interlocked.[24]

The photographer is particularly attuned to synesthesia—the calling up of one sense through the stimulation of another—since the endeavor itself is based on the thrill of observation and capturing of a subject surrounded by emotion and sensed not only through the visual but through the other sensual appeals that the visual implies. The flaneur, like the photographer, is also physically and mentally aligned with the object of observation, in a purposeful and conscious manner, while the average individual catches glimpses of objects and senses the alignment in an indirect, unconscious fashion, one that allows the contradictions to sink in yet does not acknowledge them openly in a fashion that allows for clarity through examination. This empathetic relationship between the body and the thing beyond it, that Pringle draws our attention to, is one that uncovers a particular way of sensing and experiencing the world, one in which changes in our immediate environment, whether it be human or object, are immediately sensed and more importantly, experienced in a way that changes our interpretation of the world.

Fascinated by how a society's forms of visual entertainment can offer insights into its underlying shifts and disturbances, Pringle draws our attention to the way in which modern dance, magic shows and the theater offer different spatial illusions that are particularly appealing to the modern individual. What is interesting about her examination is not so much the particular appeal that each of these forms of visual entertainment offer, but more importantly the fact that the appeal falls into a similar type: a spatial illusion of daydreaming, one that offers an escape from the rigidity of the possible, of the limited, of the real. The need for escape, in this case through the use of the visual, is particularly important as one talks about the creation of visual dreamworlds—whether it be the dreamworld of communism or the dreamworld of capitalism.

The modern visual escape that, in the nineteenth century, was limited to the indoor experience of the theater or magic shows, is now taking over a different, larger horizon, that of the streets, the common places, the everyday: the enchantment, the dreamworld, the escape is constructed in a conscious and direct way in a manner that manipulates and takes over the everyday visual horizon. By taking it out into the streets, this dreamworld inevitably clashes with the inescapability of poverty, pain, contradictions, dirt or rage, creating a disconcerting montage in which everything is apparently possible, yet nothing is certain. The dreamworld that takes over the street, introduces a different rhythm into modern spatial existence, a much faster and disjointed one. As Pringle explains:

> The interplay of physical movement, rhythmic spatial experience, and mental life is of course at play in such meditative spaces as cloisters, which work to calm the mind through quieting the body's motions. The inverse also happens, a different sort of rhythm induced by shock and movement being used to excite the physical sense and heighten a sense of unity and conviviality.[25]

That shock can excite us into a sense of unity and conviviality is however at least questionable, for the cloisters of modernity seem to have all but disappeared while taken over by malls, crowded highways and packed streets. As more and more of the spatial horizon is being captured by ads, stores and constant appeals to our wishes and wants, there is little if any room left for escape from the dreamworld. If Pringle is right in arguing that "we are linked to our times not only by the ability but also the desire to see in particular ways"[26] then it would seem that we are doing ourselves a disservice by wishing for a dreamworld that we later need an escape from. And yet we continue to vigorously construct our new dreamworld, tirelessly overwhelming ourselves with constant visual reminders of where we will soon be. The PR and visual media industry—particularly TV—have played an essential role in making this come true.

Photography, media and TV as tools of erasure and building

In Central and Eastern Europe, the rise of PR as an industry has been unprecedented, along with the proliferation of visual media, particularly TV. The thirst for images has resulted in societies whose entire visual field has changed, whose social existence has gone from spending all your time in a communal existence—both in the rural as well as the urban spaces—to spending the majority of your time engulfed in new commercials, American films and replicas of famous Italian, Spanish or Portuguese soap operas, talk shows and most recently, reality shows. While the transition towards this has been gradual, TV is beginning to play a significant role in most people's lives, particularly those who are retired as well as children and young adults. Starting with the first televised revolution in 1989, television stations have started playing a more and more important role in the lives of Romanians. Going from two hours of TV per day to non-stop cable programs constitutes a big change in a society that until sixteen years ago often did not have electricity after 10pm.

Television has become more than an escape from daily life: it is an alternative universe where one can spend hours in a row switching from one channel to another, from one world to another. Many soap operas are treated as if they were part of everyday life, where the characters come alive and become a topic of conversation for many women, who spend their time together talking about the latest thing that happened to the main character. The extent to which people become engulfed in this world speaks to the extent to which TV and the visual media have managed to capture not only the attention but also the identity of many of those who watch. The traditional gossip on the village bench has now turned into gossip over imaginary TV characters. Many of these characters symbolize different forms of hardships and difficulties, whether financial or emotional, and they provide an important outlet for many who experience a similar set of hardships yet have no other outlet for expressing their pain.

TV rates have increased exponentially: since 1990, the number of TV subscriptions has almost doubled according to official statistics, yet judging from the number of people who steal cable every day or watch TV at somebody else's house, particularly in villages, the number of TV viewers must be much higher. 50 percent of TV time is occupied by entertainment shows, 30 percent by informative shows and about 12 percent by advertisements.[27] In a country where for the majority of the population, the cost of going out into town is prohibitive, many people find refuge at home in front of the TV. The TV has replaced vacations and time spent talking to neighbors or family, as well as time spent being outside. For a society that has undergone a series of important shocks and transformations since the fall of communism in 1989, the TV provides people with a sense of support and security, often depicting a false image of a much brighter and optimistic everyday world through its reality shows and commercials. While the number of people watching TV has significantly increased, many refuse to watch news channels and restrict themselves to watching entertainment shows and talk shows. The news is oftentimes either perceived as too bleak or as the lying voice of one particular political party or another. The sense of apathy is often reflected in the refusal to watch the news any more, even in educated families, where information plays an important role. This speaks to the increasing levels of cynicism and apathy in a society where the immediate post-revolutionary enthusiasm pushed people to buy and read sometimes up to six papers a day.

Reinterpreting your everyday existence through the eyes of the media results in a series of interesting distortions, allowing you to problematize imaginary situations, to familiarize yourself with a lifestyle that will most likely never be yours, to imagine the rest of the world through the travel channel. Unlike other art forms such as photography, TV rarely offers opportunities for reflection. It exposes you to a series of new horizons, yet it does so at a highly speedy rate and it very consciously chooses the images that you will see in order to send a particular message—oftentimes a normative message. Commercials are perhaps the most obvious mechanisms for doing so: the power of persuasion lies clearly in the power to manipulate people into believing not only that a particular good is the right choice but also that the good is necessary. Appealing to the psychosomatic level, these images sell everything that post-communist societies run so short of: a sense of security, warmth, wellbeing, and depending on the audiences being targeted, a sense of tradition or the avant-garde.

The everyday as was once experienced has significantly changed: it is now dominated by a series of different levels of representation, in which the visual plays an increasingly important role. What can be seen is no longer limited by what actually exists in reality. Through new visual technologies one is allowed to let one's imagination run "free." The everyday has acquired new dimensions, where the imagination is no longer restricted to grandmother's stories or a Jules Verne novel, but instead runs free across a series of different levels of representation: from reality shows, to science fiction, to the travel channel, to abstract representations such as political cartoons. Sifting through this information is difficult enough for people who grew up with it. For those who started to experience it all at once unexpectedly, one can only imagine the kind of shock they must have experienced. Studies are only at the frontline stages in their effort to make sense of how this sudden transition has affected Romanian society, yet one is beginning to see clear signs of changes in the normative system as well as a significant increase in the general level of expectations coupled with an increase in levels of cynicism and disappointment.

Conclusion

If Benjamin was indeed right in saying that our sense of perception changes with our mode of existence, then the transition to capitalism can also be interpreted through the way in which the latter has been perceived, both by direct participants as well as by outside observers. This is precisely the kind of interpretation that this chapter has tried to achieve. Going beyond Susan Buck-Morss's idea that the "dreamworlds" or what I call illusions of communism and capitalism have been individually built using visual tools such as symbols, slogans and key imageries of success, this chapter has argued that the transition from one illusion to the other is also very much experienced through the visual.

Whether we use the visual as an escape, a promise, or simply a reflection of change, the increasing awareness of the role that it plays in helping to negotiate change has led to a series of different acts of erasure—such as the removal of statues, street names or slogans and their replacement with new ones—and powerful acts of rewriting—the building of new office and apartment buildings, the opening of shops and boutiques, or the flooding of our visual horizon with new forms of advertising. Space has become much more than a setting for daily activities: it has become a direct reflection and constant reminder of the changes that different societies are undergoing. Gazing upon this reflection allows for an interesting process of self-reflection. Whether by walking down the street—as Benjamin's flaneur would do—or looking at a photograph, watching a film or reading a novel, we are more and more exposed to reflections of ourselves. The process of change is thus directly written into ourselves, it penetrates us through visual stimuli and challenges us adapt to it. Increasing signs of nostalgia, sensual overload and visual over-stimulation speak directly to the speed of change and our ability to absorb it. As we explore new and different way of adapting to change, the visual plays an increasingly important tool for creating mechanisms of escape. This chapter hopes to have opened the door for further explorations on how the visual can be used as a powerful tool for analyzing social change, particularly in transition economies.

Notes

1   Mirjana Lozanovska, "The Architectural Edifice and the Phantoms of History," *Space and Culture* 6.3 (2003).
2   Robert Bond, "Speculating Histories: Walter Benjamin, Iain Sinclair," *Historical Materialism* 14.2 (2006).
3   I am borrowing the term from Walter Benjamin and his visual examination of the French—Parisian transition to industrialism. Benjamin used the term wish-image to express either an imagined image or an actual visual image or scene that often triggered a series of emotions and "wishes" that helped paint a particular vision—often positive—of the future as well as the past.
4   Guy Debord, *The Society of the Spectacle*, trans. Donald Nicholson-Smith (New York: Zone Books, 1994), 24.
5   Debord, *The Society of the Spectacle*, 10.
6   Benjamin, *Illuminations*, 222.
7   On a lighter note, people used to call pigs' feet "patriots" because they were the only part of a pig that was sold in Romania, the rest of it being used in meat products that were to be exported.
8   People always used to carry plastic bags with them during communism, in case stores received unexpected deliveries of scarce goods: meat, fruit or clothing.
9   Kevin Sullivan, "Out of the Darkness: Romania Tries to Shed Its Traditional Past for Entry into E.U.," *The Washington Post* March 12th, 2006.
10 Information available on their website at: www.7zile.ro (accessed March 13th, 2006).

11 This fragment has been taken from a text the group had prepared for the magazine *Lenswork*. The text was sent to me by one of the group's members, Voicu Bojan.

12 Soon enough this experience will be similar to the one that many Western kids enjoy when seeing cows and chickens at a zoo, as opposed to a traditional farm.

13 Buck-Morss, *Dreamworld and Catastrophe: The Passing of Mass Utopia in East and West*, ix.

14 Beverly A. James, *Imagining Postcommunism: Visual Narratives of Hungary's 1956 Revolutions* (College Station: Texas A&M University Press, 2005).

15 Andreas Huyssen, "Present Pasts: Media, Politics, Amnesia," *Public Culture* 12.1 (2000).

16 Huyssen, "Present Pasts: Media, Politics, Amnesia," 28.

17 Jonathan Bach, "'The Taste Remains': Consumption, (N)Ostalgia, and the Production of East Germany," *Public Culture* 14.3 (2002).

18 See Bulent Batuman, "Imagination as Appropriation: Student Riots and the Reclaiming of Public Space," *Space and Culture* 6.3 (2003).

19 See Daniela Sandler, "Incarnate Politics: The Rhetorics of German Reunification in the Architecture of Berlin," *Invisible Culture* 5 (2003).

20 See Ella Chmielewska, "Logos or the Resonance of Branding: A Close Reading of the Iconosphere of Warsaw," *Space and Culture* 8.4 (2005).

21 Noted in an article by Ion Cristoiu, "Democratia La Metrou," *Adevarul* August 11th, 2005.

22 Buck-Morss, *Dreamworld and Catastrophe: The Passing of Mass Utopia in East and West*, x.

23 Benjamin, *The Arcades Project*, "Expose of 1935," p. 13.

24 Pringle, "Spatial Pleasures," 141-2.

25 Pringle, "Spatial Pleasures," 152.

26 Pringle, "Spatial Pleasures," 155.

27 These statistics are available on the Romanian Institute for National Statistics website under the Culture and Sports Chapter at: www.insse.ro (accessed March 13th, 2006).

8
Conclusion

The road on which this project has taken me has been full of surprises and highly rewarding. Having started it with an almost intuitive approach to how people in my immediate surroundings struggled through the Romanian transition, I sought to give outsiders a chance to understand just how much this transition has affected every aspect of their lives. While I initially expected to do so relying mainly on testimonies from different groups within Romanian society, I soon realized that just another retelling of people's struggles would not be enough. In developing a new theory of illusion formation and disillusionment, drawing from studies in psychology, anthropology, urban and visual studies, I have sought to give more complexity to phenomena that would otherwise appear overly simplistic.

I have sought to dispel common assumptions that the much talked-about disillusionment haunting post-revolutionary Central and Eastern Europe was nothing more than individual pessimism related to economic shortages or a form of political apathy caused by too much governmental and institutional corruption. If anything, I have tried to point out that there is a certain sense of normality in this disillusionment: just like mourning the death of someone you have lived with for over forty years, the mourning of communism should not be surprising, nor should the nostalgic feelings that much of the Central and Eastern European population still entertain.

The loss and mourning of an illusion is always combined with the birth of another, for, both at an individual as well as a collective level, one does not let go of a past illusion until a new one is visible on the horizon. Thus, the pain and nostalgia caused by the death of one illusion is always combined with the hopes and expectations surrounding the new one. What happens in between is often a painful process of coming to terms with the past while at the same time celebrating the future. As described in Chapter 2, this does not always come easy as the process of uncovering the past is always fraught with distrust, fear and contestations. The opening of the Secret Security Archives in Romania, and across many other countries in Eastern Europe, has been a cause for great controversy, underlying the fact that many are not yet willing to live up to their own past and that history is not so easy to judge. The Romanian President's attempt to officially condemn communism, while a seemingly obvious and simple act, stirred many into a frenzy, raising fears that prosecutions would come next. The need to come clean with the past was partially justified by Romania's recent entry into the EU. Emerging as the new hope for much of Eastern Europe—Romania being one of the most enthusiastic countries in the region—the EU risks being turned into the new big disillusionment.

The transition from one illusion to another thus always carries with it a time for learning and a time for mourning. As an old illusion, such as communism, crumbles, the construction of new illusions—such as the capitalist or the EU illusion—becomes essential. Chapters 3 and 4 have tried to understand how these new illusions are built, what mechanisms are used to sustain them and how people relate to them. Focusing on the work of Susan Buck-Morss, these chapters tried to show the extent to which the communist and capitalist illusions—as modern illusions par excellence—are significantly different from previous types of collective social illusions in that they are built in direct opposition to each other, yet using very similar means of visual propaganda, promises of development and fulfillment of a certain collective ideal—of representation as well as wellbeing. Both demand high sacrifices for the achievements of the ultimate goals—of material wellbeing—at just about all costs.

The hesitant relationship that many people maintained with the communist illusion under the Central and Eastern European regimes gave birth to a new, much more pragmatic, way of relating to social illusions. Arguing that social illusions are essential for the survival of collectivities organized around nation states, this project has tried to examine the nature of this pragmatism and the extent to which it is reflected in the new relationship that people are developing with the capitalist illusion. Having been deeply disappointed once, grand dreams and promises do not carry quite the same weight in an area where people now recognize the fragility of otherwise seemingly permanent regimes. This pragmatic approach allows for the Central and Eastern European enthusiasm for joining the West, entering the European Union or enjoying the benefits of a capitalist economy, to be perceived as a sign of unquestioned support for the new capitalist illusion and its democratic dream. Yet one needs to be very careful with such assumptions, for societies that have struggled for so long are often more concerned with basic survival strategies and making the best of the situation that one finds oneself in, rather than with a particular moral stance—which capitalism certainly entails.

The transition from communism to capitalism thus involves a series of contradictory tendencies of regret and nostalgia, excitement and cynicism, pragmatism and unbounded self-sacrifice. Maneuvering these different tendencies and looking for logical connections between them can prove to be quite difficult when one does not keep an open mind about the extent to which the post-communist environment remains a very fickle one, in which the commitment to the new capitalist illusion has not fully solidified, despite the fact that there are few, if any, other options on the horizon. This democratization by default, as Tamas calls it, makes the new capitalist illusion in many ways very fragile. Its main solidifying element is perhaps the material goods that it has helped bring in, although lack of access to these goods for the majority of the population makes them seem even more surreal, despite their overwhelming presence in shop windows, commercials and advertisements.

Understanding the sometimes very mundane things on which collective social illusions are built—such as familiarity with a particular product, building or even street name—helps us better understand the process of change and the extent to which the traumatizing effects of change are just as easily felt by so-called major reforms as well as by small changes—such as the removal of a statue, the changing of a street name or the introduction of unfamiliar products on the market. Chapter 4 dealt directly with the trauma associated with the process of change or transition, using the concept of shock. When expanded to a notion of collective shock, this concept can be particularly helpful for understanding how people deal with change. Noting that in recent times there has been a significant transition from a negative connotation of shock to a positive one, the chapter argued that the trauma of change today is to a large extent intensified by an expectation that change should be celebrated as opposed to feared. This overemphasis on celebration and on imposing an overly positive look towards transitions and change in general, not only increases expectations but also takes away otherwise naturally occurring opportunities for collective grieving. The chapter clearly suggested that a collective self-recognition of the trauma imposed by the transition as well as an acknowledgement of the "sacrifice" would do more good than forcing an overly positive image of it.

Using Walter Benjamin's creative engagements with the concept of shock, the chapter was also able to draw up some possible explanations for the relationship between intense feelings of nostalgia—in situations where these would not necessarily be warranted—and periods of transition and social change. Under particular circumstances, shock becomes much more than trauma to guard against: it becomes essential for self-reflexivity as well as raised awareness about the nature of change, which in turns makes possible the enjoyment not necessarily of the shock itself, but rather the possibilities that it opens up for oneself. Given that we live in times that are constantly fraught with change, learning how to take some pleasure in the process is essential, while at the same time recognizing the normality of pains associated with it as well.

Seeking to understand more specifically how the questions of illusion formation, disillusion and the shock of transition from the communist illusion to the capitalist illusion played out in real terms, Chapters 5, 6 and 7, provided three very different mechanisms of examining change. Chapters 5 and 6 chose more classic sites for examining change: the 1989 Romanian Revolution and the formation of the first civil society group in post-revolutionary Romania; while Chapter 7 adopted a more innovative approach by looking at how the transition is reflected, constructed and experienced in the visual realm. Each of these chapters has hopefully offered a different perspective for understanding the nature of the transition from the communist to the capitalist illusion in the Romanian context and provided some inspiration for those who are interested in doing similar analyses in other parts of the world.

Chapter 5 sought to use the particular experience of the 1989 Romanian Revolution leaders as key to understanding the hesitations involved both in the proactive, yet not necessarily intended, destruction of the communist illusion, as well as in the building of the new capitalist illusion. The personal disillusionment experienced by each and every one of these revolution leaders speaks to the significant gap between their initial expectations and what they saw happening more than fifteen years after the revolution. A closer examination of the revolutionary ideals that helped support the popular ethos responsible for the fall of the Ceausescu regime reveals a very different and much less ambitious set of demands from the assumed radical democratic ones. Understanding the extent to which the transition to a capitalist democracy occurred almost accidentally, for certainly the Timisoara Revolution leaders did not dare dream that far, speaks closely to the oftentimes arbitrary nature of change. The chapter does indeed try to focus on the elements that are oftentimes overlooked yet proved to be quite essential for the success of the revolution: such as the particular location of the industrial platform where most of the demonstrators came from, a series of acts and events that gained a mystical interpretation, and the location of the famous balcony from where the leaders of the revolution were able to address thousands of people.

Looking at how the experience of the revolution is perceived by its leaders more than fifteen years into the transition, the chapter also provided an interesting perspective, allowing the revolution to be stripped of its aura and analyzed through the lenses of what came afterwards. The pervasive disappointment of the revolution leaders speaks not only to the challenging nature of the transition but more importantly to the extent to which that initial impetus that made everyone go out onto the streets and risk their lives, that incredible sense of solidarity amongst strangers, is now entirely gone. That initial solidarity is something that is still mourned as people find themselves increasingly alone and self-oriented.

If Chapter 5 examined the point of origin of the new capitalist illusion, the foundation on which it started to be built, Chapter 6 looked at some of the tools that were employed in order to justify it. The birth of civil society in Romania, while initially inspired by the same revolutionary ethos that made the transition possible in the first place, served the purpose of justifying and in many ways ensuring the democratic turn in post-revolutionary Romania. Civil society thus became a recruitment ground for new government leaders, a think-tank meant to organize the new reform process, as well as a mechanism for reassuring the population at large that their voice would continue to be heard even in the middle of political power infighting.

Following the trajectory of the first self-proclaimed civil society group in Romania—the Group for Social Dialogue—this chapter sought to better understand the role that the group played in popularizing democratic reforms and challenging neo-communist tendencies in the newly elected government. Focusing on a series of different gaps between common assumptions supported by the larger civil society discourse and the particular development of civil society in Romania, the chapter also tried to argue that the concept of civil society needs to be much more flexible in order to better understand the different roles that so-called civil society groups play in particular contexts. Allowing for this flexibility can keep us away from theoretical and empirical traps—such as making unquestioned assumptions that civil society groups are always "civil" or weighing up the "strengths" vs. "weaknesses" of civil society—while also opening a space to creatively engage with different forms of civil society.

If revolutions and examinations of civil society have by now become common sites for examining social change, Chapter 7 tried to introduce a new approach for looking at transitions, by focusing on the increasing role that the visual plays in the formation of new social and political illusions. Following the discussion opened up in Chapters 1 and 2 about the formation of the new capitalist illusion, this chapter sought to express precisely how this illusion is constructed, experienced and expressed through a series of different images. The visual is presented as much more than a new and more intense way of experiencing transitions, but also as a tool that is increasingly manipulated to serve a number of different purposes. Within this manipulation however, people have learned to use the possibilities opened up by different forms of visual representations as escape mechanisms and comfortable corners of retreat. The chapter does however seek to draw attention to the dangers that some of these comforts pose, by examining some of the effects that they have on the relationship between "dream" and "reality" and the conflation of the two to a point where "real" and immediate consequences are downplayed or ignored as if they were imagined. This particular shift in behavior poses real challenges to the way in which modern societies are built and "imagined," creating both a sense of over confidence—everything is possible—as well as a sense of inevitability—we watch disasters as if they were on TV as opposed to trying to do something about them, even when it is within our means.

By following a group of Romanian photographers throughout their travels within northern Romania, the chapter also tried to examine the extent to which different forms of representation, such as photography, can open up much-needed spaces for self-reflection and create new forms of interaction between the subject and the photographer. By displaying some of the pictures taken by the 7 Days Group, it sought to point to the extent to which visual narratives can serve both as a tool of analysis as well as a means to understanding the subjects of many of our studies as "real" and living things, as opposed to distant and easily forgotten ones. Given that, to a large extent, the shock of transition is experienced visually, the chapter tried to emphasize the extent to which putting oneself in somebody else's shoes when examining a transition, very much requires a good understanding of the visual horizon that people undergoing it are facing on a daily basis.

In conclusion, this study has attempted to provide an alternative way of looking at periods of transition from the perspective of those who are directly experiencing them While much work remains to be done to develop some of the creative ideas that were explored—the theory of collective illusion formation and disillusionment, the concept of shock and its relation to social change, and the increasing role of the visual in processes of transformation—I can only hope that these will serve as inspiration for others who are asking similar questions.

Bibliography

Adrian, Sanda. Interview by author. Tape recording, Timisoara, December 20th, 2004.
Alexe, Vladimir. "Agentul Volodea." *Ziua* May 13th, 2006. Available at: www.ziua.ro/display.php?id=199511&data=2006-05-13. Accessed March 29th, 2007.
Andreescu, Gabriel. Interview by the author. Tape recording, Bucharest, January 20th, 2005.
Armanca, Brindusa. "Brindusa Armanca in Dialog Cu Mariana Celac." *Ziua* August 25th, 2004.
Armstrong, Tim. *Two Types of Shock in Modernity*. Available at: http://personal.rhul.ac.uk/uhle/012. Accessed May 15th, 2006.
Asociatia Civic Media, *Ucis De Comisia Tismaneanu* 2007. Available at: http://civicmedia.ro/acm/index.php?option=com_content&task=view&id=63&Itemid=1. Accessed March 29th, 2007.
Bach, Jonathan. "'The Taste Remains': Consumption, (N)Ostalgia, and the Production of East Germany." *Public Culture* 14.3 (2002): 545–56.
Badescu, Gabriel, Paul Sum, and Eric Uslaner. "Civil Society Development and Democratic Values in Romania and Moldova." *East European Politics and Society* 18.2 (2004): 316–41.
Badilescu, Nicolae. Interview by author. Tape recording, Timisoara, December 13th, 2004.
Badilita, Cristian. "Visez Un Singur Gest De Razbunare—Ca Peste Douazeci De Ani Piata Universitatii Sa Se Numeasca Piata Ion Iliescu." *Adevarul* June 15th, 2005. Available at: www.adevarul.ro/articole/visez-un-singur-gest-de-razbunare-ca-peste-douazeci-de-ani-piata-universitatii-sa-se-numeasca-piata-ion-iliescu/135429. Accessed March 29th, 2007.
Balint, Costel. *1989: Timisoara in Decembrie*. Timisoara: Editura Helicon, 1993.
Barker, Adele Marie (ed.), *Consuming Russia: Popular Culture, Sex, and Society since Gorbachev*. Durham and London: Duke University Press, 1999.
Batuman, Bulent. "Imagination as Appropriation: Student Riots and the Reclaiming of Public Space." *Space and Culture* 6.3 (2003): 261–75.
Baudelaire, Charles. *Paris Spleen*. New York: New Directions Publishing Corporation, 1970.
——— *Les Fleurs Du Mal*. Boston: David R. Godine, 1985.

Bauman, Zigmunt. *Liquid Modernity*. Cambridge: Polity Press, 2000.
—— *Liquid Life*. Cambridge: Polity Press, 2005.
Beck, Brittney, Steen Halling, Marie McNabb, Daniel Miller, Jan O. Rowe and Jennifer Schulz. "Facing up to Hopelessness: A Dialogal Phenomenological Study." *Journal of Religion and Health* 42.4 (2003): 339–54.
Benjamin, Walter. "The Work of Art in the Age of Mechanical Reproduction." Trans. Harry Zohn. *Illuminations*. Ed. Hannah Arendt. New York: Schocken Books, 1968.
—— *Illuminations*. Trans. Harry Zohn. Ed. Hannah Arendt. New York: Schocken Books, 1968.
—— "A Small History of Photography." Trans. Edmund Jephcott and Kingsley Shorter. *One-Way Street*. Ed. Walter Benjamin. Frankfurt: Suhrkamp Verlag Press, 1970.
—— *One-Way Street*. Trans. Edmund Jephcott and Kingsley Shorter. Frankfurt: Suhrkamp Verlag Press, 1970.
—— *Reflections*. Trans. Edmund Jephcott. Ed. Peter Demetz. New York: Schocken Books, 1978.
—— *The Arcades Project*. Trans. Howard Eiland and Kevin McLaughlin. Ed. Rolf Tiedemann. Cambridge, MA: Belknap Press of Harvard University Press, 1982.
—— "Critica Violentei." *Despre Violenta*. Ed. Ciprian Mihali. Cluj: Idea Design and Print, 2004.
Bercea, Maria. "Condamnarea Communismului Romanesc: Comisia Prezidentiala." *22 April 28th-May 4th*, 2006.
Berger, John. *Ways of Seeing*. London: British Broadcasting Corporation and Penguin Books, 1972.
—— *About Looking*. London: Writers and Readers Publishing Cooperative Ltd., 1980.
Bertschi, C. Charles. "Lustration and the Transition to Democracy: The Cases of Poland and Bulgaria." *East European Quarterly* 28.4 (1994): 435–45.
Blaney, David and Mustapha Pasha. "Civil Society and Democracy in the Third World: Ambiguities and Historical Possibilities." *Studies in Comparative International Development* 28.1 (1993): 3–24.
Bleiker, Roland. "The Aesthetic Turn in International Political Theory." *Millennium: Journal of International Studies* 30.3 (2001): 509–33.
Blum, Martin. "Remaking the East German Past: Ostalgie, Identity, and Material Culture." *Journal of Popular Culture* 34.3 (2000): 229–53.
Boia, Lucian. *Mitul Democratiei (the Myth of Democracy)*. Bucharest: Humanitas, 2003.
Bond, Robert. "Speculating Histories: Walter Benjamin, Iain Sinclair." *Historical Materialism* 14.2 (2006): 3–27.
Booth, John A. and Patricia Bayer Richard. "Civil Society, Political Capital and Democratization in Latin America." *International Congress of the Latin American Studies Association*. Guadalajara, Mexico, 1997.
Booth, W. James. "The Unforgotten: Memories of Justice." *American Political Science Review* 95.4 (2001): 777–91.
Borza, Ioana. *Decommunization in Romania: A Case Study of the State Security Files Access Law*. 2007. Available at: www.polito.ubbcluj

.ro/EAST/East6/borza.htm. Accessed March 29th, 2007.

Bourdieu, Pierre. *Algeria 1960: The Disenchantment of the World, the Sense of Honour, the Kabyle House or the World Reversed*. Cambridge: Cambridge University Press, 1979.

Boym, Svetlana. *Common Places: Mythologies of Everyday Life in Russia*. Cambridge, MA: Harvard University Press, 1994.

—— *The Future of Nostalgia*. New York: Basic Books, 2001.

Bozoki, Andras (ed.) *Intellectuals and Politics in Central Europe*. Budapest: Central European University Press, 1999.

Brecht, Bertolt. *Brecht on Theater: The Development of an Aesthetic*. Trans. John Willett. New York: Hill and Wang, 1964.

Buck-Morss, Susan. *The Origin of Negative Dialectics: Theodor W. Adorno, Walter Benjamin, and the Frankfurt Institute*. New York: The Free Press, 1977.

—— "Aesthetics and Anaesthetics: Walter Benjamin's Artwork Essay Reconsidered." *October* 62.Fall (1992): 3–42.

—— "The City as Dreamworld and Catastrophe." *October* 73.Summer (1995): 3–26.

—— *Dreamworld and Catastrophe: The Passing of Mass Utopia in East and West*. Cambridge, MA: MIT Press, 2000.

Burawoy, Michael and Katherine Verdery. *Uncertain Transitions: Ethnographies of Changein the Postsocialist World*. Lanham, MD: Rowman and Littlefield, 1999.

Calhoun, Craig. "Imagining Solidarity: Cosmopolitanism, Constitutional Patriotism, and the Public Sphere." *Public Culture* 14.1 (2002): 147–71.

Cassegard, Carl. "Shock and Modernity in Walter Benjamin and Kawabata Yasunari." *Japanese Studies* 19.3 (1999): 237–52.

—— "Murakami Haruki and the Naturalization of Modernity." *International Journal of Japanese Sociology* 10 (2001): 121–6.

Celac, Mariana. "An Elite That Did Not Take This Country for What It Really Was." *22 January* 25th-31st, 2000: 6–7.

Cernat, Paul, Ion Manolescu, Angelo Mitchievici and Ioan Stanomir. *In Cautarea Comunismului Pierdut*. Pitesti, Bucharest, Brasov, Cluj-Napoca: Paralela 45, 2001.

Cesereanu, Ruxandra. *Decembrie '89: Deconstructia Unei Revolutii*. Bucharest: Editura Polirom, 2004.

Chandhoke, Neera. *State and Civil Society: Explorations in Political Theory*. New Dehli and Thousand Oaks: Sage Publications, 1995.

Chauffour, Celia and Henri Tincq. "Les Fantomes De L'eglise Polonaise." *Le Monde* February 1st, 2007: 20–1.

Chmielewska, Ella. "Logos or the Resonance of Branding: A Close Reading of the Iconosphere of Warsaw." *Space and Culture* 8.4 (2005): 349–80.

Cionoiu, Gheorghe. *Procesul Tranzitiei Sau Punctul Meu De Vedere*. Bucharest: Editura Brumar, 1996.

Colas, Dominique. *Genealogia Fanatismului Si a Societatii Civile (the Geneology of Fanatism and Civil Society)*. Trans. Cristina Arion, Mircea Secure and Alina Vasile. Bucharest: Nemira, 1998.

Cornea, Andrei. Interview by author. Tape recording, Bucharest, January 20th, 2005.

Cramer, Phebe. "Defense Mechanisms in Psychology Today." *American*

Psychologist 55.6 (2000): 637–46.

Crisan, Gheorghe. "Interviu Cu Domnul Ioan Lorin Fortuna, Liderul Frontului Democrat Roman Din Timisoara." *Victoria* Anul I, Issue I 1989: 3.

Cristoiu, Ion. "Democratia La Metrou." *Adevarul* August 11th, 2005.

Culik, Jan. "Profound Disillusionment." *Central Europe Review* 1.20 (1999). Available at: www.ce-review.org/99/20/culik20.html. Accessed January 10th, 2007.

Czajkowska, Beata Barbara. "From Tribunes to Citizens: Polish Intelligentsia During and after Communism." Unpublished dissertation, University of Maryland, 1999.

Czesnik, Mikolaj. "Voter Turnout and Democratic Legitimacy in Central Eastern Europe." *Polish Sociological Review* 4.156 (2006): 449–70.

Dahrendorf, Ralf. *After 1989: Morals, Revolution and Civil Society.* New York and Oxford: St. Martin's Press and St. Antony's College, 1997.

Dakova, Vera, Bianca Dreossi, Jenny Hyatt and Anca Socolovschi. *Review of the Romanian NGO Sector: Strengthening Donor Strategies, September 2000,* 2004. Available at: www.donorsforum.ro/download/RomNGOreview_En.doc. Accessed March 1st, 2007.

Davis, Fred. *Yearning for Yesterday: A Sociology of Nostalgia.* New York: Free Press, 1979.

Debord, Guy. *The Society of the Spectacle.* Trans. Donald Nicholson-Smith. New York: Zone Books, 1994.

de Certeau, Michel. *The Practice of Everyday Life.* Trans. Steven Rendall. Berkeley, Los Angeles and London: University of California Press, 1984.

Dehejia, Vivek. "Will Gradualism Work When Shock Therapy Doesn't?" *Economics and Politics* 15.1 (2003): 33–59.

Desai, Padma. "Beyond Shock Therapy." *Journal of Democracy* 6.2 (1995): 102–12.

Desteapta-Te Romane (Awaken Thee, Romanian): Romania's National Anthem. Available at: www.national-anthems.org/anthems/country/ROMANIA+. Accessed March 29th, 2007.

Durkheim, Emile. *Suicide: A Study in Sociology.* Trans. John A. Spaulding and George Simpson. New York: The Free Press, 1951.

—— *The Division of Labor in Society.* Trans. W. D. Halls. New York: The Free Press, 1984.

Eagleton, Terry. *Walter Benjamin or Towards a Revolutionary Criticism.* London: Verso Editions and NLB, 1981.

Eckstein, Harry. "Civic Inclusion and Its Discontents." *Daedalus* 113.4 (1984): 107–45.

Efimova, Alla and Lev Manovich (eds). *Tekstura: Russian Essays on Visual Culture.* Chicago and London: University of Chicago Press, 1993.

Eisenstadt, S. N. "The Paradox of Democratic Regimes: Fragility and Transformability." *Sociological Theory* 16.3 (1998): 211–38.

Eliade, Mircea. *The Sacred and the Profane: The Nature of Religion.* Trans. Williard Trask. San Diego: Harcourt, 1987.

Esbenshade, Richard S. "Remembering to Forget: Memory, History, National Identity in Postwar East-Central Europe." *Representations* 49.Winter (1995): 72–96.

Fairbanks, Charles H. Jr. "Ten Years after the Soviet Breakup:

Disillusionment in the Caucasus and Central Asia." *Journal of Democracy* 12.4 (2001): 49–56.

Feichtinger, Claudia and Gerhard Fink. "The Collective Culture Shock in Transition Countries—Theoretical and Empirical Implications." *Leadership & Organization Development Journal* 19.6 (1998): 302–8.

Filipescu, Radu. Interview by author. Tape recording, Bucharest, January 19th, 2005.

Fisher, William F. "Doing Good? The Politics and Antipolitics of NGO Practices." *Annual Review of Anthropology* 26 (1997): 439–64.

Foran, John. *Teoretizarea Revolutiilor*. Trans. Radu Pavel Gheo. Bucharest: Polirom, 2004.

Fortuna, Lorin. Interview by author. Tape recording, Timisoara, December 14th, 2004.

Foster, Hal (ed.). *Vision and Visuality*. New York: New Press, 1999.

Foucault, Michel. *Madness and Civilization: A History of Insanity in the Age of Reason*. New York: Pantheon Books, 1965.

Frank, Leonard Roy. *History of Shock Treatment*. San Francisco: Leonard Roy Frank, 1978.

Fraser, Nancy. "Rethinking the Public Sphere: A Contribution to the Critique of Actually Existing Democracy." *Social Text* 25/26 (1990): 56–80.

Freud, Sigmund. *Beyond the Pleasure Principle*. Trans. C.J.M. Hubback. The International Psycho-Analytical Library. Ed. Ernest Jones. London and Vienna: The International Psycho-Analytical Press, 1922.

—— *Civilization and Its Discontents*. New York: J. Cape and H. Smith, 1930.

—— "Creative Writers and Day-Dreaming: Leonardo Da Vinci and a Memory of His Childhood." *The Freud Reader*. Ed. Peter Gay. London: Vintage, 1995.

—— "The Moses of Michelangelo." *The Freud Reader*. Ed. Peter Gay. London: Vintage, 1995.

—— "Mourning and Melancholia." *The Freud Reader*. Ed. Peter Gay. London: Vintage, 1995.

Fritz Plasser, Peter A. Ulram and Harald Waldrauch. *Democratic Consolidation in East-Central Europe*. New York: St. Martin's Press, 1998.

Fromm, Erich. *Man for Himself: An Inquiry into the Psychology of Ethics*. New York: Henry Holt and Company, 1947.

—— *The Revolution of Hope: Toward a Humanized Technology*. New York, Evanston and London: Harper and Row Publishers, 1968.

Galloway, George, and Bob Wylie. *Prabusirea*. Trans. Constantin Sfeatcu. Bucharest: Editura Irini, 1991.

Gans-Morse, Jordan. "Searching for Transitologists: Contemporary Theories of Post-Communist Transitions and the Myth of a Dominant Paradigm." *Post-Soviet Affairs* 20.4 (2004): 320–49.

Gardiner, Michael, E. "Marxism and the Convergence of Utopia and the Everyday." *History of Human Sciences* 19.3 (2006): 1–32.

Gasset, Jose Ortega Y. *Omul Si Multimea*. Trans. Sorin Marculescu. Bucharest: Humanitas, 1980.

Gellner, Ernest. *Conditions of Liberty: Civil Society and Its Rivals*. New York:

The Penguin Press, 1994.

Gerber, Theodore P. and Michael Hout. "More Shock Than Therapy: Market Transition, Employment, and Income in Russia, 1991–1995." *American Journal of Sociology* 104. July (1998): 1–50.

Glenn, John. *Framing Democracy: Civil Society and Civic Movements in Eastern Europe*. Stanford: Stanford University Press, 2001.

Goldfarb, Jeffrey C. "1989 and the Creativity of the Political." *Social Research* 68.4 (2001): 994–1010.

Gregg, Samuel. "Markets, Morality and Civil Society." *The Intercollegiate Review*. Fall 2003/Spring 2004 (2004): 23–31.

Grossman, Richard (ed.). *The God That Failed*. New York: Harper & Brothers Publishers, 1949.

Group for Social Dialogue, Founding Members. "Founding Declaration of the Group for Social Dialogue." *22* January 25th-31st 2000: 4.

Hall, Richard Andrew. "Theories of Collective Action and Revolution: Evidence from the Romanian Transition of December 1989." *Europe-Asia Studies* 52.6 (2000): 1069–93.

Havel, Vaclav. *The Power of the Powerless: Citizens against the State in Central and Eastern Europe*. New York: Palach Press, 1985.

—— "The Velvet Hangover." *Harper's Magazine* October 1990: 20.

—— *Summer Meditations*. New York: Alfred A. Knoff, 1992.

Hay, Colin. *Why We Hate Politics*. Cambridge UK and Malden US: Polity, 2007.

Heller, Agnes. *Everyday Life*. Trans. G.L. Campbell. London and New York: Routledge and Kegan Paul, 1970.

—— "Between Past and Future." *Between Past and Future: The Revolutions of 1989 and Their Aftermath*. Ed. Vladimir Tismaneanu and Sorin Antohi. Budapest and New York: Central European University Press, 2000.

Hermochova, Sona. "Reflections on Living through the Changes in Eastern Europe." *Annals of the American Academy of Political and Social Science* 552 (1997): 107–13.

Holc, Janine P. "Liberalism and the Construction of the Democratic Subject in Postcommunism: The Case of Poland." *Slavic Review* 56.3 (1997): 401–27.

Howard, Marc Morje. *The Weakness of Civil Society in Post-Communist Europe*. Cambridge: Cambridge University Press, 2003.

Huntington, Samuel P. *The Third Wave: Democratization in the Late Twentieth Century*. Norman: University of Oklahoma Press, 1991.

Huyse, Luc. "Justice after Transition: On the Choices Successor Elites Make in Dealing with the Past." *Law & Social Inquiry* 20.1 (1995): 51–78.

Huyssen, Andreas. "Present Pasts: Media, Politics, Amnesia." *Public Culture* 12.1 (2000): 21–38.

Ionescu, Ghita. *Politica Si Cautarea Fericirii*. Addison Wesley Longman: London; Bucharest: Bic All, 1999.

Iordache, Claudiu. *Romania Pierduta*. Bucharest: Editura Irini, 1995.

—— *Clasa Nevrednica*. Bucharest: Editura Irini, 1997.

—— *Polul De Putere*. Bucharest: Editura Irini, 2002.

—— Interview by author. Tape recording, Bucharest, January 15th, 2005.

Jackel, Anne. "Romania: From Tele-Revolution to Public Service Broadcasting, National Images and International Image." *Canadian Journal of Communication* 26 (2001): 131–41.

Jaguaribe, Beatriz. "The Shock of the Real: Realist Aesthetics in the Media and the Urban Experience." *Space and Culture* 8.1 (2005): 66–82.

James, Beverly A. *Imagining Postcommunism: Visual Narratives of Hungary's 1956 Revolutions*. College Station: Texas A&M University Press, 2005.

Janos, Andrew C. "From Eastern Empire to Western Hegemony: East Central Europe under Two International Regimes." *East European Politics and Society* 15.2 (2001): 221–49.

Jenks, Chris. "Watching Your Step: The History and Practice of the Flaneur." *Visual Culture*. Ed. Chris Jenks. London and New York: Routledge, 1995.

Joravski, David. "Communism in Historical Perspective." *American Historical Review* June (1994): 837–57.

Jozwiak, Joseph F. and Elisabeth Mermann. "The Wall in Our Minds? Colonization, Integration and Nostalgia." *The Journal of Popular Culture* 39.5 (2006): 780–95.

Kalb, Don and Herman Tak. "The Dynamics of Trust and Mistrust in Poland: Floods, Emotions, Citizenship and the State." *Postsocialism: Politics and Emotions in Central and Eastern Europe*. Ed. Maruska Svasek. New York and Oxford: Berghahn Books, 2006.

Kaldor, Mary, and Ivan Vejvoda (eds). *Democratization in Central and Eastern Europe*. London: Pinter, 1999.

Kalekin-Fishman, Devorah (ed.). *Alienation: Exploring Diverse Realities*. Jyvaskyla: University of Jyvaskyla Press, 1998.

Keane, John (ed.). *Civil Society and the State: New European Perspectives*. London and New York: Verso Press, 1988.

Kierkegaard, Soren. *Fear and Trembling and the Sickness Unto Death*. Trans. Walter Lowrie. New York: Doubleday Anchor Books, 1954.

King, Charles. "Post-Postcommunism: Transition, Comparison, and the End of 'Eastern Europe'." *World Politics* 53 (2000): 143–72.

Kirshtner, Kelly. "Syn(Aes)Thesis: A Conversation of the Senses." *Octopus* 1.1 (2005): 3–9.

Kiss, Csilla. "We Are Not Like Us. Transitional Justice: The (Re)Construction of Post-Communist Memory." In *History and Judgement*. Eds. A. MacLachlan and I. Torsen, 2006.

Kleinegger, Thomas. Interview by author. Tape recording, Bucharest, January 21st, 2005.

Koen, Vincent. "The 'Soaring Eagle': Poland's Economic Performance and Challenges." *10 years of Polish membership in the OECD*. Warsaw, 2006. Available at www.oecd.org/dataoecd/29/0/37737384.pdf. Accessed January 10th, 2007.

Koestler, Arthur. *Darkness at Noon*. Trans. Daphne Hardy. New York: MacMillan Company, 1941.

Kolakowski, Leszek. *Toward a Marxist Humanism: Essays on the Left Today*. Trans. Jane Zielonko Peel. New York: Grove Press Inc., 1968.

— "On Collective Identity." *Partisan Review* 70.1 (2003): 7–17.

Kombinat: Industrial Ruins of the Golden Era. Bucharest: Igloo Press, 2007.

Konrad, George. *Antipolitics*. San Diego: Harcourt Brace Janovich

Publishers, 1984.

—— *The Melancholy of Rebirth: Essays from Post-Communist Central Europe 1989–1994*. Trans. Michael Henry Heim. New York: Harcourt Brace & Company, 1995.

Konrad, George and Ivan Szelenyi. *Intellectuals on the Road to Class Power*. Trans. Andrew Arato and Richard Allen. New York: Harcourt Brace Jovanovich, 1979.

Kornai, Janos. "The Great Transformation of Central and Eastern Europe." *Economics of Transition* 14.2 (2006): 207–44.

Kwon, Paul. "Hope, Defense Mechanisms, and Adjustment: Implications for False Hope and Defensive Hopelessness." *Journal of Personality* 70.2 (2002): 207–31.

Lacy, Mark J. "Deconstructing Risk Society." *Environmental Politics* 11.4 (2002): 42–62.

Latour, Bruno. *We Have Never Been Modern*. London: Harvester Wheatsheaf, 1993.

Lefebvre, Henri. *Everyday Life in the Modern World*. New York: Transaction Publishers, 1984.

Lena, Kolarska-Bobinska. "The Changing Face of Civil Society in Eastern Europe." *Praxis International* 10.3-4 (1990-1991): 324–36.

Levi-Strauss, Claude. *Myth and Meaning*. New York: Schocken Books, 1979.

Levy, Robert. "Review of Tismaneanu's Stalinism for All Seasons: A Political History of Romanian Communism." *East European Politics and Societies* 18 (2004): 717–19.

Los, Maria. "Lustration and Truth Claims: Unfinished Revolutions in Central Europe." *Law & Social Inquiry* 20.1 (1995): 117–61.

Lozanovska, Mirjana. "The Architectural Edifice and the Phantoms of History." *Space and Culture* 6.3 (2003): 249-60.

Luke, Timothy, W. "The Things of Order: The Nature and Practice of Knowledge for International Relations." *International Studies Association Annual Meeting*. Hawaii, 2005.

—— *Scanning Fast Capitalism: Quasipolitan Order and New Social Flowmations*. Available at: www.uta.edu/huma/agger/fastcapitalism /1_1/luke.htm. Accessed May 15th, 2006.

—— "Technology as Metaphor: Tropes of Construction, Destruction, and Instruction in Globalization." Paper presented at the International Studies Association annual conference. San Diego, 2006.

—— "Transnationalities: Embedded, Imagined, and Engineered Communities." Paper presented at the conference "Rethinking Spaces: Transnational Representations." McGill University, 2006.

MacKenzie, Jean. "Were We Really That Naive?" *Moscow Times* March 10th, 2003.

Malcomson, Scott. "Romania: Philosophical Fragments." *Transition* 62 (1993): 80–8.

Marangos, John. "Was Shock Therapy Really a Shock?." *Journal of Economic Studies* 37.4 (2003): 943–66.

Marcuse, Herbert. *Eros and Civilization: A Philosophical Inquiry into Freud*. Boston: Beacon Press, 1966.

Marx, Karl. "Economic and Philosophical Manuscripts." *Karl Marx: Early*

Writings. Ed. T.B. Bottomore. New York: McGraw-Hill Book Company, 1963.

Michnik, Adam. *Restauratia De Catifea*. Bucharest: Polirom, 2001.

Michnik, Adam and Vaclav Havel. "Confronting the Past: Justice or Revenge?" *Journal of Democracy* 4.1 (1993): 20–7.

Michnik, Adam and Ira Katznelson. "Gray Is Beautiful." *Dissent* 44.2 (1997): 14.

Militaru, Ana. *Europa De La Capatul Sforii (the EU at the End of the Rope)*. 2007. Available at: www/iqads.ro/Analize_Reclame_read_6362/europa_de_la_capatul_sforii.html. Accessed February 15th, 2007.

—— *Prea Multa UE Strica (Too Much EU is Bad for Us)*. 2007. Available at: www.iqads.ro/Analize_Reclame_read_6321/prea_multa_ue_strica.html. Accessed February 15th, 2007.

Milosz, Czeslaw. *The Captive Mind*. [1951.] New York: Vintage International, 1981.

Modak, Jeffrey and Adam F. Gearing. "Civic Engagement in a Post-Communist State." *Political Psychology* 19.3 (1998): 615–37.

Mungiu-Pippidi, Alina. "10 Years of Illusions." 22 January 25th-31st, 2000: 15.

—— *Politica Dupa Comunism*. Bucharest: Humanitas, 2002.

—— "Culture of Corruption or Accountability Deficit?" *East European Constitutional Review* 11/12.4/1 (2002–2003).

Nancy, Jean-Luc. *Comunitatea Abstenta (The Absent Community)*. Trans. Emilian Cioc. Panopticon Collection. Cluj: Idea Design & Print, 2005.

Nietzsche, Friedrich. *The Birth of Tragedy and the Genealogy of Morals*. Trans. Francis Golffing. New York: Anchor Books, Doubleday, 1956.

Norem, Julia K. and Nancy Cantor. "Defensive Pessimism: 'Harnessing' Anxiety as Motivation." *Journal of Personality and Social Psychology* 51.6 (1986): 1208–17.

Orru, Marco. *Anomie: History and Meaning*. Boston: Allen and Unwin Press, 1987.

Ost, David. "The Politics of Interest in Post-Communist East Europe." *Theory and Society* 22.4 (1993): 453–85.

Palade, Rodica. Interview by author. Tape recording, Bucharest, January 20th, 2005.

Pamfil, Eduard. "Comunismul S-a Nascut Pe Malurile Nevei Si a Murit Pe Malurile Begai." *Victoria* Anul I, Issue I 1989.

Pasha, Mustapha and David Blaney. "Elusive Paradise: The Promise and Peril of Global Civil Society." *Alternatives* 23.4 (1998): 417–50.

Pasti, Vladimir. *Romania in Tranzitie: Caderea in Viitor*. Bucharest: Nemira, 1995.

Pearlin, Leonard. "Social and Personal Stress and Escape Television Viewing." *The Public Opinion Quarterly* 23.2 (1959): 255–9.

Plesa, Carmen and Daniela Sontica. "Icoana-Minune, Pricina De Scandal." *Adevarul* August 11th, 2005.

Plesu, Andrei. "Post-Totalitarian Pathology: Notes on Romania Six Years after December 1989." *Social Research* 63.2 (1996): 559–71.

—— *Obscenitatea Publica*. Bucharest: Humanitas, 2004.

Pringle, Patricia. "Spatial Pleasures." *Space and Culture* 8.2 (2005): 141–59.

"Proclamatia Frontului Democratic Roman Constituit La Timisoara." *Victoria* Anul I, Issue I 1989: 2.

Proust, Marcel. *À La Recherche De Temps Perdu*. Paris: Gallimard, 2002 (new edition).

Roman, Denise. *Fragmented Identities: Popular Culture, Sex, and Everyday Life in Postcommunist Romania*. Lanham, Boulder, New York, Toronto and Plymouth: Lexington Books, 2003.

Roncea, Victor. "Tismaneanu Contestat De Dobre." *Ziua* January 15th, 2007.

Rupnik, Jacques. "The Politics of Coming to Terms with the Communist Past: The Czech Case in Central European Perspective." *Transit online* 22 (2002). Available at: www.iwm.at/index.php?option=com _content&task=view&id=286&Itemid=464.

Sachs, Jeffrey. "Shock Therapy in Poland: Perspectives of Five Years." Lecture, *The Tanner Lectures on Human Values*. University of Utah, 1994.

Sandler, Daniela. "Incarnate Politics: The Rhetorics of German Reunification in the Architecture of Berlin." *Invisible Culture* 5 (2003). Available at: https://urresearch.rochester.edu/retrieve/2167/IVC_iss5 _Sandler.pdf. Accessed January 10th, 2007.

Schaff, Adam. *Alienation as a Social Phenomenon*. Oxford: Pergamon Press, 1980.

Schiopu, Madalina. "Interviu Cu Alin Teodorescu: Triumful Diversitatii." *22* January 25th-31st, 2000: 2–3.

Schumacher, Bernard N. *A Philosophy of Hope: Josef Pieper and the Contemporary Debate on Hope*. Trans. D.C. Schindler. New York: Fordham University Press, 2003.

Simmel, Georg. *The Sociology of Georg Simmel*. Trans. Kurt Wolff. Cambridge: Free Press, 1964.

Singer, Daniel. "Europe's Crises." *Social Justice* 23.1–2 (1996): 91.

Skocpol, Theda. *States and Social Revolutions: A Comparative Analysis of France, Russia & China*. Cambridge: Cambridge University Press, 1979.

Sloterdijk, Peter. *Critica Ratiunii Cinice*. Trans. Tinu Parvulescu. [1983.] Iasi: Polirom, 2000.

Sontag, Susan. "Under the Sign of Saturn." *Under the Sign of Saturn*. New York: Anchor Books, 1972.

Sorel, George. *The Illusion of Progress*. Trans. John and Charlotte Stanley. Berkeley: University of California Press, 1969.

Stanciu, Alina. "Publicitatea a Aderat O Data Cu Romanul (The Publicity World Acceded to the EU Along with the Romanians)." *Cotidianul* January 19th, 2007.

Stanculescu, Manuela Sofia and Ionica Berevoescu. *Sarac Lipit, Caut Alta Viata! Fenomenul Saraciei Extreme Si Al Zonelor Sarace in Romania 2001*. Bucharest: Nemira, 2004.

Stavrakakis, Yannis. *Lacan and the Political*. New York: Routledge, 1999.

Stolyarova, Galina. "De-Stress with Shock Therapy." *Moscow Times* September 11th, 1999.

Stone, Richard. "Stress: The Invisible Hand in Eastern Europe's Death Rates." *Science Magazine* 288.5274 (2000): 1732–3.

Sullivan, Kevin. "Out of the Darkness: Romania Tries to Shed Its Traditional

Past for Entry into E.U." *The Washington Post* March 12th, 2006: A12–A13.

Svasek, Maruska. *Postsocialism: Politics and Emotions in Central and Eastern Europe.* New York and Oxford: Berghahn Books, 2006.

Tamas, G.M. "The Hungarian Revolution." *The Spectator* 1989: 12.

—— "A Disquisition on Civil Society." *Social Research* 61.2 (1994): 205–22.

—— "The Legacy of Dissent." *The Revolutions of 1989*. Ed. Vladimir Tismaneanu. London: Routledge, 1999.

—— "Victory Defeated." *Journal of Democracy* 10.1 (1999): 63–8.

Tanase, Stelian. "22 Was from the Beginning in the Opposition." *22* January 25th-31st, 2000: 8.

—— *Zei Si Semizei: La Inceput De Secol*. Bucharest: Curtea Veche, 2004.

Taylor, Charles. *The Malaise of Modernity*. Toronto: Anansi Press, 1991.

Teitelbaum, Stanley H. *Illusion and Disillusionment: Core Issues in Psychotherapy*. Northvale: John Aronson Inc., 1999.

Teodorescu, Alin. Interview by author. Tape recording, Bucharest, January 23rd, 2005.

Terzani, Tiziano. *Goodnight, Mister Lenin: A Journey through the End of the Soviet Empire*. Trans. Joan Krakover Hall. London: Picador, 1994.

Tismaneanu, Vladimir. *The Crisis of Marxist Ideology in Eastern Europe: The Poverty of Utopia*. New York: Routledge, 1988.

—— *Condamnati La Fericire: Experimentul Comunist in Romania*. Sibiu and Brasov: Fundatia Exo, 1991.

—— "Dialectics of Disenchantment." *Debates on the Future of Communism*. Ed. Vladimir Tismaneanu and Judith Shapiro. New York: St. Martin's Press, 1991.

—— *Reinventing Politics*. New York: Free Press, 1992.

—— (ed.). *Revolutiile Din 1989: Intre Trecut Si Viitor*. Bucharest: CEU and Polirom Press, 1999.

—— "Civil Society, Pluralism and the Future of East and Central Europe." *Social Research* Winter (2001): 977–91.

—— *Stalinism for All Seasons: A Political History of Romanian Communism*. Berkeley: University of California Press, 2003.

—— *Comisia Prezidentiala Pentru Analiza Dictaturii Comuniste Din Romania: Raport Final*. Bucharest: Romanian Presidency, 2006.

Tiu, Ilarion. "Crimele Comunismului 'Marca' Tismaneanu." *Jurnalul National* December 20th, 2006. Available at www.jurnalul.ro/articole/5589/crimele-communismului-%22marca%22-tismaneanu. Accessed January 10th, 2007.

Vasquez, Rolando. *Poetry and Modernity: Walter Benjamin's "On Some Motifs in Baudelaire."* Working draft, 2006. For more information contact author.

Verdery, Katherine. "Faith, Hope, and Caritas in the Land of the Pyramids: Romania, 1990 to 1994." *Comparative Studies in Society and History* 37.4 (1995): 625–69.

—— "Anthropological Adventures with Romania's Wizard of Oz, 1973-1989." *Focaal: European Journal of Anthropology* 43 (2004): 134–45.

Vogt, Henri. *Between Utopia and Disillusionment: A Narrative of Political*

Transformation in Eastern Europe. Oxford: Berghahn Books, 2005.
Welsh, Helga A. "Dealing with the Communist Past: Central and East European Experiences after 1990." *Europe-Asia Studies* 48.3 (1996): 413–28.
Wexler, Philip. "'Re-Selfing' after Post-Modern Culture: Sacred Social Psychology." *Alienation: Exploring Diverse Realities*. Ed. Devorah Kalekin-Fishman. Jyvaskyla: University of Jyvaskyla, 1998.
Zizek, Slavoj. *The Sublime Object of Ideology*. New York: Verso Press, 1989.
——— *For They Know Not What They Do: Enjoyment as Political Factor*. London and New York: Verso, 1991.

Index

(nb. 'n' after a page number indicates a note on that page)

aesthetics 85n, 86n
  aestheticization 63
  aestheticize 36
alienation 4, 31, 80, 86n, 178, 220n
anomie 4, 31, 222n
apathy
  political 1, 4, 73, 140, 145, 170, 202, 206
  social 4, 29, 121, 140, 202
architecture 62, 93, 150, 177, 179, 181, 185, 196, 205n
archives
  Group for Social Dialogue 149
  secret security 4, 6, 7, 14, 27n, 106, 135n, 154, 207
artist 40, 152, 183, 184
aura 56–58, 68, 210

Basescu, Traian 7, 26n, 27n
Baudelaire, Charles 55–6, 84n, 85n, 177
Benjamin, Walter 4, 36–7, 55–7, 61–3, 68, 84n, 85n, 176–7, 180, 198, 203–4, 205n, 209
Berlin Wall 29, 87, 91, 96
Brasov 49, 53n, 90, 93–5, 113, 132n, 216n
Buck-Morss, Susan 35–7, 52n, 53n, 193, 197, 203, 205n, 207
built environment 35, 193
Bulgaria 17, 27n, 37, 70

capitalism
  disillusionment with 42, 49, 64, 70–1, 116
  fast-capitalism 59, 65, 85n
  illusion of 4, 26, 35–6, 38, 45, 90, 100, 171, 178–9, 193–4, 197–9
  transition to 1–4, 38, 69, 116–17, 186–8, 203, 208
Ceausescu, Nicolae 9, 43–5, 49, 88, 90–5, 98–9, 101–6, 108, 112–14, 116–21, 124–9, 131, 133n, 147, 151–2, 155, 167, 172n, 193, 196–7, 210
civil society 1, 5, 6, 30, 35, 83, 137–50, 153, 155, 157–71, 172n, 209, 211
  disillusionment with 137–50
  illusion of 132, 137–50, weakness of 5, 34, 69, 131,
  see also Group for Social Dialogue
collective memory 8, 80
commercials 25, 60, 174, 180, 197, 201–2, 208

communism
  crimes/condemnation of 10, 15, 16, 18–19, 27n, 53n, 207
  disillusionment with 26, 35–37, 39–41, 43–8, 51n, 61, 71, 87, 89, 93, 100, 159, 161, 204n
  illusion of 20, 25, 26, 35–7, 39–41, 43–8, 50, 51n, 94, 98, 112, 123–4, 140–1, 181, 186–7, 193, 198–9, 203, 206
  transition from 1–4, 7–8, 12, 16, 122, 173n, 202, 205n, 208
consumption 31, 57, 79, 205n
corruption 1, 7, 26, 27n, 29, 71, 100, 121, 123, 131, 140, 145, 161, 163, 169–70, 182, 197, 206
culture shock 50, 55, 72–3, 85n
cynicism 4, 12, 22–3, 31, 144, 175–6, 202–3, 208
Czech Republic 151

decommunization 14, 16–17, 27n
demonstration 33, 49, 87–8, 90, 92, 95–7, 100–1, 104, 111, 116–17, 125–8, 130, 133n, 152
dissident 1, 8–10, 12, 93, 100, 113, 138–9, 141–2, 147, 151–2, 155–6, 161–2, 171n, 172n
Ditchev, Ivailo 37, 53n
dreamworld 35–6, 52n, 53n, 178–9, 183, 187–8, 193, 195–200, 203, 205n
Durkheim, Emile 31, 51n

East Germany 30, 205n
emotions 51n, 58, 151, 204n
European Union (EU) 4, 6, 13, 23–6, 28n, 29, 167, 208
everyday life 2, 31–2, 51, 64, 73, 76, 82, 176, 201
expectations 1–2, 11, 16, 26, 32–4, 48, 63, 88, 99, 100, 125, 131, 148–9, 160, 164, 184, 203, 207, 209, 210

fear 12, 44, 48, 61, 68–9, 76, 88, 91, 95–6, 98, 102–4, 117–19, 144, 195, 207, 209
flaneur 56, 177–8, 188, 199, 204
Foucault, Michel 67
fragmentation 30, 78
freedom 29, 32, 42, 49–50, 61, 73, 79, 88, 98–9, 109–11, 116–17, 121, 125, 139, 159, 185–6
Freud, Sigmund 35, 52n, 55–56, 63, 79, 84n, 86n
Fromm, Eric 32, 52n, 80

Group for Social Dialogue (GDS) 5, 30, 137–8, 147, 158–9, 162, 172n, 173n, 211
  see also civil society
guilt 8, 11–12, 20–1, 35, 106, 119, 164

Havel, Vaclav 15–16, 27, 32, 37–8, 51n, 53n, 88, 139, 141, 145, 148, 161, 170–1, 172n
hope 1, 25, 32, 34–5, 37, 40–1, 43, 45, 63, 76, 81–2, 92, 94, 97–8, 103, 114, 116, 137, 148, 164–6, 169, 171, 173n, 176, 196–7, 204, 207, 210, 213
hope capital 32, 146–7
hopelessness 29, 33, 38, 51n, 52n, 90, 140, 145, 176

Hungary 17, 100, 173n, 205n

identity 27n, 37, 63, 152, 173n, 195, 201
ideology 3, 32, 35, 37, 38–40, 45, 47, 52n, 117, 151, 159, 193
intellectual 1, 18, 29, 34, 37, 39–40, 42, 44, 46–8, 50n, 51n, 57, 93, 101, 109, 113, 116–17, 124–5, 135n, 136n, 141–2, 147, 150–2, 154, 157, 159–61, 165

justice 7, 13, 15–16, 18, 20–1, 23, 27n, 28n, 30, 79, 85n, 100, 118, 121, 147, 194

Koestler, Arthur 39–43, 51n, 53n

lustration 14–18, 20–2, 27n, 28n

malaise 4, 52n
Marx, Karl 31, 52n, 80
media 23, 58, 77–8, 86n, 93, 116, 155, 168, 171, 180, 184, 197, 200–2, 205n
see also television
memory 8, 19–21, 23, 27n, 46, 62, 79–80, 84n, 195
Michnik, Adam 15, 27n, 162
modernity 32, 36, 52n, 56–7, 59, 64–5, 67–80, 84n, 85n, 86n, 179, 183, 188, 193, 198, 200
morality 11, 38, 100, 121, 139–40, 149, 160–3, 165–6, 170, 171n, 172n, 173n, 208
myth 2, 18, 34–5, 51n, 52n, 102, 126, 135n, 139–40, 198

narrative
  written/spoken 51n, 64, 77, 85n, 87–9, 133n, 134n, 174–5, 183, 196
  visual 78, 171, 174–5, 182, 196, 205n, 212
National Salvation Front (NSF) 90, 107–8, 113, 116–17, 161–2, 167
nationalism 36, 46, 68, 168
nomenklatura 11, 14, 134n, 167
normalization 48, 64–7
nostalgia 4, 19–20, 31, 59–63, 73, 76, 85n, 175–6, 188, 193, 195, 204, 208–9

photography 5, 58, 112, 121, 152, 159, 171, 175, 183–8, 199–200, 202, 204, 212
Poland 16, 27n, 51n, 70–1, 85n
popular culture 31, 51n
psychology 2, 30, 32, 51n, 52n, 86n, 206
publicity 23–4, 28n, 58, 179–80

religion 39, 51n, 52n, 76, 80–1, 96–7, 111, 119, 127–8, 160, 168, 184–5
Romanian Communist Party (RCP) 9, 13, 44–8, 154
Romanian Democratic Front (RDF) 108–15, 117, 122–3, 129, 134n

sacrifice 14, 36, 38, 45, 48–50, 99, 117, 165, 207–9
Secret Security 4, 6–7, 14, 18, 21, 27n, 135n, 151, 154, 207
Slovakia 17, 30, 141
Socialism 35, 38, 51n, 94
solidarity 3–4, 35, 122, 140, 210–11

Sontag, Susan 61–2, 85n
spectator 175, 177–8, 196
stability 3, 17, 48–9, 62, 69, 83, 117, 125, 147, 195
Stalinism 43–4, 47, 53n
stimuli 55–7, 60–1, 63, 76, 175, 199, 204
symbol 6, 24, 37, 84n, 88, 91, 94–5, 121, 126, 128–31, 148, 158, 172n, 188–93, 196, 201, 203

Tamas, G.M 37–8, 53n, 100, 133n, 139–140, 171n, 208
technology 55, 64–5, 74, 85n
Teitelbaum, Stanley 32–3, 51n, 52n

television 95, 102, 113–14, 122, 129, 201
see also media
Tismaneanu, Vladimir ix, 9–10, 12, 27n, 43, 51n, 53n, 132n, 133n, 135n, 165, 173n
Tokes, Laslo 96–8, 101, 127, 133n
trauma 21–2, 50, 55–6, 58, 78, 83, 106–7, 208–9

utopia 29–30, 35–6, 40, 51n, 52n, 53n, 85n, 198, 205n

Valea Jiului 49, 90–3
Velvet Revolution 91, 96, 102

EU authorised representative for GPSR:
Easy Access System Europe, Mustamäe tee 50,
10621 Tallinn, Estonia
gpsr.requests@easproject.com

www.ingramcontent.com/pod-product-compliance
Ingram Content Group UK Ltd.
Pitfield, Milton Keynes, MK11 3LW, UK
UKHW021942200326
4879IPUK00004B/52